Public Library Services
for Children

Public Library Services
for Children

Barbara T. Rollock

With a Foreword
by
Augusta Baker

Library Professional Publications 1988

First published as a Library Professional Publication,
an imprint of The Shoe String Press, Inc.,
Hamden, Connecticut 06514

Printed in the United States of America

Library of Congress Cataloging in Publication Data

Rollock, Barbara.
  Public library services for children.

  Includes index.
  1. Libraries, Children's.   2. Children—Books and
reading.   I. Title.
Z718.1.R65   1988   027.62'51   88-12863
ISBN 0-208-02016-0

Reprinted with permission of the American Library Association,
"Services to Children and Young Adults"
edited by Diana Young from *Public Libraries*,
Fall 1986; copyright © 1986 by ALA.

The paper used in this publication meets the
minimum requirements of American National Standard
for Information Sciences-Permanence of Paper for
Printed Library Materials, ANSI Z39.48-1984 ⊗

"Behind the work of the children's librarians there is a fine spirit of optimism—not blind to difficulties, but courageous, ardent and hopeful."

—Henry Edward Legler,
Library Work with Children

Dedicated to my colleagues at
the New York Public Library
who taught me so much

Contents

Foreword

This is a wonderful book, and an important contribution to the professional literature. I am proud, of course, that it was written by one who has exercised leadership of the children's services program of the New York Public Library, and I am pleased also that it is so much more than just a recital of that program's history. Instead, the subject of children's services has been approached from a national viewpoint, and it is many years since we have had any book so comprehensive about our field.

Public Library Services for Children should, in my opinion, be required reading for every person who is undertaking professional library education for public or school library services. I mean by this not only those who intend to specialize in these areas of complementary services to children, but those also who will become administrators, branch supervisors, and those in charge of adult and reference services. I say this because I believe that it is increasingly important that *everyone* who works in a library system understand what library work with children encompasses, its goals, and its implications for society's future. The book should be read and studied also by those who are preparing to be the future teachers and school administrators, and those presently concerned with curriculum in the schools, so that they too will comprehend the vast potential for collaboration that exists between schools and public libraries in enabling parents/families and community agencies to reinforce children's learning and to contribute to their lifelong competence and self-fulfillment.

There are so many high points in this book that it is hard to choose which ones to cite and to reaffirm. Overall, one of the book's great strengths is that while it is certainly forward-looking and up-to-date in terms of management concerns and program objectives, it conveys a sense of the importance of the traditions of work with children which endure and provide a strong base for the present and future. For instance, while discussing the need for better statistics and quantitative measures for evaluation purposes, the author emphasizes also designing better ways to evaluate quality in the program that is being produced. Although attention is paid to reaching out to more children in the population, there is strong recognition that the impact of books and of programs for groups is highly individual, affecting children one by one. The extent, and the duration, of beneficial influence on a child of a particular book, story, puppet play, or librarian is at the heart of quality in public library programs for children. It is this quality which is so difficult to evaluate, but Barbara Rollock encourages fellow children's librarians in their effort to try to find ways to validate quality even as they try also to muster quantitative "proof" of effectiveness for administrators.

Listen:

> Measurement of the library's raw product, its output . . . is still far from satisfying to most of us. It leaves the question of what effects, *long-range effects*, on imagination, self-identity, ability to communicate, learning capacity, development of intelligence, even, our children's materials and programs really have. Maybe one day soon, one of us, or someone else who is skilled in research, will devise a study taking into account all the variables, and prove that library services to children and youth *make a difference*, and that those who have them early and richly fare better in their lives than those who are cheated of them. Meanwhile, a considerable body of ethnographic or experiential study shows that this is indeed so. . . . The indisputable relationship between library services to children and the national interest in lifelong literacy and continuing learning has . . . been drawn and dramatized as never before.

All three of the chapters on management concerns are immensely valuable; chapters 3 and 5 especially should be read many times, absorbed and internalized and acted upon by everyone responsible for policy-making and implementation of library services for children.

The whole section in chapter 5 on goals and objectives should be studied and applied to current, particular situations, and discussed formally and point by point with administrators.

A continuous theme throughout the book which cannot be affirmed strongly enough, is that the chuldren's department staff must draw upon the support and assistance of a great variety of allies: parents, child-serving agency staffs, friends' groups, local businesses and organizations—more than ever they have in the past. Children's librarians have always been greatly abetted in their efforts by the help of their friends. I cannot emphasize strongly enough, reinforcing the emphasis of the book, the importance of working closely with friends' groups and volunteers of all kinds. Those who work with children in libraries have been greatly stimulated and inspired by the natural allies in "the community of the book" and in "the community of the child."

Authors, illustrators, editors, and reviewers and teachers have played an intimate part in the development of children's library services. "Crossover" roles are common: librarians were among the greatest of the early children's book editors; editors became authors, authors became editors, librarians became famous illustrators, and many people in the field have had a hand in reviewing, critiquing, and interpreting books for children. Some of the greatest and most influential "enhancers" of library services for children were not librarians at all—people like Frederic G. Melcher of *Publishers Weekly*; booksellers like Frances Chrystie of F.A.O. Schwartz and Quail Hawkins (both of them authors as well); and May Lamberton Becker, writer, editor, and newspaperwoman long associated with the *New York Herald Tribune*. Legions of others like Professor of Children's Literature May Hill Arbuthnot, and Bertha Mahony Miller who started *The Horn Book*, have given their energies and loving commitment to books, libraries, and children.

I firmly believe that there are more like them everywhere—all over the country. It is up to us to find them, invite them to come and help us, respect their creativity and expertise, and encourgage them to share the problems and rewards of our work.

Two very important issues are raised and discussed in the marvelous chapter 5, and I urge every administrator and every practitioner to study and discuss them fully. They are the vital responsibility of public relations, and the importance of *public* funding for children's services. Included in the list of management functions encompassed by "the greatly misunderstood and underrated term public relations" are "reporting to the top management and governance; communications—always two way, and involving reading and listening as well as writing and talking—with staff and public, child-serving agency personnel, organizations and business contacts, and the media; and continuous, constant promotion of library services to children and youth, not just in terms of what they are and when they take place, but in terms of their larger meaning for individual children, families, the community, the nation, and the future. The manager consciously builds that meaning into every program, every contact, and the use of every piece of material; fervently believes in its importance; and leads staff members and patrons into that belief also."

This significant chapter also deals with the issue of public funding versus private funding of children's library programs and services. The book cites, quite correctly, the fact that all libraries, in the face of shrunken library budgets, have been looking for and utilizing "alternate sources of funding." The negatives associated with attempting to *substitute* private funds for on-going allocations of tax-based funding are clearly identified and set forth. Rollock urges managers of children's programming to think in terms of "additional, program-enhancement, rather than alternative, sources of funding." She points to the fact that "private funding sources will almost never provide funds for basic, on-going operations," and the second concern, that "private funds almost always come with strings attached and may tempt the library manager to undertake projects and programs that are not really in line with priority goals and objectives. This may skew the program in subtle and not always beneficial ways, causing undue emphasis on one area over another or on one group of children over another." Barbara Rollock continues:

A third and most serious concern is that in operating too much of its program on private funds, the library may encourage certain elements in local government or the community to think of library services—in this case, those for children—as something that should be paid for by those who use them, i.e., out of private rather than public funds. It must be constantly drummed into community awareness that public library services—especially those for children—are for *everyone*, not just for those who can afford to pay for them or those who compose a desirable customer group for advertisers (which, in effect, business donors are). Library programs for children are in the public interest, and should therefore be supported chiefly out of public funds.

In response to the question of why the illiteracy problem obtains, Barbara Rollock minces no words:

It relates directly to the low priority accorded to children's services in public libraries: there is not enough support for them to enable them to reach out to all the children—especially the preschoolers who need them. It is the children's librarians who emphasize the enjoyment in reading, and foster the love of books and the desire to read them. It is the children's librarians who can work with the parents of young children (or their surrogates) to instill the desire to read, the habit of reading, without which decoding skills will not be sustained by practice and will deteriorate with disuse in after-school life. The love of reading, the motivation to read, that has been fanned successfully for a comparatively few children by children's librarians for the past hundred years, is now seen as economically and socially desirable for all. It is not necessarily seen as desirable for all children because it will enrich their lives, offer them ideas and possibilities, and help them to escape from lack and limitation. It is seen as necessary for those children to read competently—computer screens, manuals, instructions—so that they can be productive for the economy when they grow up.

Does this have a huge potential for beneficial impact on the fortunes and development of children's services? It does, but only if we are alert enough and energetic enough to exploit it vigorously . . . tying these and all other issues raised here to the need for support of children's library services and resources.

To all of this, Amen!
There is a whole chapter devoted to the recent burgeoning of the preschool programs and especially those addressed to parents and

other caregivers. This now highly visible and specialized interest owes much to the programming in this area which had its beginnings in the 1940s and '50s. Here again, we see the glory and the great strength of public library work with children—its evolution growing out of experience and true effectiveness. I am reminded, in this connection, of the administrator of a large public library who hired a brilliant specialist in work with children to change what he conceived to be some of the "outmoded traditionalism" of the children's room. After a suitable length of time had passed, she had not done what she had been brought in to do. Asked why, she replied that she found that the work, its momentum, and its strong roots were stronger than any individual and his or her ideas because they represented the creativity, the dedication, and the vision of not just one, or a handful, of people, but many of them. These many had observed children, worked for them, planned for them, and seen them launched on a lifetime of love for story and character.

I suggest, apropos of this, that we examine carefully any and all new directions and priorities before making drastic changes—thinking always not of how "modern" we are looking to others with our microcomputers and other hardware, but how well we are serving the long-term interests of each child, and successfully supplying for each one experiences, hopes, values, and aspirations to which they may not be exposed anywhere else.

Children's librarians should endeavor to bring to the attention of administrators, policy makers, and organization leaders, the discussion of "program" found in this book. Here, point by point are the elements, including one aspect of program that is "hard to define exactly, but terribly real and important nevertheless. It can be summed up as library environment and librarian attitude, and it manifests itself as acceptance and respect from intelligent, educated people who are working at jobs they obviously like. It is a great builder of self-esteem in child patrons. It is part of the atmosphere of the library and the expectation of the librarians that you are a responsible and trustworthy person, a thinking person whose thoughts matter. . . . Very often early impressions remain through adulthood, and the library and its books have been recorded by many as having helped them to transmute certain of their negative life experiences into positive ones."

Finally, I share so strongly the belief expressed at the end of this outstanding book: "Library services for children have a glorious potential. But nothing 'just happens' no matter how right it seems. We must forge coalitions and attract allies who will help us to state our issues and concerns in every available public forum. Only in this way will we gain public support for improved library services for children. These issues must be put in a context of everything that affects the lives of children both directly and indirectly. . . . Our concern that children shall have quality library services is nothing less than our concern, and our responsibility, for our society and its future."

AUGUSTA BAKER

Acknowledgments

Grateful acknowledgment is made first to Martha Barnes, formerly children's consultant of the Westchester library system, for access to the files she had begun on preschool and early childhood and parenting programs in libraries. I also wish to acknowledge Elizabeth Huntoon, children's consultant of the Chicago Public Library, and Leslie Edmonds, project librarian at the Multicultural Project at the Chicago Public Library, now on the staff of the graduate school of Library and Information Science at the University of Illinois, for information they have supplied, as well as to Grace Ruth, book evaluation librarian at the San Francisco Public Library. Thanks are due Diana Young, children's consultant for the state of North Carolina, and editor of the "Children's Services" column in *Public Libraries;* to Faith Hektoen, children's and young adults' consultant at the Connecticut State Library; Dr. Margaret Mary Kimmel, of the University of Pittsburgh, Graduate School of Library and Information Science, and editor of *Top of the News;* Art Plotnik, editor of *American Libraries;* and to Dr. Ellin Greene, formerly of the University of Chicago, Graduate Library School, for information and permission to excerpt material from their publications. Thanks are due also to Dr. Frances A. Smardo of the Dallas Public Library for her help.

Special acknowledgment is made to Doris Thompson for volunteering assistance in the preparation of the manuscript; to Virginia H. Mathews, my editor, for faith and patience; and to my family, Howard, David, and Phillip, for their encouragement and indulgence.

Introduction

Even the pioneers in this area of work could not pinpoint the very first time libraries were open to children. It may have been in West Cambridge, Massachusetts, to fulfill the bequest of Dr. Ebenezer Leonard; in the basement room opened in 1890 in the Public Library of Brookline, Massachusetts; or in 1893 in the separate room designated, and staffed with an assistant, at the Minneapolis Public Library. In any event, by 1896, more than a dozen reading rooms or circulating libraries for children were reported to be in operation. Mary Wright Plummer, librarian of the Pratt Institute Free Library at the time, observed that those "libraries report crowding and lack of time and space. . . . Turning from these reports to a general consideration of the subject, we must admit, first, that a definite decision as to the object of a children's library is the first thing needful."

A little less than a century later, library administrators are still searching for a definition or "decision as to the object of the children's library" which will justify its place in an institution that is striving for efficiency of operation amidst revolutionary changes in the educational, technological, and socioeconomic character of the society it serves.

From its inception, the public library movement in America has indulged in a great amount of introspection and soul-searching as to its purpose, goals, and objectives. Part I will examine briefly some recent and relevant studies which have had a noticeable impact on library service to children. Significant among them have been *The Public Library in the United States: The General Report on the Public Library Inquiry* by Robert D. Leigh; *The Report of the National Commission on Libraries and Information Science; The State of New York's Report of the*

Commission on Education's Committee on Library Development; and *The Philadelphia Study* by Lowell Martin.

Nineteenth-century librarians, probing the reading needs of the library's clientele, viewed youth as the prime period for developing literary and cultural tastes. Only those books which stimulated mental growth or had "something positively good about them" were suitable, asserted W. I. Fletcher, ALA president in 1891–92, and an early advocate for the removal of age restrictions in libraries. From the earliest days it was considered of utmost importance that the children's librarian really *know* the books. For that reason, few books on children's library services have been written without major attention to what has been considered the primary responsibility of practitioners: quality selection of books and other materials for child patrons and of related activities for children. Programming was seen by Anne Carroll Moore and other pioneer leaders in the movement, as correlated with the child's exposure to the best in books. To insure availability of the best books possible they became—Miss Moore especially—influential forces upon the publishing industry, and on the special juvenile book departments of major publishers that began to be organized in 1918 and throughout the 1920s.

This book will focus from a practitioner's point of view on the state of the art in children's public library services in the mid-1980s, and on at least some of the social forces in this century which have combined to alter the perspectives and potentials of library services to children. Among these have been the child welfare laws, the shorter work-day and -week for parents, and the growing expectation of high school and even college levels of education. There has been, too, the evolution of the electronic age, specifically the invention of television and its all-pervasive presence in homes and in the life of the child. Most significantly, there has been the changing structure of the family and the home, as well as the wide availability of effective contraceptives, which have reduced family size and contributed to the recent decline in school populations and in public library use by children. Directly affecting public libraries has been the establishment and rapid development of school libraries, starting in the secondary schools, and more recently the growth of library media centers in the elementary schools.

The first library doors opened to youth admitted older children, many of them apprentices or employed youth who were ambitious for advancement or eager for the diversion books could offer. Quite soon, however, those librarians in the forefront of the new work in public libraries began to reach out to children of all ages. Their book selection policies reflected their awareness that young children, too, needed to be introduced to books, and choices ranged from picture books to titles for older readers.

The interrelationship of the public library service with the work of other community agencies was from the beginning considered an important factor in work with children. Therefore, in the 1960s, when national interest turned to the preschool child and the development of the Head Start program (originally intended for disadvantaged children), the library was seen as one of the natural community resources available for implementing or enriching the program. The subsequent success of television's "Sesame Street" also highlighted the need for good and more expansive programs for pre-elementary schoolchildren. Children's departments in public libraries began to produce innovative means of introducing the library's resources to many new groups of library users, including those who brought with them demands resulting from changing family patterns, and the electronic media. Most especially in recent years, librarians have bent their efforts toward attracting the pre-reading child and his/her parents and other caregivers.

Although introducing literature to preschool children was the object of many an early twentieth-century story hour in the library, concentration on total programs to encompass parents and other adults who work with children increased from the 1960s on. In 1974, at least fourteen such library programs around the country could be identified. More than a decade later, some programs have expanded in depth, quality, and emphasis, as early childhood education, information about how young children learn, and awareness of the importance of parenting have grown. The ways in which children's librarians are making a significant contribution in these areas will be fully explored in part II, in which a number of exemplary programs from various libraries will be outlined.

Library service for children seems to have changed relatively little from the vision of its founders. This vision was centered around the development of a constituency for libraries starting with people during their "impressionable years." Perhaps because children's needs and growth patterns remain in large degree constant, despite drastic social change, the objectives of the work have remained basically the same: to meet and serve the child as an individual, and to collaborate with others in the general community to which the child belongs. Possibly, out of this wider community will emerge a network of adults who will become advocates for lifelong mental stimulation and search for knowledge on behalf of a new, upcoming generation, and the library will have played a significant role in developing that network.

This book will attempt to show that public library service to children is alive and well, but because its benefits and productivity are largely undocumented, it is most vulnerable to budget cuts and personnel shortages. Library service to children *can* be a viable part of the total library program, equal to the challenges of change with each new generation it encounters. In order to be so, however, it must be nourished by adequate resources, properly respected, and neither taken for granted nor smothered with benign neglect. A community's future, a nation's future, are its children and young people, and we shortchange or ignore library services to them at our peril. Tomorrow's solution to a highly technical and economically critical problem may likely spring from the very same imagination that was stimulated long before by a library storyteller's tale.

B. R.

1

Library Services for Children:
A Historical Perspective

In 1906, in one library, a report that the reading room tables were occupied with one man, one woman, and fifty-one children, prompted library administrators to set aside a separate room for the children.[1] From the beginning, children's work in libraries came in for more than its share of criticism, and its practitioners became subjects of caricaturing by others. Some attributed the ridicule to the usual "growing pains" of this new phase in library work. As one librarian described it, "We children's librarians, in the past fifteen or twenty years, have had to take a good many knocks more or less facetious from spectators of the sterner sex who are worried about the 'feminization of the library.' "[2]

However, persistence in providing library services for children drew many to their doors and this sustained the early children's librarians. These dedicated, and for the most part strong-willed women, and a few men, saw the purpose of their work on two levels: directly with the individual child and through cooperation with other civic agencies. Both modes would further reinforce the library's unique place and its importance in the community.

Of paramount importance to their pursuit of spreading the library's influence was the principle that good books had substantial moral and mental benefits for those who read them. To this end, book selection was stressed above all else. Many a prominent librarian felt that a librarian's primary duty lay in making discriminating choices which would eliminate such trivia as the widely circulated "dime novels" and leave only the best for young eyes and minds to absorb.

Anne Carroll Moore, previously mentioned as one of the early architects of library service for children, allowed for a breadth and quality in selection, recommending ,"variety to meet the needs and desires of boys and girls from the picture book age to that experience of life which is not always measured by years nor by school grade . . . the selection of classed books [should be] less like those of a school room."[3] Citing specific adult titles which she thought should also be included on the children's shelves she stated further, "The principle of selection should be to provide the best standard novels . . . without lowering the standard of that taste for good reading which is the chief purpose in shelving such a collection in a children's room."[4] The children's librarian in such instances was expected to have a thorough knowledge of these titles in order to guide the child's reading intelligently.

Second only to the literature was the concern that the library assume a role in the community among other agencies serving the child. Its role was not that of a "detached social force"[5] and therefore did not exempt it from active work with people in the schools, including the teachers and parents. At the turn of the century, every effort was made particularly to reach the immigrant population which had settled in the urban areas. Work with children of immigrant and working parents was especially vigorous, since these parents were often the most reluctant to visit the public library. There was a two-pronged goal in relation to the foreign born: to keep children, through books, in contact with their heritage, and to use books as a means of assuring their assimilation into a new culture. In one informal survey at her library, Mary Wright Plummer informed her audiences at the Friends' Library Association of Philadelphia and at the New York Library Club that "of one hundred children [questioned] sixty-eight reported that other members of the family used the library . . . thirty-two reported themselves the only borrowers . . . fifty-seven children reported that they were read to at home [or that they read to younger siblings.] Seventy out of the hundred children answering, used no libraries also."[6] Sunday school libraries, the precursors for many families of the public library children's rooms, were also concerned with establishing reading habits and proper book selection, but by the nature of their association they were more limited in the scope of the materials they made available.

Methods of presenting the literature to children were no less novel than contemporary practices, with book talks and storytelling, lantern slides, exhibits, reading clubs, and "quiet" games in some libraries. Periodicals were seen as natural additions to the book collection and were considered useful not only for their articles, but for their illustrations, which could sometimes be displayed on a bulletin board.

As work with children progressed, practical aspects of administration had to be considered. The most complex of these was the development of the job description for the person who would work with the children and the subsequent making of an assignment to the position. All agreed that the children's librarian should first of all be knowledgable in the literature, have some acquaintance with child psychology and educational principles, love children, and be specially trained to work with them. Ideally, she would also be thoroughly familiar with the school curriculum, since children and their teachers used the public library to supplement their school work. It was considered desirable that the librarian possess some degree of technical skill in order to organize the collection and administer the program.

There seems to have been no question about the library's important civic function in the democratization and social development of the individual. Like the public school, it was free to all, rich and poor alike. It was felt that the library conferred a special passport to citizenship through the medium of the printed word, affording an entree and encouraging assimilation into American society and culture. For this reason, both schools and the homes of working parents and the poor were targeted recipients of book deposits, as were playgrounds and recreational centers. If the library stressed first the influence and value of "good" or "the best" books, reaching out to parents, teachers, and other adults in the lives of children was a closely related second imperative. Both the books and the adult models and motivators were understood to be central to helping children to develop discriminating literary tastes, and to promote a lifelong love of reading and the "library habit."

It appears to have been an unwritten objective of the early days, too, that public library use would supplement school work and enrich learning, an acknowledgement of the fact that the school was the primary institution of formal instruction. It was readily recognized also that the school was the most significant agency with which the public librarian assigned to children's services must certainly cooperate.

It is interesting to note that those who shaped children's library services at their beginning did so with a broad vision: while embracing the library's overall traditional objective of selecting, preserving, and providing materials in order to produce a "more enlightened citizenry" they, at the same time, advanced the contemporary objective of serving as a source of information in the community. They reached out to the schools, the playgrounds, and recreational centers to find the underserved and the unserved.

The best and the brightest of those who pioneered library service, and those who followed them, maintained this balanced concern, not just for the criteria and qualities of the books they would select, but for the children who were to be introduced to them. Anne Carroll Moore, in the forefront of those who insisted on the best in books for children, was also among the first to endorse extending the work outside of the library and initiating unique and innovative approaches to book-related programming for children. Commenting at an American Library Association meeting on "how far the library should go in relating its work to that of other institutions," she advised that "a firsthand knowledge of the aims, objects and method of work of all the forces at work in a given community and a perception of their interrelationship is essential if we wish to do away with the present tendency to duplicate work which is already being carried on by more effective agencies. . . . The aim should be to make [the library's] own work so clear to the community in which it is placed, that it will command the respect and support of every citizen."[7]

Harriet Long, one of the great library school teachers of children's literature and children's services in the School of Library Science at Western Reserve University from the early 1930s through 1957, confirmed in *Rich the Treasure*, the importance of guidance to children in their reading choices, but also the need "to encourage lifelong education . . . to help the child develop to the full his personal ability and his social understanding, and to serve as a social force in the community together with other agencies concerned with the child's welfare."[8]

Unfortunately, for a considerable period of time, the heavy emphasis on "the book" and its quality was interpreted by many, both inside and outside of the children's work specialization, to mean that selection criteria were the means, end, and almost sole preoccupation of children's librarians. This led to the perception by some observers that children's librarians were inclined to be "precious," elitist, and more interested in their own reaction to books than in those of the children for whom the books were intended. It is perhaps due to such misperceptions, and also to a lack of clarity in interpreting purpose, goals, and benefits, that those who engage in children's library services have endured, and continue to endure, varying degrees of conflict, antagonism, or belittlement. This is for the most part internal, born of a fight for status and resources within institutions—public libraries—that are facing the challenge of supporting an information revolution while being ever more constrained by the lack of funds. Externally, in the community, children's services are usually taken for granted. Greatly appreciated by those whose children use them, their broader, long-range implications for a literate workforce and citizenry are probably little understood in most communities.

2

The Impact of Four Studies/Reports on Library Services for Children

The Public Library Inquiry (1950)

Several studies of the public library have provided, periodically, a perspective on the institution at various points in its history. These have charted, and indeed recommended, shifts in goals, administrative perceptions, or directions for future growth and management. No other study has produced the long-lasting sense of security and accomplishment of that engendered by the one in which Robert D. Leigh described the children's room and librarians as "the classic success of the public library."[1] This oft-cited phrase became a proud testimonial in defense of children's services in public libraries that was used well into the opulent 1960s.

However, sometimes overlooked in the report were some other conclusions which suggested imminent challenges to these very classically successful services to children in the public library. Leigh noted the coming to an end of a past in which the reading-learning practices in elementary and secondary schools had limited students almost entirely to required texts with the result that "the public library had a free field in which to encourage and serve the voluntary reading opportunities from a wide range of children's books, a practice which eventually contributed to the appearance and growth of school libraries."[2]

The Public Library Inquiry examined existing patterns of delivery of library services to children then available through both school and public libraries. There were "unified systems" in which public libraries adopted school libraries as branches, with attendant administrative problems. There were instances in which local boards of education functioned as the library board or the public library board was appointed by the community's board of education. Where school and public libraries operated as separate entities, there were instances of voluntary cooperative activities in some situations, while in others neither institution communicated with or seemed to know of the other's existence. Exemplary ways of communicating were discovered in some communities, where the two agencies effectively complemented each other's work in providing library services to children. In these instances, personnel held joint book selection sessions, shared a unified cataloging system, or provided in either location a parents' or teachers' collection.

The failure of the school library to enlarge its concept of curriculum needs to include "all children's literature" was seen as one of its limitations, as was its lack of accessibility to parents and children after school hours or during vacation periods.[3] Reference is made to an influential corps of administrators in large city schools and colleges of education who viewed public library–school cooperation "as a transitional phase in the transfer of a function from one institution to another."[4] These people anticipated that the advent of the year-round school would eventually lead to the school as the site of all library services to children.

The State of New York, Report of the Commissioner of Education's Committee on Library Development (1970)

The sense of pride in achievement enjoyed by children's librarians in public libraries brought about by the accolade in the *Public Library Inquiry* report was disturbed, if not visibly shattered, by the recommendations made by a committee on library development in its report to the State Commission of Education in New York. Taking into account new advances in communication, it strongly advocated resource sharing and networking, which would facilitate delivery of information services and accessibility to all library users in the state. It deplored the lack of clear definition of the mission of public libraries as compared to school, college and university, and special libraries.

In identifying categories of library users, children were set apart by reason of their age. The committee's first statement under the heading "Library Services to Children" was: "The elementary school media center should have the responsibility and the capacity to meet *all* the library needs of all children except those in health, welfare and correctional institutions. (The term "children" in this context is defined as that group of users now served by children's rooms in public libraries—usually pre-school through grade six.)"[5]

The committee outlined methods of implementing this basic premise, recommending more extensive state budget support for school library resources, subsidies for nonpublic schoolchildren, extension of the traditional open hours of school, sufficient resources to cover assignments, accessibility to the school media center by the community, and a statewide media network to meet the needs of students and teachers.

It was suggested that the media centers could make available nonbook materials, plan and operate cooperative projects with other libraries, and provide advisory services to parents concerned with children's individual reading needs. Some of the legal and administrative details would involve the school administrative staff locally and on the state level; restrictions on all children being served in the public schools would be removed. The public library's province was seen to be the acquisition of children's materials for adult use or to provide services to children who needed access to adult materials. Rare or historical collections of children's literature in which adults are interested could be located in any type of library and accessible through a networking system. Above all, the report strongly deplored competition for library funds between the public library and the schools.

The chief justification for the recommendations was economic efficiency, since duplication of funding would be eliminated and the public library freed to improve services to young adults and adults. Other factors on which the recommendations rested included: the greater number of school library outlets available to children; the wide range of equipment and media in schools; the curriculum oriented context of the library program; and the school's resources for gathering information on children's interests and special needs.

Problems raised at preliminary hearings in 1969 before its official publication were considered and noted in the final report. Among these were the compulsory, school-related use versus the voluntary use of library facilities; the possible diminution of parent involvement in and sharing of library experiences with children; and a "concern that the doctrine of pluralism will be seriously violated . . . by placing so critical a social function . . . in an institution which already shapes an increasingly large proportion of the lives of children as the school inevitably does."[6]

The National Commission on Libraries and Information Science (NCLIS) (1975)

Access and networking were the key considerations in the commission's proposal to develop a national program for libraries. The National Commission viewed the aggregate resources of libraries in the United States as a totality of the nation's recorded cultural and intellectual achievement and growth; it perceived in the development of new technology the potential for unifying these information resources. The commission's plan was developed to facilitate access and coordination of information through a nationwide network. Its major program objectives were "to strengthen, develop or create where needed, human and material resources which are supportive of high quality library and information services; and to join together the library and information facilities in the country, through a common pattern of organization, uniform standards, and shared communications."[7] The commission's program particularly underscored the realities of changing conditions and the inability of many libraries to manage the mounting information explosion. Its proposed national plan would, the commission believed, incorporate timely technological knowledge and systems of sharing resources, which would reduce costs while providing maximum access to library units of all sizes.

Existing public libraries were characterized in the NCLIS proposals as being closely involved with community residents but beset with multiple problems, financial and otherwise. The child was seen primarily as a user of the school library, which the commission said is "often . . . his [the child's] first exposure to information resources and molds his information behavior for the future. Thus, the school library plays an essential part in readying the child for his adult role in society. . . . Access to the broad resources of a nationwide network would provide added value by increasing the child's opportunity for independent study and adding to his ability to become a literate, well-informed citizen."[8]

The statement above is worth noting, even though the commission acknowledged the deficiencies among school libraries which exist "in most cases." Operation of school libraries at a level below ALA/AASL standards, book and audiovisual collections too small to support school curriculum, and inadequate staffing and space are among the deficiencies specifically cited. The report, however, commended school libraries for their impressive sets of standards or guidelines, which are in fact goals for most schools.

Many of the conclusions stated in the NCLIS plan of 1975 reflected those of the New York State report. This may have been because public library administrators did not make a strong case for the importance and viability of public library services to children during the information gathering stage of either report. Perhaps some were hesitant about coming out strongly on the matter because the absence of good cost–benefit measures made it difficult to justify an advocacy role for children's services.

The Free Library and the Revitalization of Philadelphia: A Program for the 1980s (1981)

Dr. Lowell A. Martin, a prominent library consultant who had completed a most detailed study of the Chicago Public Library (published as *Library Response to Urban Change*) conducted the Philadelphia study also. In it, he cites statistics and discusses the problems inherent in assuring the healthy survival of this traditionally splendid library. Recommendations are made not only for bare survival, but for maintenance of programs within Philadelphia's budget constraints. Goals and objectives are defined and priorities assigned. Some shifting of former objectives and priorities was deemed necessary to allow the library to meet the challenges of change and to allow for the depletion of budgets. Although Dr. Martin does not give in the study a very detailed presentation of population statistics or characteristics, except as they relate to the use of the library at the time of the study, he profiles a nearly archetypical large urban library situation in a city with a large inner-city population and a declining school enrollment.

One significant statement about reading and public library service to children emerged from the study in Philadelphia: "Unless reading is nurtured by stimulation and guidance that shows its rewards, the skill is little used except under compulsion, and for many it becomes a facility employed only when there is no alternative. Children's librarians in public libraries have demonstrated that they can maintain reading interest in many youngsters, and with more time and resources they could reach more of the younger generation."[9]

Martin and his associates recommended that the school library's role be that of sole source for study materials, and that the Free Library should avoid duplication in this area. If this were the case, the implication is that the public library would be freed to pursue its mission of promoting reading enjoyment and the habit of leisure reading. Statistics given in the 1981 study show that the Free Library's circulation had, in 1965, almost doubled from 3,894,029 to 6,313,822. During the next fifteen years, except for a brief period in the 1970s, a steady loss in circulation—attributed largely to a loss in juvenile use—resulted in a drop of fifty-three percent.[10] The exodus of middle class families from the city and a lower birth rate were among the contributing factors. The growth of school libraries and the impact of television had also played a part. Nevertheless, the study recommends that the branch libraries in the system remain as the neighborhood outlets for library service to children and young teenagers, and even suggests expanding space for them in areas previously allotted to adult readers. With expanded service and space in these neighborhood units, and adequate staff (with at least two professional librarians) to operate a branch, Philadelphia Free Library, Martin believes, should be able to maintain its commitment to good library services to children. Priorities outlined for this approach to service for children include activities or programs such as story hours, reading clubs, multimedia and preschool programs. The recommendations suggest greater use of audiovisual materials and childhood "classics," as well as subject content relevant to the children's own experience by librarians in programming, and greater direct use of these materials by children and young adults themselves.

The report advocates a team approach to their common clientele by school and public librarians. With shared knowledge of individual children's capabilities, characteristics, and interests available and shared by both professionals, and with joint program planning, there would be reinforcement of both programs, benefits to the children, and new dimensions added to the professional status of the librarians. A strong case is made for supplementing or complementing, without duplicating, school-related materials, since the public library cannot possibly satisfy all student demands. All of this would require a concerted effort between school and public library administrators and an acquisitions policy that would result in the desired collection for each institution. The intent is that budgets would go further if allocated toward general or pleasure-reading materials in the public library, once they were relieved of supplying materials for school assignments.

A major problem with drawing the line between what is and what is not school-related material is, in this writer's view, that this very much depends on the interests and predilections of a given child, and the expectations and the kinds of assignments given by individual teachers. Assuming that we are talking about trade or "library" books, as opposed to text materials, one child's school-related book may be another's pleasure reading, or the same book may be both to a given child at different times or at the same time, depending upon context and occasion. These would not be easy decisions to make or to write policies about.

Other recommendations, although somewhat unique to the situation of the Free Library, nevertheless relate to concerns elsewhere. Questions exist about the relative value of nonprint media in public library collections, and also about the extension of preschool programming at a time when the enrollment of school-age children has declined. The Free Library has been noteworthy for its large percentage of children registered—at the time of the study some forty-three percent of the population, as opposed to twenty-eight percent of the adult population. Children's books have circulated at a rate of 3.1 books per child, as compared with 2.0 books per adult.[11]

By reaffirming the neighborhood branch as the logical place for emphasis on services to children and youth, Martin has recognized the generally limited mobility of children in their communities, as well as their need for intellectual and recreational opportunities as close to home as possible.

Echoes of the 1950 *Public Library Inquiry* can be heard in this study as Martin discusses objectives: "Children's librarians are an exception . . . they do not say they give the children 'what they want' . . . but [try] to open the joy of reading to youngsters . . . to develop their understanding of people and the world . . . to stimulate their imaginations. . . . What remains of the past aura of the public library is being satisfied by the juvenile program."[12]

The implication here of reader development objectives contrasts with the emerging patterns of service in libraries where administrators see demand as the overriding book selection criterion. Statements of purpose and benefit by children's librarians are considered to be ineffective and unconvincing in the absence of quantitative measurements that show the cost-effectiveness of services.

The full impact of the Philadelphia study and the more recent San Francisco study by Dr. Martin still lies ahead. However, Martin's recommendation to close some branches in the San Francisco area produced, in 1981 and 1987, an immediate public reaction which applied sufficient pressure on the legislators to cause them to supply adequate funding to prevent the closings.[15] The effect of these studies so far has been to alert the public to the present, and possibly future, plight of the library, and to sharpen awareness of an institution vital and unique in the individualized cultural, educational, and informational opportunities it offers.

3

Management Concerns:
External Non-Library Issues

Management of any enterprise, if it is to be effective, requires a great variety of skills as well as a range of background information on the part of the manager. Management concerns are broad in scope and of many kinds, but generally speaking they fall into two main categories: those which impact the organization or program from the outside and those which affect it from within. External concerns themselves are of two kinds: the economic, political, and social trends and climate within which the library functions, especially demographics, legislation and funding appropriations, and national and state priorities; and professional matters, such as state and national standards and guidelines. These, with the goals and objectives of the parent organization, become internal guidelines for the program manager.

Examples of some external trends and issues of the economic, social, and political variety, and their influence upon the operation of the children's library services of the public library are discussed in this chapter. Those cited are by no means all that must be considered.

The Political and Economic Powerlessness of Children

In an era of high-pressure lobbying, political action committees, and single issue voting, children and youth have few effective advocates. Organizations like the Children's Defense Fund, steered by the redoubtable and tireless Marion Wright Edelman, gather facts, testify, and lobby on behalf of children, as do a number of education-oriented groups. None of these, however, can make the major political contributions of which big business and many large organizations are capable. Children do not produce; they do not influence foreign trade or jobs or the stock market. They cost money. They do not have clout or the means to strike or to close down workplaces. They do not even vote, and many of the parents and other adults who should be representing them at the polls do not bother to vote either.

The number of births has been smaller over the past decade or so. At the same time, other groups have gathered numbers and risen to power: older people who are learning to flex their political and economic muscles; the young two-income professional couples, urban and suburban, who have often elected the perks of "the good life" over a major commitment of time and money to children.

Does all of this have an impact on children's services in the public library? Certainly it does. There are no funds especially earmarked for public library service to children and youth at the national level. City managers, trustees, and many library directors see children's services as a low-priority item on their agendas, an area that can be, and often is, cut at budget time. There seems to be the impression that the program can muddle along with inadequate staff and far fewer other resources than should be available to do the job right. Children's services, being largely traditional, are thought of as being "old hat." They have always been, as has been stated earlier, such an area of strength in most public libraries that the idea seems to be that they will keep going on their own without much support. Unless the user group—or its adult representatives—are unusually knowledgable about what they should be able to expect the library to be doing for the young, and unusually articulate in demanding it, children and youth in the community often get the leftovers.

The Lives of Millions of Children in the United States Are Ridden With Disaster

According to the Statistical Abstracts for 1985 (the latest available figures at the date of writing), 20.9 percent of the child population (under eighteen years of age) lived in homes headed by a single, usually female, head of household. The vast majority of these are living in poverty. Twelve and a half million children altogether are living in poverty, or one in five, according to Marion Wright Edelman in an October 1984 article in the *American Journal of Orthopsychiatry.*

She states also that thirty-five states as of that date had reported an increase in child abuse cases, and that fourteen states had an increase in death from child abuse. As of that date, too, about three million families were homeless, and the number of these has risen substantially since then because of lost jobs and depressed industries.

Does this have an impact on children's services in public libraries? Indeed it does. Children's librarians in communities across the country are finding themselves with a child and family clientele quite different from the old one composed of mother, father, and the standard two or three children, properly bathed, dressed, fed, and sheltered. Single mothers—an increasing number of whom are teenagers themselves—struggle for survival with insufficient skills. More than half a million babies were born to these adolescents in 1985.[1] The mothers are often unable to get even the basics done, let alone read aloud at bedtime, be the child's first teacher, motivator, and intellectual stimulator.

Librarians are seeing many more emotionally disturbed children, as well as victims of drug and other abuses, and are increasingly becoming more involved with child care personnel, provider mothers, and other surrogate parents. More requests for information and program assistance are coming in from institutions, underscoring the necessity for more community contacts, adaptation of programming hours and content, and knowledge of referral resources in the community where parents and other concerned adults can get help for children. The children's librarian is being forced to function more as part of a team, to accumulate community information and to share it on behalf of these millions of troubled children and young people. At the same time, the library experience for children must be geared to trying to stimulate imaginations and to expand horizons and hope through often traditional and effective elements: the story hour, the singing game, and the characteristic order and quiet.

But while the children's library service staffers perform these functions, they must be newly conscious of doing so in a context of their awareness of political strategies. They must realize that *public* understanding of these services is not only of major importance in the total scheme of public library service, but in terms of the future for the individual children and for the society.

Mothers Working Outside the Home

According to figures cited in the American Statistical Index (from the U.S. Bureau of Labor Statistics *News Bulletin* for 1987), 34,066,000 children in the nation had working mothers in 1986. Of these 8.8 million mothers, 6.6 million had children under six years of age. This compares with 27,500,000 children just seven years earlier, a jump of nearly a million a year during this period.[2] Obviously, this has changed the way in which libraries perform their functions, as well as the hours and days of the week in which mothers can be expected to participate in programs in any numbers, or even to bring children to the library. It has wrought drastic changes in family eating habits (more fast food, more meals out, meals not eaten together); in perceptions of family life which children bring to their library and reading experiences; in the home reinforcement of reading and other learning habits. Most significant, it has spawned the "latchkey" children, children who are on their own between the end of school and the time one or both parents come home. These children either let themselves into their homes to be alone and watch TV, visit with friends, or hang out on the street, or, possibly go to the library. Figures released in the fall of 1987 show that twenty-five percent of children in this country qualify as latchkey children.[3]

Illiteracy and the Drive to Overcome It

Instead of going away, as it was supposed to do in a country which devotes significant resources to universal education, the incidence of functional illiteracy and semi-literacy has worsened in the past several decades. The often-quoted and generally accepted figure—since exact figures can never really be known—is that at least one-fifth of adults in this country cannot read at a level consonant with their own expectations of entrepreneurial or even skilled jobs, or the needs of an increasingly technological society. The "sustain" rate of reading capability (maintenance of literacy after leaving school), even of those who have graduated from high school, is woefully low. Parents who cannot read, and the millions more who can but don't—thus allowing their skills to atrophy—cannot be expected to model reading enjoyment for children or to be able to reinforce good reading habits at home. All of the recent reports on improving education and the importance of early reading development, among them *A Nation at Risk*[4] and *First Lessons*[5] (both issued by the U.S. Department of Education), stress the necessity of reading-behavior modeling and reinforcement by parents.

Why, ask the educators, does this situation obtain? The answer comes back loud and clear in the reports themselves. It relates directly to the low priority accorded to children's services in public libraries: there is not enough support for them to enable them to reach out to all the children—especially the preschoolers—who need them. It is the children's librarians who emphasize the enjoyment in reading, and foster the love of books and the desire to read them. It is the children's librarians who can work with the parents of young children (or their surrogates) to instill the desire to read and the habit of reading without which decoding skills will not be sustained by practice and will deteriorate with disuse in after-school life.

The love of reading, the motivation to read that has been fanned successfully for a comparatively few children by children's librarians for the past hundred years, is now seen as economically and socially desirable for all. It is not necessarily seen as desirable for all children because it will enrich their lives, offer them ideas and possibilities, and help them to escape from lack and overcome limitation. It is seen as necessary for those children to read competently—computer screens, manuals, instructions—so that they can be productive for the economy when they grow up.

Does this have a huge potential for beneficial impact on the fortunes and development of children's library services? It does, but only if we are alert enough and energetic enough to exploit it vigorously. For example, the second national White House Conference on Libraries and Information Services will probably now take place in the early nineties; it will be a public forum for tying these and all the other issues raised here to the need for support of children's library services and resources.

Television/Video and Related Electronics

Television has changed society, childhood, and the climate in which libraries must operate in so many ways that it is not possible even to name them all, let alone discuss them. It has altered and limited vocabulary, concepts of sequence and passed time, the concept of death and its finality, and the image of human relationships generally. It has brought violence, crime, urban decay, cruelty, drug addiction, rape, and suicide into view as everyday, familiar, even normal, events. It has introduced children early to "situation ethics" and fostered superficial perceptions, along with the belief that the "quick fix" is the best, and perhaps the only, one. It has bred intolerance for anything that does not happen immediately. Constant viewing has led to a shortened attention span in many children, disinclination to commit self or time to any one thing for very long, and confusion about cause and effect. Most significant of all, perhaps, children have been subject to constant sales pitches and been trained from infancy to see themselves as voracious consumers, rather than contributors or idea generators.

In fairness, something must be said for the benefits that television has bestowed upon the now nearly two generations which have been reared on it. People born since the middle of this century have been exposed to a smattering—actually disconnected fragments—of information about people, places, and events undreamed of by children of an earlier time. They have been "present" at occasions like that of man walking on the moon. They have had a great variety of human behaviors modeled for them, and have had the opportunity at least to see and hear sports of all kinds from tennis to wrestling, natural history and exploration, concerts, operas, and "live" theatre performances. They have even been introduced to books by some of the better children's programs, as well as to basic word and number skills and positive ethical concepts. But these benefits have outweighed the negative messages, by and large, only for those children who have been prepared for positive planned viewing by and with parents and other adult family members, who could help them to put it all together.

Whatever television has done for good or for ill, it is here, and everywhere, to stay. The managers of library services for children must take into consideration its power and its influences. They must make use of the valuable and positive, and counteract the bad to the extent possible, offering alternative forms of entertainment and information, discussion of what is viewed, and criteria for discriminating viewing.[6]

Demographics

A group of other significant factors affecting the lives of children and having, therefore, a major impact on library services for them, can be dealt with under the heading of demographics.

In addition to the overall aging of the population, there is now an established trend toward more children being born to women between the ages of twenty-eight and thirty-five. These women, having started their careers, have elected to have their children at a later age, and will be responsible for a new generation of preschoolers. The declining teenage and young adult population may suggest to many libraries that attention be turned to the thirty-five to fifty-four-year-old age group, as well as to the under-four-year-olds. The resurgent birthrate will demand increased support for all facets of service to young children in the near future, as well as to their older parents.[7]

There is the matter of highly mobile populations, also. Workers, no longer tied to the economy of a physical place, such as a family farm or particular plant, follow the jobs. In recent years, we have seen a surge of population to the Sun Belt states of the south and west, and now we see it reversing itself in part for a new surge to the northeast. The latest figures show that 12,000,000 children, one through nineteen years of age, move annually.[8] Such frequent uprooting has an obvious impact on children and on the fabric of family life, and many implications for library services.

An Influx of Immigration and an Increase of Minority Populations

Children in nearly every region of the country, even in the smallest towns and most rural areas, are now more conscious than ever before of cultural plurality—languages, customs, food, skin tones different from those to which children were previously accustomed. The Task Force on Library and Information Services to Cultural Minorities, convened by NCLIS, chose to limit its study and recommendations to the four major cultural minority groups in the United States: Afro-Americans, American Indians, Asian-Americans, and Hispanic-Americans—all of them primarily nonwhite and comprising altogether about one-fifth of the nation's population.

Among its findings, the NCLIS Task Force pointed out that "minorities are growing at a faster rate than the population as a whole, and during the next three decades, the proportion of the American population of white and of European ancestry will decline at a rapid rate." These demographics, said the task force, have "serious implications for America's economic planning, the educational system, and library and information services. . . . Since minorities will constitute a major segment of the work force and will contribute substantially to the economic well-being of the nation, the United States government must be certain that its minority populations

receive quality education and are guaranteed access to library resources and information."[9]

It is useful to note that since 1960, Hispanics have averaged forty
percent of the total immigration to the United States and are expected
to account for fifteen percent of the population of the United States
by the year 2020. Asians are the second major minority group which
is immigrating at an increasing rate into this country.[10]

Health Problems—Physical, Mental, and Emotional

This cluster of health problems will demand closer attention from
library program managers in the future. The effects of poor nutrition
both before and after birth are now, and will continue to be in the
future, factors to be considered by all who serve children. Inherited
addictions and predisposition to addictions will take their toll. Depression and alienation among children has increased at an alarming
rate, as have alcoholism, drug abuse, and suicide. All of this underscores the need for children and young adult librarians to take greater
initiatives in making common cause with all other youth-serving
agencies that are on the front lines of the fight to counteract the
causes of the need children feel to escape life, instead of meeting it
with anticipation.

*   *   *   *

We conclude this selection of broad, societal, external factors
which have an impact on children's library services with a quotation
from an article in *Top of the News* by a children's librarian reacting to a
talk at the first White House Conference on Library and Information
Services in 1979:

"The scope of knowledge in children's service is larger than the
content of children's books. It extends to knowledge of society and
its concerns. . . . Acquisition of reading skills and a lifelong reading
habit have long been goals of children's service, but do we really
understand the relationship of those important goals to the well-
being of the larger society?" Pauline Wilson sees the children's
librarian's role "heightened because of the emphasis on the electronic
medium, television." She concludes, "We need to know what we are
doing when we prescribe for the child. We need to have at least some
notion of what the consequences of our prescription might be, its

social, political, economic consequences; we need to know what kind of world we may be helping to bring into being."[11]

It is important to have a keen and current grasp of the national and state framework for services to youth and of every trend and political nuance that will affect their future. Says Regina Minudri, director of library services in Berkeley, California, president of the American Library Association in 1986, and a former youth services librarian, "It is equally important that you know what is going on in your own local situation. You should be aware of the political context which surrounds your library. It is important that you be cognizant of changes in income levels, education levels, populations changes, things which can be predictors of future trends."[12]

Growing concern about all of these matters has spurred existing leadership in the children's field into more intensive action over recent years. There has been a good response by children's librarians to the planning process proposed for public libraries; it has prompted assessment of roles and goals, and formulation of guidelines and plans for implementing them. We will deal now with this next set of external factors which have an impact on management of children's library service programs.

4

Management Concerns:
External Professional Factors

A primary responsibility for the manager of the program for children's services in the public library is to keep in active touch with the best creative thinking, forward planning, and recommendations of the profession's leadership including, of course, but not limited to, youth services. What is new and interesting in reference services for adults, for example, will have its impact also on services to children and youth; what's happening in college libraries will affect the not-too-distant futures of today's preschool patrons. It should go without saying—but unfortunately experience has proved that this is not always the case—that children's and young adult library profession-als in public libraries should be deeply and intensely interested in every development affecting school library media programs, as well as in educational policy and trends in general.

Naturally, library professionals serving children are inclined to be most concerned and knowledgable about professional matters bear-ing directly on their own jobs, those having to do with standards and guidelines, goals and objectives, performance measurements, confer-ences and reports. There is a vital and symbiotic relationship among these that it is helpful to understand clearly.

A "standard" is, according to *Webster's New Collegiate Dictionary*, a "means of determining what a thing should be," and also "some-thing established by authority." A standard of library service adopted by a state agency or by a professional organization implies that that agency or organization expects compliance with that standard, and may even intend to enforce such compliance if in a position to do so.

Adherence to a standard may be a requirement for accreditation, or even a legal matter. Too often, unfortunately, standards relating to library services and resources are couched in terms of bare minimums, and in very vague and ill-defined terms at that. They are based, generally speaking, on the average past performance of a cross-section of libraries, rather than on the performance of only the very best ones, and thereby are considered "realistic." They deal for the most part with the quantitative elements that go into the library's performance.

A "guideline" or "set of guidelines" carries the connotation of recommended standards or ways of proceeding. Confusingly, the terms are often used interchangeably, although they mean different things to different people and in different situations. In general, however, we see that guidelines deal more with goals—that is, higher levels of attainment—than do standards. This is true especially of documents prepared by professional associations, as opposed to those set forth by an official governing body such as a state agency or school district.

"Performance measurements" or "output measures" are data showing what actually takes place in a given area of activity. Performance measures can be wisely used as a precursor to the development of standards in order to judge what it takes in personnel, materials, facilities, and budget to produce certain results in the running of the library or its program. Output measures are used in evaluating progress toward the achievement of goals and objectives.

"Goals" are the broad, overarching attainments desired. They may be of short-term or long-range variety. They are defined in the dictionary as "the end toward which effort is directed." They are reached through gaining sequential measurable objectives—stepping stones to attainment of the ultimate goal.

Statewide Leadership for Development and Coordination of Services to Children through Local Public Libraries

A 1981 survey by a committee of the ALA's Public Library Association attempted to assess the amount of leadership offered and the responsibility taken for the development and coordination of library services to children by the state library agency. The survey revealed that at that time fourteen states had a children's specialist serving full time as a consultant in that area of work. Twenty states had a general consultant on the state library staff who devoted some time to children's services, and in ten states the state librarians themselves were said to assume responsibility for overseeing this area. Four states reported a position vacant, and the remaining two assigned responsibility to the assistant state librarian. The survey also found that only four states indicated that they had developed written standards or guidelines for children's services.[1]

Efforts to update this information failed to clarify, at least in terms of numbers, the present status of consultants at the state level trained in children's services. From informal information-gathering efforts, however, it became clear that more attention was being paid to children's and youth services by several members of the state agency consultant staff—at least in some states. Faith Hektoen, a longtime state agency consultant in Connecticut with a strong background in children's library work, now provides across-the-board consultant services and no longer devotes full time to youth services alone. She offered the view, in an August 1987 telephone conversation, that this is far better, because it gets the consultant "out of isolation" and forces attention to the overall program of the public library in which children's services play an important role. In this way, she can bring to children's librarians with whom she works increased awareness of some of the external factors that have an impact on the entire library program, and can also reinforce concern for children's services in directors and other staff members with whom she works. William Asp, director of the Office of Library Development and Services in Minnesota, would like to have, and is still working on getting, a children's services-trained member of the consultant staff, but he agreed that if such a consultant were hired he would probably want her special expertise applied to the library program overall. Meanwhile, according to an August 1987 telephone conversation with Mr. Asp, Suzanne H. Mahmoodi, full-time continuing education specialist on the state agency's staff (one of the few such positions), is working with children's and young adult librarians in the state to develop a list of competencies and skills required by them for quality services to youth.

It would seem, perhaps, that integration of awareness and responsibility for consultation in children's services may be the wave of the future. New Jersey's document, a combination of state-of-the-art findings and a goals- and objectives-oriented action plan which will be further discussed in the next section defines the work of a consultant with a major recommendation for its action plan that "the New Jersey State Library should assume responsibility for the development and support of children's and young adult services. It should designate research/resource centers for interlibrary loan, supplemental reference, and preservation of historical and research materials in children's and young adult services. It should gather, prepare and disseminate statewide information, data and research relative to youth services. It should provide consultative services, sponsor continuing education activities, and focus grant programs to foster library development. It should assign responsibility for the specialty field to qualified staff and involve that staff in overall Library Development Bureau activities so as to bring the specialist perspective to them. It should provide leadership and coordination in youth services for the state."[2]

The detail for this recommendation includes the statement that "the New Jersey State Library should have consultants for children's and young adult services who work with public libraries and related organizations and who participate in the overall activities and planning of the Library Development Bureau. The time devoted solely to youth services should be no less than twenty-five percent and no more than fifty percent of a full-time position."[3]

A good part of the problem of lack of leadership and apparent listlessness, at a time when development of children's services should be moving strongly ahead, lies in the serious scarcity of children's specialists graduating from library schools. Many factors have been blamed for the fact that there are few children's librarians available for positions at *any* level: state, regional, or local. They include: the current and projected decline in births and the child population; the growing emphasis on data transferral and computerized services; the services, often seen as competitive, of the school library; the fact that service to people, especially small, "powerless" people, is out of fashion; the lower salaries generally to be expected for those who serve people rather than machines; and the lack of a planned career ladder in the field. Related to all these is the fact that the graduate library schools—many of them hovering on the brink of extinction, in addition to several distinguished ones which have already closed— have seen what appeared to be the handwriting on the wall, spelling out, "No students interested in children's services," and dropped the courses in that specialty.

But the fact is that without new, energetic leadership at the local

system and state levels, the thrust for school–public library cooperation (or any other forward movement) to a meaningful, substantive
level can only stagnate. For the public library systems to deal effectively in a partnership with the district school system, there must be
something approaching equality of contribution, creativity, and clout
in the personnel involved from each agency. Without public library
children's services leadership at the state level, there is little hope for
in-state coordinated development, interstate liaison, or national input. In addition, there is the fact that many rural areas in most states
rely, when they can do so, on a state consultant's stimulus and
support for program planning, ideas, materials selection and evaluation, and the implementation of guidelines and standards. This is
especially true in areas where trained specialists in children's services
are lacking, and professional or even nonprofessional staff are expected to provide all the specialized services while they organize and
operate the agency.

State Standards, Guidelines, and Goals for Children's and Youth Services

At the time of the PLA's 1981 survey, four states responded that
they had in place standards for children's services in public libraries.
They were California and Illinois, Vermont and Virginia. Vermont's
and Virginia's standards were designed under state agency auspices,
while those of California and Illinois were developed by the children's
services sections of their respective state associations. Among the
recurrent topics covered by those standards, and ranked among those
of the highest importance, were:

- Equal access to materials, facilities, and service hours for children
- Children's services programming
- School and public library cooperation
- Clearly identified specialty areas for children
- Budget support for staff development among professionals who
  work with children
- Regular allocations for materials
- Cooperative plans with other youth and community agencies

- Outreach
- Written materials selection policy
- Statistics and record keeping concerning services to children
- Access for children to networking services

Since the time of the 1981 survey at least five more states have produced a draft or completed standards or planning guidelines for service to children and youth. They are Ohio, Michigan, Wisconsin, New York, and New Jersey.

In 1984, New York published its *Standards for Youth Services in Public Libraries of New York State*. Past presidents of the New York Library Association's youth services section, and others, formed the committee to provide "a guide by which librarians and administrators may assess the strengths and weaknesses of their youth services."

These standards address well the philosophy of service to children, collection standards, and community services, including programming and facilities. The standards were designed to cover service to both children and young adults. Staffing, management, and the specialist's role are also part of the booklet. An appendix enumerates competencies for librarians serving youth, and includes "Restricted Access to Library Materials: An Interpretation of the Library Bill of Rights," and "Free Access to Libraries for Minors." The standards are strong on philosophy, but do not fully specify quantitative measures to substantiate resource needs or the impact of the service in the public library. There are simply statements about collection size: "Approximately thirty percent of the library materials budget should be spent for children's materials. Of that amount ten to twenty-five percent should be spent on audiovisual materials for children." Under the heading "Maintenance" the standards further state, "Of the total children's materials budget, twenty-five percent should be spent for replacement." No justification for these percentages is given.[4]

The Ohio Library Association's *A Guideline to Planning Public Library Service to Children in Ohio* (adopted by the board of directors, February 10, 1984) starts off with the "Ohio Children's Library Bill of Rights" and "Free Access to Libraries for Minors." Under the heading "Personnel," a standard based on population is outlined for central services departments to follow: for populations of 30,000 and over, for 10,000 to 30,000 populations, and for under 10,000 populations. Recommendations are made as to the responsibilities of the children's librarians, with the overriding principle stated, "In every library there should be at least one person who is responsible for library services to children." In the section on materials the principle is stated as: "The library should have a written selection policy for children's materials," and the materials selected should meet community needs and interests. Sections on facilities and programming complete the roster of the main topics covered. There is an outline form for noting "Current Status," "Goals—Short Term," and "Long Term Goals."[5]

A draft has been prepared of *Standards for Public Library Service to Children and Competencies for Children's Librarians,* and issued by the Michigan Library Association's children's services division. The draft suggests standards for a budget; competencies; management and administration; facilities; materials; services, including programming; staffing; and definitions of children, "from birth through age 14, persons of age 14 and under," and of other terminology used in the document. Under goals, these standards involve basic principles as well as an outline for recording quantitative measurements in terms of specific goals. For example, the first goal listed in the section on management states, "The library shall base its program of service to children on a thorough knowledge of the needs and interests of the children it serves [according to]:

- The number of children in the library's service area who are ages five and under; four through fourteen
- In-library surveys and questionnaires
- Visits to area schools
- Output measures for children"

The second goal listed is, "To maintain accurate and up-to-date records [with regard to]:

- Percentage of children's circulation in proportion to the entire library collection
- Number of children registered as borrowers
- Number of reference questions asked and answered
- Children's collection maintained outside of the library"[6]

Sets of goals or long-range planning documents from two states are particularly notable because they incorporate or are based upon two important aids to the measurement, goal-setting, and planning process for libraries produced by the PLA. They are *A Planning Process for Public Libraries*, published by ALA in 1980,[7] and *Output Measures for Public Libraries: A Manual of Standardized Procedures*, published in 1982.[8] Both documents were refined and updated in the light of user experience in 1987. Essentially the planning process in the 1987 version remains similar,[9] "but the 1987 manual has an increased emphasis on reviewing the library's role in the community."[10]

The two states which have made full use of the basic procedures are New Jersey and Wisconsin. There is an interesting difference, however, between the two. New Jersey's, as its title indicates, deals solely with services and youth,[11] while *Wisconsin Public Library Standards* are organized by role and mission and do not treat services to children separately.[12] This means in effect that standards for service are expected to be at the same level all across the age spectrum.

The output measures for public libraries as they relate to children's services will be discussed in greater detail later in this chapter, but for now we shall examine the recommendations and standards for the two states.

New Jersey's document in terms of both its format and its content, is a work in progress. It is the result of a study conducted under the auspices of the New Jersey State Library. "It analyzes the strengths and weaknesses of [children's and young adult services] in New Jersey, drawing upon the research conducted and the experimental projects undertaken to recommend a plan for statewide action." Librarians throughout the state were involved in the process which gave particular attention to the question, How does the program of the individual library fit into the context of the statewide, multitype, cooperative network?

"The document is divided into two major sections: a State of the Art analysis of the current provision of children's and young adult services in N.J. and an Action Plan for goals, objectives and activities to improve and strengthen those services statewide." Three areas are discussed in each section: library services, program development, and resources. The following are among weaknesses identified in the state-of-the-art analysis: approximately half of the libraries in New Jersey have written plans for children's services and virtually none for young adult; children's services programs appear to emphasize

programming at the expense of collection development and information services; continuing education for children's services librarians
is required at intermediate and advanced levels, also, but most of
what exists relates to basic skills; outreach services and the related
provision of information and referral services are the weakest element
in the service plan for both children and young adults; there are
limited interactions between public libraries and other community
agencies on the local level and the bulk of these interactions are
initiated by the agencies.

Among the important objectives is to develop and strengthen
information services for youth at all levels of the network, through
supplemental reference services, interlibrary loan, and careful evaluation of pertinent statistics such as frequency, fill-rate, and turn
around time. A related objective is "to improve the provision of
community information and referral to youth," with librarians being
specially trained to provide this service. Under the goal of "Provision
of Library Services to All" is the objective "to provide direct library
services to unserved young people especially in urban areas." A
second objective here is "to stimulate communication, cooperation,
and coordination between libraries and youth-related organizations."
Action under the objective of "promot[ing] long-range planning activities for children's and young adult services in public libraries," calls
for 1) statewide guidelines for children's and young adult services to
be developed and maintained on a current basis, 2) training in
management and research skills to be provided for children's and
young adult librarians, and 3) long-range planning efforts to be
undertaken by public libraries should include youth services. The
New Jersey guidelines make an important recommendation for library staff, calling for "developing and endorsing a promotional scale
and career ladder that allows children's and young adult librarians to
advance while retaining their specialization."

This well-thought-through and well-designed set of guidelines, in
which, in its own words, "the action plan builds upon the state of
the art analysis, drawing upon the strengths to address the weaknesses," can serve as a model for others.[13]

The *Wisconsin Public Library Standards* is a formal, printed document which "incorporate[s] the very latest developments in public
library planning into our standards. As a result, there is an increased
commitment to local-level planning and evaluation."[14] Recommended
quantitative standards represent minimum levels of effort. The stan-

dards are structured in terms of the local library's selection of its
mission and the role it is gearing itself to emphasize.

Traditionally, public libraries have seen themselves as providers of all things to all people as an informational, educational,
and recreational institution. The 1987 planning manual ex-
pands these three functions into eight distinct roles or service
profiles that public libraries may carry out in their communities. [These include]:

- Community Activities Center. The library is a central focus
  point for community activities, meetings, and services.
- Community Information Center. The library is a clearinghouse for current information on community organizations,
  issues, and services.
- Formal Education Support Center. The library assists students of all ages in meeting educational objectives established during their formal courses of study.
- Independent Learning Center. The library supports individuals of all ages pursuing a sustained program of learning
  independent of any educational provider.
- Popular Materials Center. The library features current, high-
  demand, high-interest materials in a variety of formats for
  persons of all ages.
- Preschoolers' Door to Learning. The library encourages
  young children to develop an interest in reading and learning
  through services for children, and for parents and children
  together.
- Reference Library. The library actively provides timely, accurate, and useful information for community residents.
- Research Center. The library assists scholars and researchers
  to conduct in-depth studies, investigate specific areas of
  knowledge, and create new knowledge.[16]

It is evident that with the exception of the "preschoolers' door to
learning" role, these roles are not age specific and can be carried on
in terms of children, young adults, or adults. As the standards say,

"Every library varies in its ability and need to carry out all eight roles; it is critical to determine which roles the library will emphasize. This decision is based on information about the community, as well as library conditions such as size of budget, facilities, and so forth."

Standards are then laid out in this document for staffing, collection, services, public relations, and access and facilities—all of these in terms of role requirements. Certain quantitative standards relating to population are given for staffing, collection, reference services, and access. Qualitative standards are clearly spelled out. For example, "Staff in charge of a library that emphasizes its role as a Preschooler's Door to Learning [should] have formal training in child development, selecting and using materials, and planning and implementing appropriate programs and services for preschoolers, parents, and adults working with preschool children." And again, under the heading "Services—Reference and Readers Advisory": "The library cooperates with all other types of libraries in the local area to offer information service to all residents." Public school libraries are specifically mentioned earlier in this section. In the section on access and facilities, populations between 8,000 and 25,000 should expect to be able to use the library no less than fifty-six hours per week. In the same section we find the statement, "The library has allocated space for child and family use, with all materials readily available, and provides furniture and equipment designed for use by children."

Two further points should be made in reviewing this state-of-the-art set of standards, which projects expected excellence in library services to children and young adults as well as to other segments of the community. One concerns the continuing education for staff, stating: "The library annually provides opportunities for ten (10) contact hours for staff continuing education and professional activities for each full-time employee (prorated for part time employees)." The other concerns public relations, which has a full chapter of its own in the standards. An annual budget for public relations, designation of a staff member to coordinate activities, and professional quality of all printed materials and graphics are among the standards to be met. Special efforts are outlined for those libraries intent on fully implementing the role of preschoolers' door to learning.

Both of the above, continuing education and public relations, are of special importance to librarians serving youth. Keeping up with the fast-changing world of children and families requires constant attention and effort, and publicity and public relations for children's and young adult services has been nonexistent or casual at best in most libraries. Especially is it essential not only to tell about the programs and services, but to explain their full significance. At least one administrator has gone on record recently to talk about "the mind expanding activity" for which children's librarians can provide guidance,[18] but who nonetheless have failed to communicate their effectiveness to the community or even to the library administration. The Wisconsin standards indicate strongly that this must change.

These new sets of standards and guidelines emphasize building on strengths, eliminating weaknesses, in part through coordination and pooling resources, and integrating service to children and young people into the total planning and evaluation process. They can herald a new day for children's services in public libraries. Here is an opportunity for librarians serving youth to involve themselves in challenging management functions and thereby to gain visibility and dignity for their departments and for themselves on a equal footing with other managers.

Performance Measurement and Statistics

In preparation for development of the *Wisconsin Public Library Standards*, the Wisconsin division for library services conducted a study of output measures for children's public library services under the guidance of Douglas Zweizig, senior author of *Output Measures for Public Libraries*. Results were published in *Output Measures for Children's Services in Wisconsin Public Libraries: A Pilot Project—1984–85*. This study proposed the following seven output measures for children's services:

- juvenile circulation per capita juvenile
- in-library use of juvenile materials per juvenile capita
- juvenile library visits per juvenile capita
- annual juvenile program attendance per juvenile capita
- reference fill-rate for juveniles (numbers of reference transactions completed for juveniles divided by the number of reference transactions for juveniles.)
- library registration of juveniles as percentage of juvenile population.

• turnover rate of juvenile materials (annual circulation of juvenile materials divided by holdings of juvenile materials).[17]

An article prepared by the PLA's Committee on Service to Children points out that "the use of output measures for children's services is controversial. The measures raise questions about the purposes of children's services as well as their measurement."[18] The committee suggests establishing a community profile that details demographics, type, size, and availability of educational, recreational, and cultural facilities, other community information resources, transportation facilities, and other agencies in the community concerned with children. It suggests a survey of library use by adults and their awareness of the existence of services for children; a survey of children who use the library (conducted with suitable caution); and a survey of the library staff. Statistics and performance measures geared to the children's department should include the number of staff members assigned to this area. Collection size, circulation, information questions answered (type and number), number and nature of programs, number of registered borrowers, proportion of population served, and the size of the facility are also telling factors in statistics gathering. The committee reminds us that "performance measures are linked to goals and objectives, to determine what progress is being made."

In referring to the use for children's services departments, the PLA committee warns that the manual "includes information about collecting the data, but these measures and data collection techniques are intended to be used with adult services. Adapting them to measure children's services requires a precise definition of 'child' and some consideration of service patterns in which children use adult collections and services while adults borrow children's materials (for classes, for their own children, etc.) and seek guidance from children's librarians." Some strategies for appraising services for children include: recording per capita counts for circulation of materials; in-library materials use; library visits; program attendance; reference transactions; reference fill-rates; user satisfaction rates; turnover; documents delivery; and registration and use as a percentage of population.[19]

Measurement of the library's raw product, its output, in these terms is the best perhaps that can be done for now. It is more than has ever been done for most children's library services, and it is a giant step in the direction of showing something of what is accomplished with the resources devoted to this service. But it is still far from satisfying to most of us. It leaves the question of what effects, *long-range effects* on imagination, self-identity, ability to communicate, learning capacity, development of intelligence, even, our children's materials and programs really have. Maybe one day soon, one of us, or someone else who is skilled in research, will devise a study taking into account all the variables and prove that library services to children and youth *make a difference,* and that those who have them early and richly fare better in their lives than those who are cheated of them. Meanwhile, a considerable body of ethnographic or experiential study shows that this is indeed so. The U.S. Secretary of Education's recommendation, expressed in *First Lessons,*[20] that every child be signed up for a library card and the use of libraries encouraged, was launched as the National Library Card Campaign, a joint effort of NCLIS and ALA, late in 1987. The indisputable relationship between library services to children and the national interest in lifelong literacy and continuing learning has thus been drawn and dramatized as never before.

Seeking Directions Toward Excellence: Other Reports

As more state and national groups convene to examine the status of children's and young adult services in libraries, often now referred to simply as youth services, more objective studies and solutions will emerge and will help to provide adequate, even overwhelming, justification for excellent library services to youth.

Good examples of such productive meetings took place in 1986 and 1987: one in New York State called, "Libraries Serving Youth," and the other in Illinois—the Allerton Park Institute, a national conference sponsored jointly by the Graduate School of Library and Information Science of the University of Illinois at Urbana and ALA's three youth-serving divisions (AASL, ALSC, and YASD.)

The report of the New York conference, which included 160 state-based participants from a variety of library structures and types concerned with youth services, plus nationally known speakers from outside the state, is entitled *Libraries Serving Youth: Directions for Service in the 1990s.*[21] Participant discussion was based upon advance reading of a discussion paper and four documents referenced in the paper:

Standards for Youth Services in Public Libraries of New York State,[22] *Becoming a Nation of Readers,*[23] *A Nation at Risk,*[24] and *Realities.*[25] The conference announcement cited elements of the "steady erosion over the last twenty years in our capacity to deliver the service":

- No state-level youth consultant for public libraries
- Forty percent of school librarians eligible to retire in the next five years
- Fewer library school courses in youth services and materials
- Inadequate salaries and absence of career ladders
- Steady erosion of youth service positions in libraries, schools and systems

Ten points summarizing the common concerns of the small discussion groups became the action agenda, with strategies for implementation being enlarged upon in later discussions. The points were as follows:

- Stimulate, encourage, support, and nurture the young in their efforts toward literacy
- Recognize and serve the needs of young people
- Build strong local collections of materials
- Provide library staff who are responsive to, responsible for, and trained in youth services
- Serve all young people through outreach
- Create networks of all types of libraries and community agencies, communicate with peers, share programs and resources.
- Articulate to the administration the need for library service for youth
- Stimulate, nurture, and support the ability of youth to become their own information managers
- Market library service for youth—at every level
- Actively work for legislation and adequate funding

Public relations, and all that largely misunderstood term implies, runs as a strong thread through the report of this conference, its exhortative speeches, and its action plan: marketing, articulating, communicating, becoming politically active, building coalitions with other youth agencies. Developing both management skills and research expertise are also very much in the forefront, with injunctions like: "learn management jargon," "make statistics work for youth services," "don't whine," "start the action: don't wait for administrators to do it," and "management is a constant exercise in coping skills."

Regina Minudri, a former youth services librarian, now a library system director and a speaker at the New York conference on "The Management Perspective," spoke plainly about what many youth librarians, both in New York State and outside of it, see as their greatest stumbling block, saying: "Many librarians serving youth complain that they aren't taken seriously by their administrators, managers or supervisors. It seems to me that we still suffer from some of the myths about youth services librarians. Following are some common myths, all stated in negative terms. . . . Sadly, some of these are self-perpetuating. Youth services librarians:

- are childlike, overly identified with client group
- are incapable of seeing "the big picture"
- don't see beyond their own services
- are emotional
- can't be reasoned with—are stubborn
- live in an ivory tower
- are inflexible
- fluster easily
- don't understand budgets
- don't know how to justify requests (because they only ask for what is right, true, just, and good)
- can't estimate or forecast
- refuse to listen to reason, won't compromise
- won't set priorities, because *everything* is important."[26]

Participants, spurred by this and other challenges have written an action agenda that will be useful for many youth services librarians who plan to celebrate a renaissance of image and success in the 1990s!

The Allerton Park Institute in Illinois which drew from youth services leadership around the country, also focused on improving image, not only for the purpose of increased clout with the administrators and the public, but also for greatly stepped-up recruitment of new professionals in youth services. Pay equity, mentoring programs, systematic training for paraprofessionals, development of career ladders, and systematic continuing education for all youth practitioners were topics discussed with great intensity.

Much attention was given also to coalition building and to all the kinds of efforts implied therein: shaping legislative policy at all levels; being effective politically at all levels; use of assertive skills and willingness to take responsibility for leadership outside of as well as inside of the profession; demanding that ALA adopt a "youth agenda"; developing cohesive national standards for youth services from all types of libraries which clearly show differences among complementary services and the mission and role of personnel; adapting and improving existing output measures (basically planned to measure adult service performance) to more effectively evaluate youth service efforts.

Participants in this national conference held in Illinois set themselves the task of being much more aware of demographics and their impact on youth services: mothers in the workforce, immigration patterns, and population shifts, among others. Literacy—facts, levels, and its relationship to the social and individual welfare, as well as how to motivate toward it—came in for its share of discussion, as did the task of taking some responsibility for the removal of barriers which deny access to information and materials in any and all formats and for all ages. There is in both these points, as indeed in most of the others, a large share of responsibility for public information and education.

And finally, this cross section of youth services leadership focused on the importance of greatly enhanced management skills for youth services librarians, as well as a growing expertise and awareness of research needs and potentials relating to the great range of possible library services and experiences for youth from preschool to older teenage. Research relating to the possibility of national certification of youth services librarians was discussed. Concern for revision and rethinking of the education and continuing education of personnel came in for discussion, as did the felt need for training in evaluation procedures.[27]

The report of this conference was not ready for publication at the time of this writing, but it is evident that its agenda and recommendations for action reinforced those not only of the New York state conference but of the guidelines and standards discussed earlier in this chapter. The picture that emerges is one of a youth services profession in ferment: visionary in terms of its broad mission, practical in terms of how to accomplish its goals, and eager to provide a high-expectation framework for local communities where children meet librarians and—it is to be hoped—have their lives changed for the better.

5

Management Concerns:
Internal and Operational

"Well-managed media programs do not just endure whatever comes their way; they prevail over circumstances because they are led by managers who understand the nature of shifting priorities and changing program focus."[1]

This is the ideal, of course. But whether managers do indeed manage whatever comes their way or just manage to endure it, each day's quota of details must be coped with and the problems met and dealt with. A major proportion of the manager's day-to-day work deals with resources, chief among them, budget and staff. Another large portion should deal with evaluation of how those resources are spent and the quality of what they buy; and still another—a most vital one—deals with public relations. This last, greatly misunderstood and underrated term, covers a multitude of responsibilities and management functions. They include: reporting to the top management and governance; communications—always two-way, and involving reading and listening as well as writing and talking—with staff and the public, child-serving-agency personnel, government officials, organization and business contacts, and the media; and continuous, constant promotion of library services to children and youth—not just in terms of what they are and when they take place but in terms of their larger meaning for individual children, families, the community, the nation, and the future. The manager consciously builds that meaning into every program, every contact, and the use of every piece of material; believes fervently in its importance; and leads staff members and patrons into that belief also.

Costs and Budgets

There are many statistics which must be compiled for internal use or for making reports to funding sources in order to justify budgets. These include data about the extent of the library's collections and the use of materials; the number of persons registered; expenditures in relation to delivery of services; acquisitions and costs of maintaining facilities; and circulation figures. Without a good showing when these measures of cost-effectiveness and others are applied, priorities which are likely to slip lower in times of budget shortages are those which do not measure up well statistically. Subjective statements without sufficient documentation have been, in all too many libraries, the chief means by which the value of library services to children have been judged, and resources allocated.

Resting too comfortably, perhaps, on a tradition of success, practitioners of services to children have failed to offer objective proof of their effectiveness and productivity by using accepted and recognized techniques for measurement and evaluation. So generally is this the case that the term "evaluation" as applied to children's library services is usually used only in the context of criticism of literature and other materials for children. Rather than being eager to evaluate how specific activities, such as reader guidance or group programming, contribute both to short-term objectives and long-range goals for the children (and thereby for the library's program), some children's librarians still insist that although they *know* that what they are doing brings benefits, these benefits cannot be measured. It has been observed that "library service to children is based upon predominantly untested assumptions."[2] One library administrator states the case this way: "Budget cuts are determined by identification of areas where the impact on total public service will be the least felt. . . . Most traditional children's service can be updated in today's terms as valuable, but you must look at when and how you render it most effectively. . . . Seriously, push the value and uniqueness of your service."[3]

During the mid-1970s, a compilation of library data showed a twelve percent increase in library expenditures with a mere one percent increase in circulation in public libraries. Since then, escalating costs and inflation have continued the upward spiral in costs as budgets have eroded for most libraries.[4]

On a graph and box chart, Professor Herbert Goldhor of the

Library Research Center at the University of Illinois at Urbana, compared increases in public library circulation and library expenditures from 1976 to 1985. Figures were based on reports from the 1985 Index of American Public Library Circulation and from the Index of Expenditures taken from a sample of fifty-three public libraries in the United States serving populations over 25,000. Circulation was up 1.8 percent, or two points, from 1984 and 9.7 percent, or fourteen points, from 1979.

The 1986 Index of American Public Library Circulation remained at 111, the same as in 1985. Operating expenditures for the total sample of libraries also remained almost the same with sixty-one percent allocated for salaries, two percent less than in 1980; sixteen percent for materials; and twenty-three percent for all other costs. The year's index values reveal the low increase in salaries with a corresponding high increase in all costs since 1980.

While an increase in the U.S. population from 1977 to 1986 was almost ten percent, the Index of American Public Library Circulation increased over twelve percent in this period, and the Index of Expenditures rose from twenty-five percent in 1980 dollars. The 1986 circulation in public libraries was estimated to be the same as in 1985 (1,154,400,000). The total operating expenditures in all U.S. public libraries in 1986 was estimated as about $3,051,000,000, or between $2.64 and $3.45 billion. Significant changes in 1986, based on the sample of fifty-three public libraries, indicated that forty public libraries, or seventy-five percent of the sample, had an increase in juvenile circulation. Adult circulation was recorded as a nine percent increase since 1980, and juvenile circulation twenty percent more than in 1980.

A devastating budget experience for libraries began with the first of the so-called citizens' tax revolts in California in 1977. This was known as "Proposition 13," and its effect was to cut library budgets for almost all libraries and schools by as much as between sixty-seven and ninety percent. Libraries were forced to close immediately in some communities throughout the state and children's librarians and media specialists, with others of their colleagues, were suddenly jobless. Fortunately, in 1978 there were some surplus state funds available to fill some of the shortfalls. Startled voters, who declared later that they never meant for libraries to be affected, were spared prolonged closings of their libraries. A survey of fourteen libraries in California revealed that the impact of Proposition 13 was indeed widespread; it caused 10,877 fewer hours each week of public service,

Public library circulation and expenditures

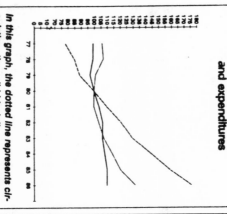

In this graph, the dotted line represents circulation; the solid black line represents expenditures in current dollars; and the line of dashes represents expenditures in constant 1980 dollars.

Annual indexes for a sample of American public libraries: 1977–86
(with 1980 = 100; for 1980–86, N* = 53)

	'77	'78	'79	'80	'81	'82	'83	'84	'85	'86
Circulation	99	99	97	100	104	107	107	109	111	111
Expenditures	78	85	89	100	110	121	130	145	159	176
In 1980 dollars	106	107	101	100	100	104	108	115	121	133

Circulation percentages

	1980 (N=34)	1986 (N=40)
Adult	69%	66%
Juvenile	31%	34%

Expenditure percentages

	1980 (N=53)	1986 (N=53)
Salaries	63%	61%
Materials	16%	16%
Other	21%	23%

* N is the number of libraries reporting

Annual indexes for circulation and expenditure percentages

Medians	1980	'81	'82	'83	'84	'85	'86
Adult circulation	100	95	108	111	114	112	109
Juvenile circulation	100	96	106	108	112	117	120
Expenditures for salaries	100	112	123	137	147	154	162
Expenditures for materials	100	108	123	123	141	149	174
Expenditures for other	100	113	117	120	149	150	178

Other Measures: Median	1980	'81	'82	'83	'84	'85	'86
Circulation per capita	4.7	5.2	5.2	5.4	5.3	5.4	5.6
Expenditures per capita	$7.39	$8.26	$9.49	$9.78	$10.73	$11.14	$11.61
Expenditures per circulation	$1.42	$1.56	$1.57	$1.65	$1.81	$1.84	$2.04
Expenditures per capita for lib. materials	$1.10	$1.17	$1.18	$1.27	$1.49	$1.57	$1.99

Reprinted with Permission
American Libraries, July/August 1987

a twenty-one percent staff reduction, and consequent decreases in interlibrary loan activity and outreach services. Special programming for adults and children either ceased or greatly decreased.[5]

In the succeeding years, "copycat" propositions limiting support for public services severely affected libraries in several other states. Even prior to Proposition 13, New York City had experienced, in 1975, an equally dramatic decrease in library services. An overwhelming and well-orchestrated public outcry helped to prevent some of the most extreme measures for closings and severely shortened hours in some branches. Scores of writers and other creative people reacted and caused the spotlight to be turned on the situation. Among them was novelist Lois Gould who said, "When I was a child, going to the library on Saturday afternoon was a big event . . . that doesn't happen anymore. On Saturday the library is closed, and I can't take my own children there."[6]

Decreases in funding, coupled with rising costs have mandated a corresponding change in how libraries allocate their resources, manage their operations, and deliver their services. Attendant changes have come about in management perceptions and directions. Some very outdated patterns of services, totally inadequate for today's needs, were put into place with a resulting diminution of the importance and visibility of children's services in relation to other services.

Alternate Sources of Funding

If local, state, and federal sources of funding have shrunk consistently over the past two decades, how about alternate sources for funding then, from the so called "private sector?" There are some concerns and some dissatisfactions with this route, but nonetheless, special purpose/program grants from foundations and business, as well as from public fund-raising activities, have become a permanent way of life for most library programs, including those for children. The situation is such that basic operational support for a minimally adequate program is lacking in many libraries, let alone new funding for development, innovation, or expansion of successful programs and practices.

This presents a problem because private funding sources will almost never provide funds for basic, ongoing operations. They want their support to go for something new, special, and visible, an innovative addition to an effective ongoing program. Without a demonstrably good, basic program, supported by public funds, it is almost impossible to interest private sources in additions.

A second concern is that private funds almost always come with strings attached, and may tempt the library manager to undertake projects and programs that are not really in line with priority goals and objectives. This may skew the program in subtle and not always beneficial ways, causing undue emphasis on one area over another or on one group of children over another.

A third and most serious concern is that in operating too much of its program on private funds, the library may encourage certain elements in local government or the community to think of library services—in this case, those for children—as something that should be paid for by those who use them, i. e., out of private rather than public funds. It must be constantly drummed into community awareness that public library services—especially those for children—are for *everyone*, not just for those who can afford to pay for them or those who compose a desirable customer group for advertisers (which, in effect, business donors are). Library programs for children are in the public interest, and should therefore be supported chiefly out of public funds.

The ultimate concern is the question of what will replace the grant funds in supporting a given program when the grant funds run out. Many private donors now ask, before releasing money, how the library intends to continue the program when the donor funds are exhausted. It is important that requests and proposals incorporate plans for sustaining a program once it is begun and running successfully and the grant is over. The program would have to demonstrate that it is effectively meeting a priority need and is worthy of being maintained.

Personnel costs, which are usually minimally supported by private funding anyway, should not present a problem. But materials, contract services, supplies, and equipment maintenance may become an ongoing additional expense not allowed for in the budget. If the grant could result in an income-producing product, such as a salable brochure or other publication or an income-generating conference, this would be some demonstration of the library's ability to operate the program in the future with public budgeted funds, and also a means of providing supplemental funding.

Having made all of this clear, to oneself as well as to the community, there are many perfectly legitimate ways to seek these additional, program-enhancement—rather than alternative—sources of funding.

The most efficient way to raise large sums of money usually entails hiring a fund-raising professional or consultant who will systematically address the library's financial needs and request donations from all the appropriate and possible sources. Children's services managers must be certain to put the needs of their clientele and the requirements for effective services before the fund-raising committee and the outside professionals and make certain that the children's and youth department not only plays its role in getting the money, but is also assured a share of what comes in. Professional fund-raising on this scale (that is, enlisting the services of a professional), will almost without exception be done for the library or library system overall, so that the children's program will be just one of the beneficiaries.

There are, of course, many less formal forms of fund-raising, many of them that are less direct. Libraries, even individual children's departments, have been known to hold functions or events at which people may enjoy themselves and be entertained while giving money at the same time. These usually involve a great deal of time and work by volunteers and also by the staff.

Local business concerns which are known to be donors to other organizations and usually public-spirited, are likely sources of non-specific or special-project funds. Recently, a fast-food chain gave a small sum of money to underwrite publicity for children's programs in one library. Another supplied refreshments for a library party when a mural painted by local children was unveiled at the library. These chains often issue gift certificates to exchange for soft drinks and hamburgers as prizes at the end of summer reading programs. Local banks have, from time to time, donated money to assist with children's programming. For instance, a brochure designed by children which promoted reading at home was made possible by a local bank donation. It received a budget for printing and enjoyed wide distribution in the Brooklyn Public Library's community. Department stores have financed the publication of bookmark bibliographies in return for free storytelling programs for customers' children.

A major utility company in the East now sponsors annually a series of ethnic programs in three large, urban library systems and prints bookcovers for distribution to children. While not a donor of large amounts of cash to the children's program, the utility has made it possible for the library to pay professionals to perform at library programs for children.

Although individual publishers are not as a rule good sources for direct funding to libraries, they have often been involved in very successful efforts to promote library services for children and libraries in general. There is, for example, "New York is Book Country," a gala street book-fair in September, now an annual event in New York City's midtown, which is supported largely through the sale of booth space to publishers. There is entertainment, and posters designed by children's book illustrators are sold to benefit the children's services of the New York Public Library. Money realized from these sales has extended the number and quality of programs for children in the library, especially significant in times of staff shortages. And of course, National Children's Book Week, celebrated in libraries and schools throughout the country in November, focusing widespread attention on books, reading, and libraries, is organized by the Children's Book Council. Its many activities on behalf of library services to children and reading are supported by the children's departments of the publishers, in addition to sales of the posters and other Book Week materials.

Foundations of many sizes and varieties are among the most frequently tapped sources for funding. A number of children's services managers who have sufficient initiative and persistence have been well rewarded for the amount of time and energy they have spent on researching local foundation sources, writing applications, and following through when grants are received. One such project, funded by a major, nationally known foundation for New York City's special preschool project, will be described in some detail later in this book. As a rule, however, the best sources are small foundations with strong interest in local institutions and activities. Many wealthy couples form foundations for their giving and limit their grants to certain kinds of projects, frequently those affecting children. Many businesses accept particular programs or institutions for an "annual giving" list, or set up small foundations for grant purposes related in some way to their business or business image. Most foundations and other givers require evidence of effort on behalf of the institution to match the outside commitment to a project. Often this commitment may be in "in kind" terms of staffing or use of equipment.

Although it is not a foundation, and is itself supported by grants, gifts from industry, and some government funding, "Reading is

FUNdamental" (RIF) provides libraries with the opportunity to distribute books free to children who may not otherwise be able to own a book. This enables them to make a start on building a personal, home library. This book ownership has been shown to be an incentive to read and to develop the reading habit, particularly among children in disadvantaged areas.

An important component of all fund-raising is publicity. Good working relations between the children's services department and the library's public relations or public information officer are essential. Features and stories about children's services should be among the easiest and most satisfactory to place with the local media. The manager of children's services should establish good relations also with the leadership of the Friends of Libraries group and identified library friends and frequent users, as well as the "friends of children" (youth advocates) and their organizations, mentioned earlier. There is more to be said about these friends later in this chapter, and about volunteers and their important role in publicizing and promoting, as well as in fund-raising.

Most additional funding resources are closer than they are often thought to be, located in the very community the library serves. The manager of children's services has the responsibility of organizing all the troops—staff and volunteer—to reach out for these badly needed resources. Donors and grantors of whatever kind have generally agreed over the years that money spent for library programs is some of the most carefully and productively spent of any they have appropriated. Use this fact, getting a second grant to ride upon the successful completion of the first, until the track record is so good that the children's program can get money for virtually any special need it may have. A dream? No! It just takes careful planning so that facts are all straight, needs demonstrable, proposals clear and compelling, objectives measurable. Testimonials from previous donors and grantors are most helpful, as are additional sponsors who support the library's proposal. It is often a good idea to cut a long-range or very ambitious project into steps or phases. This will show the grantor the big picture of what it is hoped to accomplish, yet offer the opportunity to fund only a smaller segment or a segment at a time.

Program Staffing and Coordination

About fifteen coordinators (managers) of children's services in large urban libraries in 1975 reported the elimination and/or downgrading of the managerial position at a time when public library collections had expanded beyond the books to include audiovisual and other materials. Services too, were being stretched to encompass children with special needs: the handicapped; learning disabled and gifted; preschoolers; daycare and other agencies that care for them; and parents. More extensive requests to meet community needs have taken children's services far beyond the traditional offerings made by the children's librarian of an earlier time. Also noted was the trend toward the use of generalists—librarians not especially trained for the work—seen by the coordinators and deplored as a de-emphasis of services to children and youth. The role for the children's services coordinator was viewed as being downgraded to one of "responsibility without authority, no [real] representation of the service at top level management and consequently no voice in policy making or budgeting."[7] The coordinators saw the loss of professionals with special interest and background in work with children as damaging. This was true not only in terms of the direct work with the children themselves, but was seen as having a negative "ripple effect" on them due to the lack of specialized help for adults who work with children: teachers, youth agency personnel, students of children's literature, and parents. Members of the coordinators group also reported inadequate statistics concerning library activities for children, and stressed the need to devise more effective measurements and methods of evaluation.

Although fewer than half of the coordinators responding to the survey reported a management proposal to introduce the use of generalist professionals to replace children's work specialists, there have been some highly visible demonstrations of this practice. Working on the premise that any librarian can work with children with only some in-service training, Charles Robinson, director of the Baltimore County Public Library, initiated a retraining program for professional staff at a new branch of the system which opened in 1977. The principle was introduced as one way to cope with decreasing budgets. Mr. Robinson stated, "This is no big deal to those of you from small libraries who have always been generalists, but it is unusual in many large libraries."[8]

Other library systems have followed Baltimore County's lead, and many children's specialists have found themselves in training to become generalists in the delivery of information to all ages, as well as becoming trainers for those who must master at least the rudiments of reader guidance for children. Of course, "information" for children may be factual material or it may be a story, a wordless picture book or filmstrip; matching interest and development level to reading level and age, and creating programs out of all the diverse materials might become nearly impossible if all the trained children's librarians were to vanish from the scene. The trend toward identifying services by function rather than by client age group seems firmly entrenched as public libraries tread the narrow route to fiscal survival.

While observing the excitement generated in the attractive and busy branches of the Baltimore County Public Library system, Dr. Margaret Mary Kimmel noted the following:

1. There seemed to be "no connection between the functions of collection development and of information and programming."
2. "Anticipated client demand is the primary criterion for the selector" and a single copy purchase is unlikely to be introduced in a book talk and therefore may never be reordered.
3. "There is still an 'obvious' dependence on the presence of former age-group specialists" in an instance where specific knowledge of book content may be required.
4. At the administrative level, the staff-training component and the dependence on former age-group specialists present particular problems, since the structure does not provide for direction, planning, or training for specialized client groups.
5. "There seems to be confusion about 'information' and the educational role of the public library . . . the generalist approach suggests a 'conversion' from professional goals to a credo based on short term objectives."[9]

It is fair to say that the majority of library directors still regard the experimental move to do without children's service specialists as a short-sighted and ill-advised expedient. Given the undoubted political attractiveness of services to children—increasing daily with the public awareness that early learning interventions and habits are the ones that count most—any actions which serve to downgrade this service appear to be at the least just plain foolish and at worst like killing the goose that lays the golden egg of public satisfaction and support. Excellent, well-trained staff remain, in the minds of many, the most important ingredient in the effective children's room. Whatever the bureaucratic personnel channels through which new recruits are acquired, it is a basic responsibility of the children's library program manager to be aware constantly of supply and demand in the area. When staff openings are imminent, likely candidates should be identified and brought into the hiring channels.

Another and most important management concern is for a planned program of continuous in-service staff development. It is the children's librarian-manager who must insist that staff members be given release time, and if possible at least a portion of expenses, to attend state and national professional conferences and workshops. Staff members should also be allowed program preparation time. It is the program or department manager who goes through the relevant professional journals with a highlighter in hand, marking significant articles, phrases, events, awards, and other happenings, and then makes certain that the material circulates to the entire staff. It is the children's services program manager who, being alert to the comings and goings of persons in the community, engineers the invitation to the famous child psychologist who is visiting at the university to meet and talk with the children's staff at morning coffee; arranges author visits; organizes a program of professional videotapes for home viewing by the staff, with follow up discussion meetings held once a month; and plans for a annual series of staff workshops. The manager does these things, of course, with the advice and consent of the library's top management and probably with the assistance of a committee and other staff members—especially the public relations or information and staff development officers—and perhaps with funding help from the Friends group. But the initiative comes from the manager. Seeing a need and taking steps to meet it is at the heart of management responsibility.

Utilizing Volunteer Staff

Library volunteers are certainly friends of the library and its programs whether they are spelled with a small "f" or a capital one! Very few libraries these days can, or should be able to, get along without them. Properly planned for, trained, supervised, and utilized they can not only far extend the reach and effectiveness of the library's program, but they can constitute the best community relations force it is possible to have. This may be especially true of the children's services program.

Volunteers usually perform specific tasks in the library and related to the library program, and generally work within a designated time frame. They are expected to undertake assignments which will supplement rather than duplicate the work of the paid staff.

Large urban public libraries have never made as effective use of volunteers as they might have, whereas small, rural public libraries and most school library media centers have relied on them extensively. One deterrent has been the position of library unions, or sometimes of individual librarians, who fear that volunteers may jeopardize the jobs of regular employees.

Children's librarians have often welcomed volunteers, especially in the area of programming. Many community members have special skills that they are willing to share with children through the library: puppeteering, arts and crafts, magic, ventriloquism. A number of experts in these fields started to build their interest and skills as library volunteers. Such program volunteers may be parents or grandparents or even siblings, ranging in age from junior high school to senior citizen. Some of the most entertaining magicians have been junior high or high school students. Musicians or students from a local dance school may want to use the library as a showcase, and the children's librarian may decide that their talents are appropriate for a library program. In discussing the preschool programs in a later chapter, professionals from other disciplines are mentioned as presenting free programs for parents and preschoolers.

In the early 1970s, the Children's Services Division of ALA (now the Association of Library Service to Children), established some guidelines for library volunteers working with young children which are still useful. Included in these is the positive statement: "An effective volunteer program can improve library service to young children . . . demonstrate, particularly to parents, the value of expanded services, show that funds for the expanded library service to young children is a needed and appropriate part of the budget."[10]

Attitude, planning, training, and recruitment are all important elements to consider in organizing a good volunteer program. An interested volunteer is a great asset, and those who exhibit positive and enthusiastic behavior will gain the confidence and hold the attention of the children. If the attitude of the would-be volunteer is important, so too is the attitude toward the volunteers as a group and as individuals as reflected by the regular staff. Enlisting of volunteers should not be undertaken unless the paid staff members understand completely the value of what the volunteers are giving in time, energy, interest, and expertise. They are not there just to do the drudge work that no one on the paid staff wants to do; they are there to be fully utilized and appreciated. "Psychic reward" is important to anyone who works hard—paid or unpaid—and it is especially important to those who receive no monetary reward.

In working with volunteers, the children's program manager must weigh the great potential benefits of having them against the substantial amount of time required from the manager and other paid staff to realize these benefits. Careful screening of would-be recruits is essential, with a clear presentation of the library's standards and expectations. Volunteers who wish to work in the library's program should know something about children, their interests at various age levels, length of attention span, and expected responses to differing types of stimulation and experience. It is helpful for them to know something about children's books and to love and be excited by reading, creative thinking, fine pictures, and the library's criteria for materials selection and presentation.

Not all volunteers by any means want to, or are capable of, making program presentations. Many just want to help behind the desk, read to children, or perhaps shelve books or type cards. Clerical jobs for which no paid clerks ever have the time, such as preparing invitations and other mailings, may fill a volunteer's time and interest in helping the library; manning the phones and doing contact work may be suited to the abilities of others, or operating equipment. For those who sign on in a regular, ongoing volunteer capacity—as opposed to a one-shot contribution—it is important to have some rules governing punctuality, reliability of attendance, and prompt communication in case of deviation from schedule. There should be some orientation to the goals of the program and the library setting. For those who want to volunteer a one-time or for occasional service—in most cases a special program—the children's librarian must be certain that the program to be presented is original and creative, appropriate for library sponsorship, and geared to the age and interest level of the children for whom it is intended. Informal discussion may often result in changes in an unsuitable program if the performer or volunteer truly wants to make a useful contribution.

In any case, library staff time is required to plan and prepare a schedule for volunteers if several are being utilized. A detailed "menu" of activities which may be properly handled by volunteers is generally the responsibility assigned to a staff member who also supervises and arranges recruitment, training, and placement of volunteers. Once the ability and the reliability of a volunteer has been established, and subject to the discretion of the department head or supervisor, that volunteer may represent the library in program activities outside the library as well as within its walls. In the Baltimore County system preschool program, for example, volunteers have worked with children by taking books and realia to provider homes and demonstrating prereading activities for very young children in the home.

As for sources of volunteer help, librarians have found that the local college or university is often a good source, since many students need practical field experiences with children in community settings other than the schools. Intern programs or work-study programs in some institutions may result in a supply of students who see the library's potential for providing for observation of children's learning habits and tutorial needs. Recent concern about low math and reading scores on national standardized tests has prompted many librarians to begin tutorial programs which will provide some type of after-school homework assistance. Some programs have attracted teachers as volunteers, as well as high school and college students.

Although parents compose a large portion of the volunteer group in school library media centers, there seems to be no parent reservoir of real significance for work in public library programs. However, parent groups working in early childhood programs have sometimes spontaneously formed their own discussion groups. This happens often at the suggestion of one who feels the need to communicate with others about mutual concerns. Some librarians have arranged regular time slots and accommodations for the meeting of such groups, and tied the meeting in with the preschool program. This generally requires little direction or intervention and is a natural extension of the program.

A community member's suggestion sparked a quid pro quo artist-in-residence arrangement in the Jackson Square branch of the New York Public Library, where artists were offered space to work in the library in exchange for a set number of hours of service working with interested children who visited the library after school. Many teachers from all types of schools in the area, public as well as private, expressed a desire to work with the children and tutor them in many areas of study.

Volunteers tend then to be utilized in several major ways in work with children: to expand existing programming which can be strengthened by the volunteers' skills and talents; to supplement with an innovative service, such as homework help; to expand work with preschoolers or young children; or to assume responsibility for some routines for which staff is unavailable.

A successful volunteer program will not only aid in maintaining and expanding library services, it may also provide for a demonstration of desirable programs and services. Recruitment of volunteers may yield new community partnerships for the library, as it puts librarians into contact with neighborhood day-care centers, colleges, schools, churches, and other agencies and service organizations. The return on the staff investment of time and energy is an increasingly large and productive one.

Setting Goals and Objectives

The previous chapter devoted a good deal of space to the subject of goals, guidelines, objectives, and evaluation—all of which are inextricably tied together. Studying the goals and objectives which have been promulgated in the several states, and the recommendations that have come out of meetings and surveys, should suggest many areas for consideration in mapping out the goals for the local library's program of children's services.

There are many factors, of course, to be considered. There are the state's goals and guidelines, if these exist in written and up to date form; and the goals and objectives of the parent organization. In addition to being in conformity with these, the manager of children's services must have a thorough understanding of the community and the clientele to be served: the work imperatives of parents; languages spoken; level of literacy and education in the homes the children will be coming from; family patterns; and much more. What are the populations to be served: toddlers, preschoolers, school-age children, parents, teachers, youth agency personnel? What present provisions are being made to serve these groups? What do evaluations of the children's services tell us about the relative effectiveness and success of various aspects of the program up to now? Are there sufficient high quality resources to meet goals for a good program? Have recent community changes and demands been factored in to the budget allocated to children's services?

After the research has been done and facts marshalled concerning the present level of performance and unmet needs, the next step in the planning process is the development of the goals and objectives that will guide the program. A plan for at least a five year period has proved to be a workable one for most libraries. This gives a chance for many of the objectives that are laid out to be achieved and even some of the goals themselves to have been at least partially arrived at. New perceptions of role and mission have made most former sets—those comparatively few that have ever been concisely set down in written form—seem vague and simplistic in the extreme. This era of world-class problems, automation, and a plethora of "sponsored information," which is really not so much information as propaganda, should give children's librarians a pause in which to reflect upon their vital role as purveyors of genuine, comparative, and often contradictory information. The aim of providing the right book for the right child is no longer enough, though it is still undoubtedly a part of the whole picture. Goals and objectives for childrens's services must now embrace the total information concept. True, library work with children has always involved the transmitting of information, but mostly in the form of stories, sharing a book or filmstrip or puppet show.

There must be new emphasis now, reflected in goals and objectives, on helping children to find out for themselves those things they need to know, and even more important to form the *habit* of inquiring, comparing facts, and using information to think before they act. In later life, this habit will translate into more informed voting and purchasing, and better decision making in all aspects of life and work. All the means and tools, all the carriers of information, must be made familiar, be they electronic or printed, and children must be convinced through their library experiences that the stimulus, inspiration, knowledge, and impetus they derive from information is an important element in shaping their self-identities and their lives.

Children's librarians must learn to shape and express their goals and objectives in terms of what they intend to produce, rather than in terms of their own wishes and processes related to books and programs. Their goals should encompass the broad issues and challenges facing public libraries in general and work with youth in particular. They will have to recognize that library services for children must earn their keep on a daily basis as competition for program survival intensifies at all levels. This means "chapter and verse" statistics about the benefits the services have produced in relation to what the program set out to do—its goals and objectives. Only in this way will the allocation of resources continue to be justified. Peggy Sullivan, in a 1979 article, called for *"measurable,* articulated goals for service" that are recognized by each person responsible for rendering children's services.[11]

Goals should be flexible as well as measurable. If a goal proves inadequate or appears to be channeling efforts in the wrong direction, it can be revised. A good deal of the flexibility comes with the necessity to prioritize, to be willing to identify some objectives which carry a higher priority than others. A system-wide survey of a library's branches may dictate different patterns in each community. In one, integrated shelving of informational or nonfiction books and a large paperback collection for children, with on-line access to other materials, may be satisfactory. In another branch, parenting collections and intensive preschool emphasis is indicated. In still another, with a high rate of drop-in groups accompanied by a teacher, some staffing schedules may need to be revised. The frequency of school-related questions in one branch may mandate that the number of reference tools and services be increased, including more frequent communication with teachers or library media specialists in neighborhood schools. In branches visited by children who lack school library services, special school-related materials and services may need to be made available.

Important goals then will be formulated relating to the tools of service: materials, staff, budget, and facilities. Other goals will be couched in terms of program and public relations activities, including: forging public library–school relationships; working with parents to help them assist children's learning; staff development; community outreach and work with child-serving agency personnel, including teachers; and community awareness of the program of children's library services and all of its larger long-term implications. As the library's degree of success in approaching its overarching goal—that of providing mind-expanding, intellect-developing exploration and independence to the greatest possible number of children—becomes evident from time to time, priorities can be shifted, the mix of activities and programs changed, and objectives and goals refined and revised.

This means then that evaluation is, as we stated at the beginning of this chapter, one of the most critical of the program manager's responsibilities. Everything else, in a real sense, depends upon it: the continuous revision of goals and objectives; the scrutiny of resources and programs and services to be sure they are geared to carrying out the objectives; and the wherewithal for justifying the existence and growth of children's services. Ways and methods of measuring have been discussed in the previous chapter, but there are countless ways to be devised, many of them geared to the workings of a specific program. Study the literature of measurement and evaluation and, above all, observe and make notes: the number of parents who accompany children to the library and leave with materials; the number of requests from teachers who want advice from the library staff about materials; the number of telephone requests for particular kinds of programs for children; the number of adults who volunteer their services; the numbers of children who are found in the library at various different hours after school. Jot down anecdotes in a daily journal: the parent or other adult who used the library as a child and liked it well enough to bring a child now; the book an adult read as a child that made a lasting impression or shaped the adult's personality or future. Such anecdotal material is all raw material for reports, for interviews, for articles on the program.

And so, without evaluation, there can be no meaningful and effective public relations. There is no story, and no pressure to fund, in a mere recital of what librarians do or want, but there *is* a story, and compelling reason to fund a program that shows evidence of the benefits it is producing for a large number of children.

Public Relations

Children's library services managers and practitioners are lucky: their client is the best kind of public relations agent any product or service could have. Watch the children selling everything from soup to nuts on television if proof is needed. In the current climate—which seems certain to continue until the end of the century at the least— of concern for the future, for literacy, for job preparedness and mobility, children's librarians have a most important and persuasive story to tell. In this context the story being told at the story hour is not just a pleasant addition to the child's life but a mind and imagination stretcher, a beginning of relating, thinking, listening, and absorbing an idea—skills to be greatly needed in later life. The habit of inquiry feeds on itself: the more one knows, the more one needs to know; the more one reads the more one needs to read. This pattern forms the basis in later life for the leadership, creativity, and competence on which our kind of society depends.

In the library with a public relations department or public information officer, publicity and public information addressed to the general public are coordinated through this office. The chief responsibility for source material about the children's program, however, rests with the manager of children programs, as does the initiative for establishing a close, working relationship with the public information officer. The manager of children's services must also be on tap and prepared with facts, details, and anecdotes not only for public consumption, but also as necessary for reporting purposes to the library's administrator and board as needed.

Effective public relations results not only in bringing children and their attendant adults into the library because they have been informed that something for them is going on there, but it also develops public awareness and support. The *Wisconsin Public Library Standards,* discussed in chapter 4, recommends that "a public library should integrate an active public relations program into its ongoing plan for operation. Public relations should be a planned, continuous effort by the library to carry on positive communications with its various publics." Every children's library services program manager should take to heart, and try to adapt as a goal, at least some of the content in the public relations standards set forth by Wisconsin, especially: "The library's annual budget allocates funds for public relations activities," and "Annually, the library implements at least four of the following generally accepted publicity techniques; the choice of which techniques to employ will be based on the library's chosen role(s) and characteristics of the community.

- Library newsletter
- General information brochure
- Newspaper articles, colums or ads
- Annual report available to public
- TV and/or radio exposure
- Posters, flyers, bookmarks

- Presentations to community groups
- Exhibits, displays, bulletin boards
- Others

The Wisconsin standards recommend also that the library, in this case perhaps the department of children's services, designate a staff member to coordinate public relations activities.[12]

Use of community talent in programming and of other volunteers is an excellent form of public relations, as is joint planning and programming with related agencies and professionals who work with children. Such outreach and collaborative programming is more fully discussed in another chapter, but it is the best kind of public relations. It is useful also for extending the base of potential users and library advocates. Other agencies may supply new audiences and expertise, as well as resources.

There is one special group with which the children's services manager should establish good communications and a working relationship: the library's formal "Friends of the Library" organization. There are some 2,400 Friends groups estimated as being active in the country; of these some 1,400 are members of "Friends of Libraries, U.S.A.," which is an affiliated organization of ALA. A staff member of the ALA's public information office provides some support services for a part-time secretariat. Not surprisingly, the more urban states are the most heavily organized with formal Friends groups, and thirty-seven of the states have statewide organizations of Friends. Although there are a good many Friends organizations attached to college and university libraries, and just a very few beginning to be organized for school library media centers, the majority of Friends organizations are attached to public libraries. According to Sandy Dolnik, in an October 1987 conversation, (a chief source of energy behind the organization of the national Friends group and still its executive director,) many local Friends groups devote a great deal of their time and money to enhancement of the library's children's services. Active involvement in children's services characterizes the Friends groups in such cities as Memphis, Minneapolis, and Orlando. In a few places, a subgroup or committee of "Junior Friends," especially concerned with youth activities and services, has been formed.

Friends groups are true friends in the sense that they will do, most of them, whatever needs doing to help their library. In recent years, during which such frequent efforts have been aimed at cutting library budgets, their activity has evolved more toward fund-raising, public relations, and the mustering of political support for libraries than toward enrichment of existing services. Both kinds of efforts are still, however, an important function of most groups. Friends have conducted library tours, sponsored book sales and fairs of other kinds to make money, hosted fund-raising parties, or sponsored exhibits and special programs to promote library visibility to the community. In addition to these traditional activities, Friends groups now form a potent political force at the grass roots level as they lobby, at the local and state level particularly, for libraries in general. They often provide the steam behind campaigns for signing petitions, writing letters or demonstrating on behalf of libraries, or actually making presentations and giving testimony at budget hearings.

Friends of Children's Services in the New York Public Library engaged a professional auctioneer from a prestigious New York auction house to conduct a successful auction on behalf of children's services at one period when they were especially beleaguered. By enlisting the help of children's book authors who autographed their books, and illustrators who donated their original art work, as well as by selling old and rare books given by friends, substantial funds were raised for the support of children's programs. One group of authors even donated two years of royalty payments from a publica-tion as one type of contribution, due to the Friends' plea for help.

Friends groups constitute a type of volunteerism that has been invaluable in maintaining library service during periods of financial stress on library programming for children.

*   *   *   *

By way of summary, it can be stated that the children's librarian as a professional in the information age will have to possess a high degree of competency in the management and administration of a program far more complex than that which the founders of the work envisioned. The many facets of the work will involve not only training of staff, selection and evaluation of material, and programming planning and implementation, but also the ability to implement the mission of the library. That mission will include the social agenda for the welfare of children, to be implemented by articulating and defin-ing specific goals and objectives which focus the use of all the available resources. To do this, the following must obtain or be carefully considered:

1. The children's librarian/department manager will have to be part of the overall library management team which plans and designs and carries out needs assessments of the community to be served.

2. The children's librarian/department manager must be politically astute, knowledgable about the clientele the library's programs are reaching or should be reaching, and active on behalf of the library in this regard. Adults and institutions which touch the child in any fashion—parents and other caregivers, teachers, or agencies concerned with child welfare—should be considered to be a part of a network in which children's librarians should interact as members of the youth advocate community. Children's librarians, following the example of the children's services manager, should hold firm and informed convictions about children's right to learning and intellectual growth, and be fully knowledgable about children's developmental needs.

3. Access for children to all the services the public library may offer should be an underlying goal and principle. Providing access to the children's services and programs may entail constant communication and adequate publicity, as well as attention to scheduling and to barrier-free facilities: bibliographies, fliers, special collections, and events designed for the various age groups and their interests. It must be remembered that the children's librarian has an important role in service to adults: as advocate for the child's interests and needs and as advisor, facilitator, and planner in expanding and extending the dimensions of the child's intellectual and social world.

4. To achieve credibility and visibility with library management, those output measures which command the most attention and respect from administrators must be employed. Youth services librarians should be ready to justify a materials budget or special program efforts by measuring the impact of expenditures on a per capita basis in an area of the community where a large, child population exists and the needs are evident, or where demands for service have been made. The "better mousetrap" inside the library doors often entices not only the child but the adult community, which may need an innovative service or a more visible and accessible source of informa-

tion. When the children's services section of the Westchester Public Library system used a modest grant to inform and train staff about learning disabilities, the project identified and met a need which extended into the community and beyond, and gained national attention.

5. An important key to securing a place for children in the library's program is a willingness on the part of the children's librarians to keep abreast of new and emerging forms of media and technological information. All should be explored for their practical application in the work. While schools are experimenting with the use of computers with disabled children, or the preliteracy learning possibilities of computer use with preschoolers, some public librarians have found the computer to be an efficient helper in such matters as recording book reviews and bibliographic data to share with colleagues in several libraries. Information gathering and evaluation is more meaningful if results can be utilized beyond a given locale. The new technology, with its potential for expanding access to information, can expedite materials selection and collection development, and facilitate information referral and services.

6. Since budget making is a sensitive part of administrative decision making, the children's specialist must be prepared to document through proper research and analyses, specific needs for the child constituency. Funding from sources outside the library can often help to supply the additional financial support needed to implement a program design. Success or failure in meeting the criteria and expectations of donors will depend on the validity of the program design and on the measures used to evaluate its effectiveness. Program strength depends in large part on efficient use of regular staff, often with the judicious use of professional expertise from outside of the library. Arrangements for outside resources—funding or personnel—entail communication with management concerning planning, proposal writing, documenting credentials, and evaluating. An important consideration is the potential for sustaining the activity when external support ceases.

7. As from the beginning, so for the foreseeable future, the professionals who work with children will be required to know the materials being used with children. As time goes by, materials may increasingly vary, but selection and evaluation principles must be clearly defined with standards delineated in terms of age groups

being served, as well as according to the goals and policies of the library. Children, like other users of the library, deserve professional respect during their most impressionable years, and the quality of service which will help them to develop their tastes and contribute to the life-long habit of learning.

8. To strengthen professional status, as well as to maintain a supply of specialists, the right of children's librarians to earn an equitable wage, comparable to that of library professionals with a graduate degree and similar managerial responsibilities, must be supported.

9. It will be increasingly urgent to demonstrate use of the library by children, as measured by circulation statistics and also by program and other attendance figures. It is certainly significant if program attendance for children's programs is three times that of adults or older youth. It will be necessary to account for and justify time and effort (both on-the-job and personal time required) for preparation of story hours or class visits and other special programs. This might be compared to time spent by colleagues in adult services who prepare for book discussions, book reviews, or film programs.

10. Successful applications for projects funded from external sources should be carefully documented, as should the evaluations of the projects' implementation.

11. A running tabulation should be kept of telephone calls, correspondence, personal interviews in which assistance is provided to other librarians or members of the public.

12. A clipping and photo file should be maintained documenting activities undertaken by the children's department or division and its personnel. A number of public libraries have become widely known and influential in the library community and outside of it because of the high quality of their children's and youth services and staffs *and* the records kept.

13. File copies of questionnaires, filled in and returned with departmental responses, sent to surveyors and researchers should be kept accessible. These show expectations of your service and the realities the outside world is seeing.

14. The formal and informal reports submitted to library top management should underscore patron needs and what is required to meet them, plans, and—most important—accomplishments.

15. Brief vignettes about satisfied patrons should be collected and kept handy for use in reports, interviews, articles, and the like: the ad agency copywriter assisted with just the right quote or a creative idea from a children's book; the letter from a mother expressing appreciation for benefits to her child; and so on. "People results" expressed by one patron can be assumed to apply to others also.

16. It is essential to be mindful at all times of making opportunities to relate areas of emphasis in materials selection and programs to current events and issues, research, and social and educational goals. This shows administrators and other "gatekeepers" and "pursestring holders" that programs are relevant and that the staff and management of the children's department are aware, for instance that recent reports from the U.S. Department of Education, the Library of Congress, foundations, and other sources have heavily emphasized the importance to later learning of early exposure to books, to storytelling and reading aloud, to games and other activities that develop prereading language skills. These injunctions should be tied to what is being done, and accomplished, with the children and parents and teachers and caregivers and other adults in the artistic and business world that the program is serving. One cannot assume that such connections will be made automatically. Library services to children, and to adults on behalf of children, are important, and it is up to us to marshal every shred of proof and every piece of evidence available to prove that this is so.

Where children's librarians make the effort to develop carefully arrived at goals and precise objectives, to evaluate in terms of these, to continuously train staff, and to gather and use evidence, they are in a position to demand an appropriate budget and to spend it effectively. They will then take a giant step toward providing the kind of services that each new generation of children needs in its particular time. We may perceive that the world has changed and find it difficult to adjust, but children see no change because it is their time and the only world they know. We have the great, the priceless, opportunity to gear our programs to where children are in time.

6

Cooperation, Networking, and Community Outreach

Cooperation

Where children and young adults are the identifiable target user group, the terms cooperation and networking imply above all some types of cooperative effort between the schools in a community and the public library system. The principal goal would be the greatest possible accessibility to resources for youth both during and after school hours, and at all times during the year, including school holidays.

The history of the public library movement from its early days indicates that the pioneers in children's work made every effort to supplement the text materials used by students. As school libraries grew and developed their own collections of supplemental materials, the cooperation continued, with each agency recognizing its common goal of serving the student in complementary ways that would satisfy a full spectrum of needs. There was tacit understanding that neither type of library could satisfy the total demand for information or for recreational reading. There came to be greater understanding too, at least by librarians, that rapid changes in curriculum and in instructional methods would require greater use by children of both school and public libraries. Librarians realized too that reading and library use for recreation could not be totally separated and relegated to one type of library or the other as its sole province.

Nevertheless, intensive scrutiny, the increasingly heavy demands upon education institutions, and the complexities of administering library services to youth from two separately funded and governed sources, brought to a head in the 1960s the question of who should serve the needs of students. The five-part response to the question by Emerson Greenaway, then director of the Philadelphia Free Library and an outstanding leader in the profession, was one solution:

1. Make library service for all students the responsibility of the schools.

2. *Or*, have the public library assume full responsibility for all library service to them.

3. Subsidize public libraries through local boards of education during periods when school libraries were closed.

4. Create a library authority to be responsible for all kinds of library service.

5. Have the state library study and make the final determinations or recommendations.[1]

Lowell Martin, mentioned earlier as the consultant responsible for the Chicago Public Library study and the later San Francisco Public Library study, was the project consultant engaged also to help design a study of the library needs of Philadelphia's student population. In 1968, a grant from the then U.S. Office of Education enabled the Philadelphia Student Library Research Center Project to get underway. Two of its objectives were:

1. To define actual library resources needed by elementary and high school students and to evaluate what was available as measured against student needs and national standards.

2. To define the roles of the school and public library in the provision of these needs and in joint planning.[2]

Most of the information on student library needs was to come directly from students drawn from elementary and secondary public, parochial, and independent schools in the city. Cosponsored by the major school and public library organizations in Philadelphia, the final report was prepared by a research unit not affiliated with either of the agencies being studied. By 1969–70, funds from the U.S. Office of Education were provided to establish a demonstration program for future implementation, to be replicated later, it was hoped, throughout the country.

Questionnaires and checklists distributed to students provided input from representatives of college, university, school, and public libraries to be included in the planning and research activities. The project received its impetus from the sudden growth of the Philadelphia school libraries due to federal funds allocated under the Elementary and Secondary Education Act of 1965. The proliferation and development of school libraries and their ability to serve students effectively almost immediately caused a loss in public library circulation to children and youth.

Some significant statistics were collected which demonstrated the decline in interest in recreational reading in students between fourth grade and the twelfth. Results of the survey, which were intended to test use and needs for library resources by students, also revealed the impact of relationships between students, teachers, parents, and librarians. A large demand for materials was related to school assignments. Students from the sixth grade used 1.9 library books per week for school work. The sixth graders seemed to require twice as much audiovisual material as did the twelfth grade students. In the inner-city areas students used 1.75 audiovisual items per week as compared to 1.24 such items by students in higher income areas. Changes in reading habits occurred as children advanced in school or completed it. Sixty-one percent of fourth graders engaged in recreational reading as compared to twenty-two percent of twelfth graders. Forty-two percent of sixth to twelfth graders used both school and public libraries; thirty-two percent only the school library; and thirteen percent used other sources, such as home libraries and book stores. There was increased use of the public library as students advanced in grades sixth through twelfth from five percent to twenty-one percent.[3]

The survey revealed also that inner-city children found it difficult to visit public libraries and that they were less interested than suburban children in print materials. One telling factor was the rate of satisfaction students experienced in searching for materials. While twelfth graders complained about their lack of success in finding materials, the librarians cited a forty-five percent fulfillment rate in contrast to the thirty-four percent estimated by the high school students. Fewer inner-city students received help from parents than did students from more economically favored areas.

The Philadelphia Project findings culminated in a decision to open a new type of community library, an Action Library sponsored by both the public library and the schools, to make library resources more accessible to students and to involve community adults in library activities. One might conclude that the Philadelphia Project was a response to the furor occasioned by New York State Education Commissioner Nyquist's committee report which questioned the need for taxpayers to support two institutions which essentially provided library service to the same clientele. Somehow the availability of dual resources never seemed troublesome when it came to the support of public high school or college and university libraries, or of the public libraries which older and more mobile students patronize.

The Philadelphia Project did provide a model for measurement and evaluation of services as well as a statement of objectives, both short-range and long-range. Overall, the experience had important implications for the urban library in terms of assessing community needs and encouraging the participatory role of parents and the professionals in the other community-based agencies. During its demonstration period, grants from the U.S. Office of Education and the Pennsylvania State Library (through the Library Services and Construction Act from the federal level), contributed to the development of the Action Library. This model library was placed in an inner-city community of Philadelphia, where it served a population of close to 20,000. It was well-equipped with a range of multimedia equipment from record players to tape cassettes, a portable TV unit, film viewers and projectors.

Another inner-city library, begun with the cooperation and support of both the city board of education and the public library system, is the Langston Hughes Community Library and Cultural Center in Queens, a borough of New York City. This center has its own board of directors and continues to serve a large number of students, as well as preschool children, parents, and older citizens.

In 1979, the Olney Community Library and Arts Center, located between the elementary school and the high school on the school campus in Olney, Texas became an ongoing experiment in school–public library cooperation. Planning and research aid came from a nearby university and funding from the U.S. Office of Education. When the center opened, library facilities were made available to both elementary and high school students, and to adults in the community. The library operated, and still does, on a year-round basis. Job sharing and the generous use of paraprofessionals have made it possible to provide service six days a week. Intershelving of junior and senior high school collections made room for growth and for expanding collections in the spacious facility. Almost a decade later, the Olney Library is going strong, serving a community of just over 4,000 and providing access, for students and adults alike, to interlibrary loan resources from a much wider world of information.

Cooperation, often seen as a more efficient way of providing effective library services, generally starts with communication, according to Diana Young, youth consultant in North Carolina.[4] Beginning a dialogue between school and public library professionals may mean more than meetings. In some cases it takes flyers and other materials to interest teachers; newsletters; invitations to events; joint meetings of faculty and staff and between administrators of the agencies; the public librarians addressing a significant meeting of parents. A grant to the New York Public Library's George Bruce branch certainly demonstrated the need for many lines of communication as necessary preliminaries to planning for cooperative action.[5]

This grant, which came from the ESEA Title II (federal funds aimed at development of school library resources), was to involve local parochial schools and a public school which had used Title II grant funds effectively to equip itself with books and audiovisual materials and to produce library media program in an inner-city area. Good communications between the staffs of the schools and the public library enabled these agencies to coordinate their assistance to teachers and parents as well as to the students themselves.

Young also describes a project in Charlotte and its surrounding Mecklenberg County where the public library system and the school library media specialists joined forces to reach teachers with various communications, among them a leaflet entitled "You Can Help Us Work . . . Together."[6] In it, the public librarians were able to air their problem with mass school assignments and suggest some alternatives to teachers.

In Colorado, a cultural-awareness project was undertaken with LSCA funds from the U.S. Department of Education's division of libraries. The agencies jointly involved were the Conejas County Library and the North Conejas School District, which together selected, processed, and circulated some 600 documents to enrich knowledge of their Spanish heritage for some 4,000 students and adults who were Spanish-speaking and, for the most part, economically deprived. The project included recording and videotaping interviews with older community leaders.[7]

In Pennsylvania, a reading-aloud project was launched cooperatively by the Dauphin County Library system—which initiated it, also with LSCA funds—and six participating school districts. In a year-long research and planning effort, "Propelling Reading" undertook work with teachers and families to ensure reading aloud both at school and at home. Participants were included in an incentive–reward program. Preliminary findings indicated that taking home a book which a child had already listened to increased the child's word recognition skill, increased ability to read with expression and understanding, increased sentence fluency, and also the frequency with which parents read to children.[8]

Another specific and recent cooperative effort between schools and public libraries took place in a rural area of California. This one was also a reading-motivation project coordinated jointly by the Kern County rural schools and county libraries, which sponsored professional artists in dance, drama, music, and creative writing in presentations geared to motivating children in geographically isolated areas to read for pleasure, self-identity, and growth. The program in the Performing Arts Libraries and schools reached some 1,500 students.[9]

Through the years, the professional literature has been filled increasingly with examples of school and public libraries engaged in informal, cooperative relationships, such as periodic meetings of staff to discuss and review materials and plan programming. These efforts at coordination and reinforcement took a big leap forward when funds for such cooperative ventures were made available under Title III of LSCA, and now, still another big leap forward with the aid of technology. We are seeing many more formal, complex, and structured multitype arrangements and electronic inter-connections. To be sure, school and public librarians still exchange and distribute summer reading lists, arrange class visits to the public library and visits by the public librarian to the classroom, and present joint programs on reading motivation and other subjects for PTA groups. But now, for a decade or more, both agencies have known that these activities, useful though they are, do not go far enough. Shortages of funds, and therefore of staff and materials, have added a new urgency and new goals to cooperative effort, and technology has made different orders of cooperation and resource sharing possible. However, as the use of technology increases, the means of coordinating acquisitions, sharing materials, and evaluating them will need to be studied. Most important will be the need for continuing education, for both professionals and support staff in the cooperating agencies, to be placed high on the agenda for future ventures.

A real challenge lies in the barriers to communication between institutions with different missions and mandates. Another lies in the temptations to plan cooperative efforts without sufficient assessment of what the clientele to be served really wants or needs. Still another challenge lies in the inability of many students to view schools, or for that matter even public libraries, as anything other than establishment environments bent on curbing, modifying, or otherwise changing youthful behavior. These and other factors often limit the efforts of librarians with potential users of library materials or information. Perhaps more library services will have to be delivered to youth in the future from neutral ground, that is, outside of schools or libraries, like the Philadelphia Action Library or the Langston Hughes Cultural Center, both mentioned earlier. Children are looking, and more will look in the future, for media outlets or environments; schools and libraries will have to learn to share the task of providing them.

There are some important questions to be studied, among them: How much by way of savings can be realized by sharing resources of materials, data bases, delivery systems, staff? Resource-sharing and networking plans in many forms are still to be explored and tried out, in order to find the most efficient means of providing optimum services to children and youth through two separately governed and funded agencies. Budget cuts and the repeated defeat of school bond issues resulted, for a time, in administrators returning many "excessed" school library media specialists to the classroom; now the tide is turning the other way as schools try to restore library personnel. Public library administrators are trying to fill long-vacant positions for professional children's librarians, and having a hard time finding them. It seems just possible that the importance of library services for children through both school and public libraries has begun to prove itself, and school library media specialists and public library children's specialists are gaining valuable insights and experience by working together in more focused activities, and in ways that are open to them without huge expenditures or technical know-how.

One good example is the citywide storytelling contests which take place both in Nassau County and in New York City itself. Children, teachers, parents, and librarians, in both schools and public library neighborhood branches, engage themselves in the coordination of a program which involves both materials and people to great advantage. Public librarians assist in the selection and introduction of story materials, in storytelling techniques and performance standards. They serve as judges as children tell the stories, and as advisers to teachers and school library media specialists. Later, public libraries provide the setting for children's performances as storytellers. Children and adults are introduced to different cultural backgrounds through the stories, to richness of language and expression, and to the ancient art of oral entertainment and transfer of knowledge. The teamwork that develops around this project between schools and public libraries takes place without the benefit of computers, or layers of bureaucratic structure.

In 1982–83, the Los Angeles County Public Library included ten schools as part of a grant project for "Stimulating Reading and Library Use by Children Through Involvement in Quality Arts Experiences."[10] The project had as its goal the motivation of children through the performing arts, poetry, and creative writing, and the public library, using live artists, tied in books and programs for the school children in the area. A product of the program is a handbook for teachers and a videotape of program events to encourage other teachers and librarians to interpret the enjoyment of literature in relation to the arts.

No discussion about school and public library cooperation would be complete without an examination of some of the barriers to access erected for children and young people. Theodore Hines observed that these "arise either from a failure to perceive properly how children's intellectual development does require access to a very wide range of titles, or from a setting of priorities which places children and young people very low indeed on the totem."[11] This lack of proper access was recognized by the 1981 State of New York Education Commissioner's Committee report on *Meeting Information Needs of the 80s.*[12] This committee on statewide library development affirmed the policy that all residents of the state be guaranteed free access to services through libraries and library systems. It recommends further that "the state should make every effort to encourage and develop the sharing of resources by all libraries (public, academic, school, special and institutional) within the state, through local, regional and state partnerships." Many children fail, however, to benefit fully from resource sharing through the systems. Dr. Marilyn L. Miller, then of the University of North Carolina School of Library Science at Chapel Hill, in her 1981 report "Children's Access to Library Systems," found that access to children's materials through inter-library loan procedures is somewhat limited.[13] She notes that only the Children's Media Data Bank, developed by Ted Hines at the University of North Carolina at Greensboro, which operated only until 1981–82, provided an extensive database of materials for children. This database contained thousands of titles and a great range of media, citing listings and annotations in well-known journals and review sources such as *Booklist, The Children's Catalog,* or the *Elementary School Library Catalog,* as well as the Library of Congress Marc records for children's books.

At this point it might be well to take a closer look at the community library's partner in the cooperative efforts we have outlined: the school library media center and its program. After all, "school is where the children are,"[14] and where they can be reached much of the time if one is considering kindergarteners and up through sixth grade in the public, private, parochial, and independent schools across the nation. If, in the future, schools were to be open year-round and daily school hours extended, libraries in schools could prove to be even more readily accessible to the children than they are now.

The fact that there are more schools than public libraries is a first point in making the case that the school library is a logical place for children to satisfy their recreational as well as their informational needs. The widespread system of busing has both advantages and disadvantages in providing access to the school library, however. It may mean library access even in an area so remote that there is no public library service; it provides access for a clientele that has little mobility on its own. However, buses leave promptly at the end of the school day, and children dependent on the school library may have no access to it in weekend or late afternoon and evening hours because of distance, even if it were open and located in facilities that could be operated independently of the rest of the school building.

Other points in favor of strong services to children through their school libraries, assuming that they are equipped to live up to their potential, are: a collection of materials geared to the school's instructional program; administrative support and commitment both to children and to education, as well as specifically to the library media program itself; and appropriate professional staff. Largely as a result of the flow of money into the development of school libraries in the 1960s, many strong, centralized library programs replaced the scattered and disorganized classroom collections of books which had been common in schools in earlier decades. These school library media centers, as they came to be called, were most fully effective when staffed by professional teacher-librarians with credentials which included degrees and certification for teaching as well as for library work. Their new designations signified not only growing inclusion of audiovisual and other nonprint materials in their collections, along with books, but an active effort to make library resources and services an integral, everyday part of the instructional program of the school—part of its curriculum, rather than just being supplemental and enriching. Although federal government funding accounted for a large part of the financing for school library development, there was enthusiastic citizen support and an increased allocation of local tax monies to the effort, too.

A national project—the Knapp School Library Demonstration Project—funded by a foundation and carried out by a specially appointed board under the auspices of the American Association of School Librarians, focused attention on good school library programs. It did this by supporting, at a cost of more than a million dollars, a demonstration of excellent, fully realized programs in selected elementary, and later secondary, schools. Team visits to these schools by educational and community leaders from around the country, paid for out of project funds, were instrumental in spreading the word and the vision of how effective a school library program could be. Various studies highlighted the role of cooperation in the efficient administration of the library media center. Teachers were the obvious first-line partners in shaping and utilizing the school library's collection and program.

The flow of diverse books and other materials into the school library coincided with new perceptions among educators about methods of teaching, learning style, and the desirability of the independent, non-lockstep learning made possible by a wealth of library materials beyond the textbook. The earlier concept that the school library's only role was to serve the instructional, curriculum-related needs of the child gave way to the realization that reading for learning and reading (and viewing and listening, too) for enjoyment cannot be strictly separated. It is still true, however, that the use of materials primarily for learning and instruction and the teaching role of the school librarian characterize the school library media specialist, as compared with the public library children's specialist. The public library children's librarian has perhaps a better opportunity to reach out beyond the child to parents and the personnel of agencies, other than the schools, that affect the community's children, and to promote pure reading enjoyment. The point is frequently made that the use of the public library is voluntary and its use may have little or no connection with school.

For all of these reasons, the concept of a single type of library service for children, lodged within the school, has largely given way to acceptance of the idea of a cooperative, complementary-services plan under which each type of institution may emphasize different aspects of service to the same child-user. It has become increasingly apparent that no one type of library can possibly meet all the demands. Ideally, sometime down the road to the future, both school librarians and public library specialists serving the children of a given community can share information about each child, his mental and physical development and needs, his family situation and background, and plan together a full range of services and stimuli for this "whole child."

Networking

Many of the technologically oriented and formal cooperative programs aimed at producing economies now involve shared computerized databases, cooperative delivery systems, film networks, joint materials evaluation, purchasing programs and staff development.

In the state of Washington, for example, the Washington Library Network includes school personnel on the governing board and provides statewide library services.[15] A regional film catalog and a file of resource persons, available to both institutions and their individual users, is part of the cooperative effort in Colorado. North Carolina lends films to both school and public libraries from the state's collection, and the use of its Department of Public Instruction's Media Review Evaluation Center is available to both types of library.[16] A statewide storytelling festival, public library workshops on preschool programming, and an element of a rural, community-sponsored project funded by the Library Services and Construction Act through the state library, are all part of the cooperative activities of the state.

Ambitious steps to improve access to materials are being taken in both Pennsylvania and Minnesota.[17] Students and teachers are able to obtain access to materials located in scores of school and public libraries through a CD-ROM catalog in each library. In Minnesota, the CD-ROM catalog will be accessible on Apple II or IBM PC micros connecting fifty-nine school districts. The catalog is expected to contain some six million holdings which represent 250,000 titles. Pennsylvania's project is part of an ongoing "Access Pennsylvania" program. The current budget will allow forty-six high school libraries to join sixty libraries which are already sharing collection data for 650,000 unique records with location data on CD-ROM.

In Wisconsin, the Cooperative Children's Book Center became an important resource in the state. It provides the opportunity for both public and school librarians to examine books before deciding to acquire them, thereby improving the selection process.

A cooperative in Rochester, New York is composed of four Boards of Cooperative Educational Services (BOCES), which serve schools in the city and in Monroe County. Governed by the Rochester Area Resource Exchange (RARE),[18] it also includes system and network representatives and operates a document delivery service, interlibrary loan, and a union list of serials.

In New York City, the four major public library systems in the city and Westchester County are part of a multitype network which includes a school system, thus uniting all types of libraries in the city environs for resource sharing. It serves a population equal to forty percent or more of the population of the entire state. One important component of New York's INTERSHARE project is the "Homework Hotline," based in the Brooklyn Public Library and utilizing a toll-free telephone to assist students with classroom assignments. The first two months of this hotline operation recorded a total of close to 3,800 calls, more than half in the area of mathematics. Forty-eight percent of the callers identified themselves as being in the fourth through sixth grades.[19]

Several examples of networking related to school and children's services found throughout the states offer a variety of activities. A library network is of course only as strong as its component partners, and their strengths often determine the areas in which the network operates its sharing activities.

Although many libraries have made a good start in using technology to gain desirable economies and more efficient services through shared databases, automated cataloging systems, and document delivery services, a survey made in 1977 revealed remaining barriers. One great hurdle in cooperative planning and implementation is the negative attitude often displayed by actual or potential participant librarians in the various types of libraries. There is, in addition, the complexity of the political and fiscal arrangements, which may affect funding sources or have an impact on the initial recipient of the grant. Several recommendations were made as a result of the study. The most important of these were that the problems of networking be carefully researched; that an investigative commission be established to study factors involving funding in state and local agencies; and that a plan for guidance to school library media specialists be provided to assist them in solving problems involved in sharing materials obtained with federal funds. Workshops organized to help librarians to study resource sharing on a state or local level, and/or to open avenues for communication among school personnel and staff in other types of libraries, were among the strongest recommendations.[20]

Networking and a range of cooperative efforts with other community agencies—including, but not limited to the schools—loom large among the challenges facing children's librarians today. Objectives for community library work should reflect the shared responsibility each cooperating partner agency hopes to assume. Cooperation and outreach go hand in hand, and for the public library children's management and staff both will mean more joint planning, more awareness, more attendance at the meetings of other agencies, shared facilities and equipment, careful assessment of jurisdictional responsibilities and barriers to accomplishment, strategies for eliminating these barriers where possible or for going around them and, most important, willingness to compromise in order to get needed forward movement.

Reaching Out into the Community

While the school can be considered perhaps the most important of the community institutions in the child's life, today's society has

	Resource Sharing	Computer Data Base for Online Search	Films Previews & Evaluation	AV Resources	Delivery Services	Selection of Examination Center
California (CLASS)	X	X				
Illinois (Regional Library Council)	X				X	
Indiana (Vigo County)			X			X
New Jersey					X	
New York (RARE)					X	
New York (INTERSHARE)	X	X			X	
New York (BOCES Consortium)			X			
Washington (WLN)		X	X			

created many more organizations in the child's immediate surroundings which exist in addition to the home or in place of the home. The playgrounds, the churches, and the settlement houses of the nineteenth century are still in place, as are day-care and after-school centers, provider homes, health and rehabilitation or correctional institutions, community centers, youth centers, headstart programs. Various other child care-giving agencies are also part of children's surroundings.

Public libraries have long recognized the importance of working as closely as possible with these community agencies which focus on the child. Public libraries have had a history of service to these agencies and through them, as well as through the schools, to their child clients. The public library provides options for self-learning at every level; for the child, the relatively unstructured and nonjudgmental atmosphere of the public library may be its greatest appeal. Most school-age children are first introduced to the public library through group contacts by the schools.

The first point of contact by the children's librarian with many community agencies may come about through attendance at local meetings as the representative of the public library. The librarian's interest in a wide variety of community problems and needs will be noted, whether in connection with a school board meeting, as co-planner for youth activities with the YMCA or 4-H Club youth leader, or as a member of the advisory board of the Police Athletic League. The children's librarian in these situations is always alert to opportunities to support mutual concerns, or to provide lists of materials or program support. For years, for example, children's librarians have worked with scout groups, acting as reading counselors to help with merit badges, and encouraging the use of library resources and facilities in connection with the arts and crafts program and exhibits. The presence of a children's librarian on a local civic or community governing board *not* primarily concerned with youth can afford the opportunity to exchange views and to think about community goals as they have an impact on youth. Familiarity with library personnel bred by such a working relationship has produced the added bonus of more advocacy for library issues, and has indeed sometimes been the source of funding for specific library projects.

The children's librarian who maintains a continuous schedule of reaching out to explore and to open communications channels will find many a forum in which to pose questions related to services to children and to public library service overall. Who composes the various adult-user constituencies of children's services in public libraries? How can thoughtful and reinforcing overlap of programs be made to replace haphazard and wasteful duplication? How can parents and other family members be more productively involved in library and all other services offered to children in the community? And how can systems of evaluation be devised that assess the benefits of the children's services program to individual children and the extent to which these programs support and reinforce community goals?

Numerous reports and studies have attempted to define the most important roles to be performed by public libraries for children—assuming that elementary school libraries are adequate to serve at least their curricular needs, which is, of course, frequently not the case. The 1970 New York State Education Commission's report suggested at least three areas which the schools are not likely to be able to address: service to very young infants and children; service to children in institutions and residential agencies; and adults, such as teachers, storytellers, authors, illustrators, creative people from advertising and from broadcasting who may be interested in children's literature.[21] Service in these areas is certainly not a new idea for children's librarians, but they have increased their outreach efforts in these and other directions for the past decade and a half at least.

The New Orleans Public Library, with support of an LSCA grant has been able to provide books and programming to link the public library with community day-care centers. In Pasadena, California, the La Pintoresa branch began circulating bilingual materials (Spanish and English), including paperbacks and audiovisuals, to day-care centers. Much more detail about early childhood programs, into which many children's librarians have invested many resources, follows in a later chapter of this book.

Storytelling in the parks, at block parties or street fairs, brings a traditional "in-library" activity out to the public. Children's library programming has included guest visits from experts associated with museums, zoological gardens, and nature centers. More and more librarians are making common cause with professionals in these other nonschool, learning-leisure institutions to plan cooperative programs and expand children's horizons.

In line with utilizing "what's out there" and linking it to books and other library materials and programming, children's librarians have for many years worked with the best children's television programs to use their stimulus and to follow up in the library and in the home. Children's librarians in countless libraries formed viewing groups for "Sesame Street" from its inception, and librarians helped parents of preschool children to follow up on skills and concepts. A committee of children's librarians, appointed by the then Children's Services Division of ALA (now Association of Library Service to Children) and working under the auspices of the National Book Committee, worked closely with the "Sesame Street" staff to select books related to the programs and to prepare materials sent out to parents. A similar activity engages librarians in the current *"Reading Rainbow"* TV program.

Since the beginning of work with children in libraries, books and storytelling programs have been taken to hospital wards to children who are confined there. An exceptionally successful program was carried on in New York, at the invitation of the New York Foundling Hospital, in which a children's librarians introduced picture books for very young children to student nurses. Bibliographies of books for preschoolers, including books of rhymes and finger plays, became part of the student nurses' equipment in hospitals. Public libraries have been utilized, too, by teachers of homebound children in preparation for home visits.

Of all the opportunities opening up for children's librarians perhaps the greatest one of all, in the last years of this century, is the opportunity to work with parents and other family members to help them to help their own children to learn. As it often has, the professional association has opened up this vital arena of operations with a national demonstration project. The Association for Library Service to Children, according to information furnished in October 1987 by Susan Roman, executive director of ALSC, received a grant early in 1987 from the Home and School Institute (HSI), a Washington-based, nonprofit, educational organization, to participate in a "New Partnerships for Student Achievement" project over a three-year period. Funding for the project is provided by the John D. and Catherine T. MacArthur Foundation.

ALSC has selected the Sulzer Regional Library of the Chicago Public Library system as its demonstration site. In the fall of 1987, a sustained program of parent workshops and home-learning activities was begun. The goals of the program are:

- To involve community organizations in helping families fulfill their educational role
- To assist middle school/junior high school students in becoming productive, self-sufficient citizens through development of good study skills and attitudes and of a lifetime interest in learning
- To help organizations to replicate similar programs in communities throughout the country.

These programs are intended to reinforce and extend what children learn in school by motivating and enabling families to become active educators of their children. After evaluation of the demonstration site program and refinements suggested by the evaluation, the program will be available for adaptation in other libraries during 1988–89, with mini-grants for implemention and materials. ALSC is one of five organizations to receive this grant and to become one of the participants in the New Partnerships for Student Achievement. The other organizational grantees in the HSI program are the American Red Cross, the American Postal Workers Union, the National Association of Colored Women's Clubs, and Parents Without Partners.

The motto of the Home and School Institute is: "Fulfilling a child's potential is a family's achievement, a community's strength, an nation's security," a motto which children's librarians should be delighted to incorporate into their own work guidelines. Children's librarians who elect to work with the project in their own communities will find themselves reaching out to and through a whole new, widening circle of partnerships.

It may be that in the future each community will have a central educational-cultural alliance or resources-coordinating unit which would harness the energies and resources of all the types of community agencies—including libraries, of course—that serve children and families. It might arrange partnerships and joint ventures, and help parents and other caring adults to make the most of opportunities. Until then, however, public library children's librarians can step up their initiatives to forge working relationships with the multiplicity of agencies that can provide for children the same diversity of resources and help in learning and in recreation that the adults of the community have come to expect.

7

Children's Services and the New Technology

We had scarcely become accustomed to the all-pervasive existence of television and its offspring (such as video games) before even newer electronic media and devices emerged. To most children born into a world of push-button entertainment, however, none of the media is either novel or exceptional. It is to adults, who are still for the most part print oriented, that the new forms for learning and communication present problems of integration among traditional materials.

A 1980 study in California revealed that that state recorded use of a proportionately high percentage of print, as opposed to nonprint materials, in library services to children.[1] The results pointed to a need for continuing training of professionals in the use of new technology and its acceptance by them as part of library programs and services. This is especially important in view of burgeoning computer and video technology. Although library use of computers is now widespread in the areas of cataloging, acquisition, inventory, and circulation, plans for utilizing technology in areas of library programming for children have moved very much slower. Children's librarians were, however, quick to incorporate earlier nonbook materials and equipment such as filmstrips, films, and recordings into their programming. Television has been the most revolutionary of the technologies in its impact on library programs for children to date. Librarians have offered reinforcement by supplying bibliographies, recommending books as tie-ins with popular TV programs, or displaying materials which promoted book-related television shows which encourage children to read as a follow up to viewing.

The continuing controversy occasioned by the mindless passivity of the viewer and the harmful effects of the content of much television due to violence, distortion, and lack of realism, did not eliminate television nor lessen its attractiveness. Television in its many forms is more popular, more influential, and more available to children than ever.

In spite of, or perhaps in some part because of, all the criticism of television, one producer, Joan Ganz Cooney, proceeded to explore television's capacity to teach children. The success of "Sesame Street" and its impact on educational television, despite some detractors, is history. The show was conceived of and started with the simple idea of providing early preparation for learning for inner-city preschoolers. Likable characters to identify with and fast action presented the skills needed to succeed in school: reading, writing, arithmetic, and concept development. With the realization that these children were often exposed to television as substitute parents or sitters, other programs directed at this audience developed. As television claimed the minds, attention, and most of the waking hours of preschoolers as well as of school-age children (twenty-seven to thirty-one hours a week), many people became alarmed about the poor quality of programming and the degree of exploitation of child viewers by accompanying advertising. One group, begun in Massachusetts, was Action for Children's Television (ACT), which began to monitor and attempt to publicize and eliminate commercial abuses on programs directed to children.

Now that cable television is providing a greater variety of viewing choices for local communities, ACT has recommended more programming for children, commercial-free viewing, and allowance for interaction by children themselves in the programming. ACT continues to urge that adult TV viewers take an activist role in securing appropriate programming for children. In some cases, librarians have taken the lead by suggesting program ideas, becoming members of advisory and planning boards for proposed programs, and making use of the medium's potential for learning and creative recreation.

The continuing concern about the effects of TV viewing by the young manifests itself in attempts to control without censoring. The librarian's role is to encourage critical viewing skills. With preschoolers and school-age children devoting more hours to watching TV than are spent in the classroom, responsible adults keep trying to find alternatives to viewing, or at least to make children more discriminating judges of what they see and hear.

Several organizations have been funded by the U.S. Department of Education to help in the development of critical viewing skills among students.[2] The Southwest Educational Development Laboratory tested materials for kindergarten through third grade. Their packet of materials, titled "Television: A Family Focus," was directed to parents with the objective of helping children to find alternatives to television viewing or to stimulate discussion about what has been viewed. New York's public television station, WNET, received a grant for $400,000 for the purpose of working with materials for grades six through eight. A workbook called *Critical Television Viewing: A Language Skills Work-A-Text* was designed to generate discussion about programs seen,[3] and a series of ten short segments called "Tuned In" has been prepared for educators to use with the text. Other components were planned for high school and college students.

A combined package of 16-mm films and videotapes with a teacher's guide accompanies "Getting the Most Out of Television," a project funded by the ABC network and developed by Dorothy and Jerome Singer, who are associated with Yale University.[4] Emphasis on the tapes and films reflects the Singers' belief that television makes it difficult for children to distinguish fantasy from reality. The guidebook is intended for use in the classroom and under the teacher's guidance. In it, discussion about the various topics developed in the film presentations are brought into focus for student evaluation and study.

Alternatives to television programming have taken the form of video technology, and one library system found new popularity when it established its video-learning sites. The Mid-Hudson system in New York state invested in videorecorders and Hitachi color television sets for nine locations. Funding was provided under an LSCA grant of federal money through the state, and trained staff selected titles for the collections. Funding from other grants made it possible for the system to do its own video production, with a Sony Portapack. All age groups have access to the centers and to the materials. Video technology seems to have satisfied many information needs in this largely rural area.[5]

Maryland followed the lead of California and Texas in networking professionally produced videotapes.[6] Seven systems in the state are responsible for a training tape and one public service announcement each for Baltimore television. This began in Baltimore County's Public Library video studio, and is a source of programming for cable TV and for instructional tapes. The Library Video Network links the Enoch Pratt Free Library with Baltimore, Carroll, Cecil, Anne Arundel, Harford, and Howard Counties. Most of the network's equipment is provided by Baltimore County. Other counties in the state are expected to contribute to the expansion of the network, which will use video for publicity and staff development projects. Funding for this project also came from LSCA funds in a grant for $130,000.

Since television continues to play a dominant role in the life of many school-age children, libraries have decided to become more involved with and supportive of telecasts which are, or can be made to be, reading-oriented. The joint CBS Broadcast Group and Library of Congress "Read More About It" project started in 1980 to feature book titles related to the various programs.[7] Titles were selected by the Library of Congress. On another front, a cable TV show, "New England Today" offered interviews with children, selected book tips for parents or suggestions for reading guidance as part of the Boston-based "Roundtable of Children's Literature," on cable channel 56.[8] "KIDSNET is a computerized clearinghouse for children's radio and television," as described by Karen Jaffe, executive director of KIDS-NET and former National Education Association's communications specialist. It has compiled data on 2,000 programs, offering free access to information on current and future programs and programs aired in the past through its active database and archive database. It has the capability of identifying programs for specific curriculum and grade levels, from preschool through high school; for children with special needs; includes program synopses; and, of particular interest to librarians, programs based on books. A project of the National Foundation for the Improvement of Education, created by the National Education Association (NEA), it is supported in part by grants from the Ford Foundation, the Carnegie Corporation of New York, and others.

KIDSNET is still in an experimental stage, and testing of the data and access methods has been in progress since 1985. Subscription information is available from NEA in Washington, D.C.[9]

The wave of the future would seem to be an *integration* of the electronic and other, newer media with books and other printed materials in the public library children's department, as has already occurred in the school library media center. The New York Public

Library is undertaking, with a one million dollar grant in private funds, a revitalization of children's reading room collections in its seventy-six branches with children's rooms. These collections are unique to each branch in terms of content, and are noncirculating, but used in the library. Also underway is the development of a videocassette collection in fifteen branches, and the provision of microcomputers for use by the children in fifteen of these neighborhood branches. Accompanying the microcomputer and videocassette collections will be selected bibliographies of software.

Computers in the Children's Program

Canada has introduced computers to preschoolers at its Oakville, Ontario Public Library.[10] Here the goal is to improve prereading skills of the children before they enter school. When home computers achieved such popularity that parents were willing to pay twelve dollars to enroll their children in the program, the library found that it needed to hire more staff on a part-time basis to help with the increased work load.

In one Chicago library, "getting to use the computer" was the incentive for reading in the "Computers Are Fun" summer reading club. Together with book reports, awards, and exposure to books and magazines about computers, children in the club were given simple instructions on the use of the microcomputer, and each child was assured time on the computer. Both learning games and games for pure recreation were available at specific times. This library, the North Pulaski Neighborhood Library, had received a grant from the Friends of the Chicago Public Library. They invested in an Apple II, a printer, and a couple of disk drives. Both young children and teenagers have been introduced to computer use, and the children's librarian, reference librarian, and others instruct and direct programs involving use of the computer. Nearly fifty percent of the patrons who have shown interest in developing computer skills through the reading club and the library's personal computer center are between twelve and twenty years of age.[11]

There is no question but that libraries have recognized that children and youth respond and learn from other media in addition to print media. Technological developments are playing a larger and larger part in the development of literacy and a life-long learning environment. The latest acquisitions in both public libraries and school libraries—as well as in classrooms—are microcomputers which are smaller and less imposing than a TV set. In schools, the use of micros for instructional purposes is expanding rapidly. Many textbook publishers are among those developing software and course materials for classroom use with microcomputers. More and more educators are looking at the potential of computers in both classroom and library, for motivational purposes. As with any format, the question of criteria for evaluation arises. The programs or software will ultimately be judged for their impact on learning, their relation to curriculum, and their effectiveness in enabling student comprehension.

As a recent *New York Times* article has stated, "Computers could alter many of the objectives of education, including the amount of material that students are expected to carry around in their heads."[12] Thomas Carpenter, mathematics professor at the University of Wisconsin has said, "Kids will need more than facts . . . they'll need to learn to deal with information, think about, analyze and organize information more than ever before."[13]

No children's librarian in the public library of the 1980s can ignore the new language their colleagues are learning. Bytes and chips, and new languages known as LOGO, BASIC, COBOL, PASCAL, and FORTRAN separate the uninformed from the knowledgable. Children's librarians are exploring the many practical uses of the microcomputer in the public library. As early as 1979, the Chicago Public Library approved for purchase 160 microcomputers to use with children to improve reading and spelling skills. As computer hardware costs become lower, the librarian's search is focused, and probably increasingly will focus, on software programs suitable for library use. Good ones are still few and far between and comparatively more expensive than the hardware.

Computers have made a significant impact on the children themselves. They have already helped to shape the communication and learning styles of a generation, and are well on the way to creating new generations of "hackers"—described as compulsive users of computers and defined by *Rolling Stone* as comprising an "intense reclusive subculture of the computer age."[14]

Children are quick to discover that a public library has computers among its information tools and resources. In a public library in Menlo Park, California, three PET microcomputers and a TRS–80 were in constant use from two to six p.m. on weekdays, and on weekends when school is out. Children waited in line outside the library until it opened to use the computers until closing time. Some libraries have begun computer clubs to help children do their own programming or to help them improve math or spelling skills. Others have found microcomputers successful in work with disabled children. In Maryland, the Montgomery County Public Library received an LSCA grant which enabled disabled children as well as their parents, teachers, and health aides, to work with the microcomputers. Both the Rolling Meadows Public Library in Illinois, and Wisconsin's Madison Public Library have launched computer training programs for their young patrons. In the Madison Public Library, the program revealed the general lack of software for use with children and the inordinate amount of staff time required for training and maintenance of computer equipment and software.[15]

Librarians who work with children are seeing more applications of microcomputer use in providing children access to other than bibliographic information. In 1979, a pizza parlor in Menlo Park, California was the site of an experiment to introduce microcomputers to the general public.[16] The idea, which culminated in a project funded by the National Science Foundation, and later housed in the Menlo Park Public Library, was called "Computer Town USA." Three years later, Computer Town became an international network, with member affiliates in the United States and around the world with the purpose of promoting computer literacy and accessibility. The computer project in the Chicago Public Library was designed to help with reading skills and centered around a reading club called "Computers are Fun." Children who attended weekly club meetings learned more each time about computers and when each book read on the subject was recorded, the reader became eligible for individual time on the computer.

Computer use is also giving new insights into the different ways people learn and suggesting new teaching methods that may be tailored to these learning styles. Some researchers are already testing computers for use as diagnostic tools to identify the reasons for student errors and the mental processes that caused them. There are still many problems and questions, however, of which one important one is the extent to which the availability of and access to computers will vary from school to school and community to community. The more affluent schools are providing computers for student use and practice; the less affluent cannot afford them, and the same is true of public libraries.

Relative to this situation, Peggy Charren, president of Action for Children's Television, is reported as having said, "Unless all children are taught to use this new technology, we are in danger of creating a whole new disadvantaged class of people."[17] Noted educator-psychologist, Dr. Kenneth B. Clark, voiced a similar concern, as well as another major one concerning the effects on the child of constant interface with a computer. Whatever the benefits, there might also be a cost—that of losing ability to make satisfactory human contacts and to undertake less structured communication.[18]

On the question of inequities of access to computers, perhaps the public library can help to close the gaps in less advantaged communities where neither parents nor schools can afford to provide each child with adequate computer-learning time. A proposal to set up a "computer bank" would well begin with the children's department of the public library, where computers could be made available for training parents, and both hardware and software could be lent for children's use.

But even more important than the access and equality of access questions are the social and educational questions still to be answered about the shift in emphasis on quantitative responses and on either "right" or "wrong" answers demanded by computers. The diminution of the importance of the humanities and the creativity of the open-ended question and response in the face of heavy emphasis on technical skills and precise descriptors is of real concern as well. We need also a clear definition of "computer literacy." Should the term apply to computer use which aids in problem solving? As computers become more and more commonplace, certain concepts and directions in education, knowledge transfer, and communications will have to be re-examined and possibly revised.

Meanwhile, despite many uncertainties, computers are being hailed as the newest "sure road" to learning as schools solicit funds for them, accept them from companies as gifts, and find ways to utilize them throughout the instructional program at all levels. Some material that once required textbooks can now be programmed into the computers and used with or without teacher assistance.

Some teachers attest that computers have reclaimed potential dropouts and have been especially helpful with the disabled, particularly the deaf or hearing impaired, who can relate well to the visual aspects. A contest called the "National Search for Applications of Personal Computing to Aid the Handicapped," sponsored by the National Science Foundation and coordinated by Dr. Paul Hazen at Johns Hopkins University, resulted in "a keyboard for severely disabled that can be controlled by eye movements and a computer that may help the deaf learn to read lips."[19] The Kurzweil machine is a computer that enables the blind to read print through the use of a speech synthesizer, and it is being used in an increasing number of libraries.

Children's librarians should, indeed must if they are to be seen as professionally viable, take an active part in discovering new uses for electronic tools and gearing technology to making information services, learning, and recreational stimulation available to children. Computers can help to improve writing, speech, and thinking skills, to build concepts, and to sharpen perceptions. Automated systems now keep track of circulation services, materials acquisition, resource sharing through common bibliographic databases, and interlibrary loan systems. However, many—even most—of these systems have placed a low priority on juvenile holdings in their databanks and have concentrated on adult, scholarly, or business users. Access for children who might wish to take advantage of interlibrary loans is severely restricted. Now that computer use is basic to virtually every aspect of society, libraries will need to explore the computer's capacity to deliver and analyze information creatively and assist the searcher to use it effectively. This will present a special challenge to librarians working with children and youth in school and public libraries.

While automation has become a given in libraries as elsewhere, technical services specialists are still struggling to bring bibliographic choas into better automated order, both for patrons and for their own needs.

Mention was made in the previous chapter of the unique project which was begun with a view to bringing bibliographic order to children's informational needs. The Children's Media Data Bank, supported by the U.S. Department of Education, included by its third year of operation, over 10,000 juvenile titles in the computer. Conversion of the data to microcomputers had started and other experiments for refining the terms of data retrieval had been done. Subject headings included nonprint materials, picture books, reference, periodicals, and more. This project, conceived by Lois Winkel and directed by the late Dr. Theodore C. Hines, gathered information from hundreds of searches related to the level of difficulty of various requests. Results indicated a need for a different indexing approach to children's materials and a more inclusive list of subject headings. As the end of the funding approached in 1980, the Children's Media Data Bank was not yet available for use by librarians and children, and work on it was halted in 1981 and has not yet been resumed. It is to be hoped that eventually this promising project will be brought up to date and put into operation when the funds and a suitable director can be found.[20]

In Illinois, the Evanston Public Library has installed a replacement for the card catalog, a "touch-sensitive online Public Access Catalog (PAC)."[21] The terminal is keyboard-free and operates with just the touch of a finger. In addition to bibliographic details for a particular book, PAC will allow patrons to know when the item was last borrowed, when it is due back, and which branch in the system has it. Children love using it to locate information. Libraries in Iowa City, Salt Lake City, Aurora, Colorado, some colleges, and the U.S. Department of Energy, among others, have all been using public access catalogs.

Librarians in Ohio have found an effective use for the computer for their Children's Book Review Project, which was funded by LSCA and administered by Ohionet (the network of Ohio libraries). An advisory committee of twenty-five coordinators from school and public libraries process reviews by the children's librarians into an MV/4000 computer. Evaluations are based on advanced review copies and are affixed to the MARC for each title. Review cards include information librarians value highly, such as the suitability of a book for use with toddlers or for reading aloud; they can show also if the book is of high-interest and low-reading level, as well as the type of format. Annual lists can be generated through the computer, and plans for the future include attachment of citations from well-known and respected juvenile review media sources.[22]

Still, many of the questions about the uses of the new technology remain unanswered, especially those relating to reading and library programming for children and youth. What exactly is encompassed by the somewhat misleading term "computer literacy"? Does it mean mere mastery of the technical skill of inputting information and retrieving it? Is its use in fact subtly intended to imply that computer literacy is the *new* literacy and replaces all that is implied in the traditional use of the word? Is there a danger that young people growing up familiar with and able to use computers effectively will think that this indeed constitutes literacy in all the depth and fullness of that term? To be sure there are many levels and degrees of understanding of literacy with regard to print. To some people, at some times, and in some situations, the word has meant ability simply to sign one's name or to function and survive at a fourth or fifth grade level of decoding skill. In other cases, and, it is to be hoped, more frequently now, it implies ability to process ideas and information, to give them varied meanings and to integrate them with the background information already held and brought to the reading process.

So, what exactly is computer literacy and where does technology fit it? Should it be expected to replace rather than to complement existing forms of intellectual exercise and growth? Librarians serving children and youth in both of the kinds of libraries available to them should feel challenged to help find some answers and sketch in some parameters.

8

The Multifaceted Services
of the Children's Department

As we have tried to make clear from the way in which this book is structured, the considerations of its first part deal with the foundations for part II. Part II concerns the heart of the matter, which is the program of services to and on behalf of children. The philosophy, the studies, the standards and goals, and all of the other management concerns are important only because they serve the end purpose of helping children to grow with discovery and joy in books and other materials. The technologies, the training, the community outreach, the budgets, and the processes of selecting and organizing result in a product for the child: an environment for listening, looking and finding, wondering, as the world opens and self-identity begins to take shape.

Increasingly, librarians serving children have become aware that serving children directly is only part of the job. The image of one fully trained, competent, confident children's librarian talking to a child about a book, or reading aloud, or telling a story for a group of children is a shining ideal, but it cannot be fully realized when the goal is to reach all children. Fortunately there are other avenues. One of them is encouraging and assisting a parent or family member, whether a mother or father, older brother or sister, grandparent or aunt or uncle to talk to a child about a character or an idea from a book, to read or tell a story for one child or a few. Still another example of children's library programming for which the children's specialist has a large responsibility is influencing the teacher's aide, the day-care or community center staff, the babysitter, or even the teacher, also to talk with a child about books to read aloud, or to try storytelling, combined perhaps with the use of other media. There are other important facets of the children's librarian's work. It is especially important if others who speak another language are able to transmit this information in the child's native tongue. The children's librarian today must take the program directly or through others to as many children as possible: in person, on television, or through video; through work with a local business which may want to place some books for workers' checkout by the time clock; or through distribution of bibliographies for the clientele of other professionals.

What do we mean by "program"? It is the word that ties together and includes many diverse presentations and activities: a puppet show, the showing of a film or videotape, a craft event; finding for a child another book as good as————, or a story about a bear, a book about shells or about the planets. It includes helping a parent who cannot read very well, but who would like to share a story at bedtime with a special child; locating information for a worried eleven year old on how to lose weight. These are all a part of "program" and the program is all these activities and more. It is assistance to the latchkey child who has no place to go but the library between school and the parents' arrival home at six o'clock; it is also listening carefully to and providing information for the oldest of four siblings who must find out where to get protection from parents who grow violent when they are drunk, but is too ashamed to say so clearly. Helping children to get facts and referrals from a computer or community file is as vital to today's programming as storytelling.

One definition of program serves quite well; "A plan or system under which action may be taken toward a goal."[1] Whatever the action, the program of services to children or for children, moves toward the goal of enlightenment, self-realization, and stimulation for the child.

Some elements of program have, of course, appeared in previous chapters, especially in examples given in chapters 6 and 7 on networking, technology, and community outreach. But here we are attempting to give a picture of the full scope of what the children's department of the public library encounters. We can categorize the activities and work in several areas, including:

- public program presentations of all kinds to children, both as individuals or in groups, through media such as film, television, or radio;
- public presentations to groups of adults about children's library services; about reading, the parents' role in modeling literacy. These could include, speeches at the Rotary Club, workshops arranged by local industry for worker parents, and the like;
- written presentations including lists, reviews of children's books in the local paper, articles, publicity round-ups about the library's role and goals;
- advice and counsel to adults—either one-to-one or librarian-to-group—as when the librarian meets with the director and staff of a shelter for the homeless to assess what the library might do to support the work with young residents in the shelter; or with a local TV station that wants help in choosing a children's book excerpt for a program, or to relate to a network broadcast;
- professional involvement and leadership—for example, the twice yearly meeting with school library media specialists and other supervisors to discuss homework resources and other assignment problems.

All of these activities come well within the definition of program given above, and all are part of a plan of action to be taken toward the goal of reaching as many children and adults as possible with services that will make a difference in the lives of the children. If one categorizes the elements of the library services program for children in this way, it is evident that a great deal of the work of the children's specialist is with adults: parents, families, and others who are concerned in some way with the well-being of children. The direct work with the children themselves relates either to preschool children or to those who are already of school age. Much that we will emphasize in detail about the program in the chapter which follows has to do with services to preschool children and those adults who shape their destiny, that is, their parents or designated caregivers.

We have chosen to do this for at least two reasons. With the growth of school libraries, as we have mentioned earlier, there is another library, the school library, which is dealing with at least some of the information needs of the children who are in school. For preschool children, there is no other agency devoted to this service except the public library. In addition, what makes the service to infant and preschooler an especially important responsibility for the public library is that there is finally some awareness among specialists in human growth and development, as well as among educators and members of the general public, that the first five years of life are "prime time" for intellectual development and for stimulating patterns of learning, thinking, and inquiry. What makes service to parents and families of these preschool children the greatest possible responsibility and challenge for children's librarians is that even more recently there has come the realization that the library is one agency outside the home that has the potential to do a successful job of stimulating, motivating, and reinforcing learning. The library's work must touch those who are with the young child most, the people in his world to whom he feels closest—parents or other caregivers.

The School-Age Child

If we conceive that the dividing line between what constitutes children's services and what constitutes young adult services is indeed the magic preteen age of twelve, we have a period of about seven years in the children's department to work with the six to twelve-year-olds and to supplement the services they are perhaps getting in the school library. The first program planning step for direct services to these children is to find out in detail what services they are actually getting in the community's schools. A second step, perhaps, is to ascertain who is in the population of six to twelve-year-olds. Is there, in fact, a high percentage of children from broken homes and troubled families who are already getting services from other community agencies? Is there a high proportion of children with two parents or just one parent who works all day, with no adult at home to receive the child after school? Are there many children of new American or foreign language origin? The school librarians can tell us, perhaps in concert with school counselors, about drug or child abuse and other problems in this group. Is there a preponderance of girls or are there many boys as well? What other activities engage them?

Once the profile of school-age potential patrons is developed, elements of the program that relate to departmental and institutional goals and objectives can be laid out, priorities sorted out, and program planning can get underway.

The elementary school child who uses the public library involves librarians with teachers. If the schools are operating without full-time professional librarians and staff, what are in effect only reading rooms or book exchange centers, the public library children's room will find itself taking up much of the slack in terms of curriculum-related assignments, reference questions, and so forth. This is of course not a good situation, but unfortunately persists more frequently than not. In this scenario, teachers and children alike consider the public library as a bottomless source of information and of a large stock of "thin" books on such topics as American Indians, explorers, and George Washington—or so it seems on a winter afternoon when all the fourth and sixth graders in the school system descend on the library with the same assignment! This happening needs to be forestalled to the maximum degree possible by a visit to each school in the library's district to discuss with principals, department heads, or supervisors, and of course any existing school librarians, how assignments can be staggered or individualized—perhaps with some choices and alternatives by way of materials being left to the wisdom and discretion of the children's library staff. Often a note to the grade teacher asking if substitute titles or another reference tool may be used will be effective and bring the desired result, but face-to-face consultation is the best way of easing the universal problem of mass assignments for which there are limited resources.

A great effort should be made to work with each school library media specialist so that programs may be jointly planned or at least made complementary. Collection development should be discussed so that needless duplication is avoided and some form of networking arrangement can be planned. In some communities, book ordering is done centrally by the schools, and the public library may be allowed to pool orders with those of the schools in the interest of larger discounts from jobbers and publishers. Special event programming, such as presentations for National Children's Book Week in the fall or National Library Week in the spring, should be at least coordinated so that there is mutual reinforcement and variety in the offerings. Many school and public libraries have instituted, on behalf of their common school-age clientele, joint materials examination and evaluation, in addition to joint ordering and processing.

What if there is not a school library professional in each of the elementary or middle schools in the library's school district? The job is obviously harder and more burdens will fall on the public library, as we have seen, but there is still room for some effective collaboration with teachers in charge of library matters, PTA library chairmen, and principals who are probably trying most valiantly to better the library resources situation they may have inherited through budget cuts and job freezes. Special opportunities will present themselves to the ready observer. For instance, one school with a large Spanish-speaking population and an active and successful bilingual program involves a bilingual storyteller from the public library staff in a yearly celebration with parents and children and an assembly featuring songs and stories with a Hispanic cultural background.

Many of the contacts the children's library staff has with the schools are with school personnel, but parent-teacher meetings are occasions for the public library to be visible to parents and to teachers as a library partner adjunct to the learning process.

The traditional class visit to the public library should continue to be part of the regularly scheduled program the library conducts in conjunction with the school. When a group of children come to the public library by grade, orientation is in order. It may be the first visit for many of the children who have not been brought there by parents or other adults. Library requirements for borrowing books and other materials, use of computers and other equipment, location of materials and services such as reference, microforms, and inter-library loan will be introduced. Also, there will be a rundown on types of library activities such as storytelling, reading aloud sessions, writing seminars, book discussions, and family nights. Emphasis should be put, from the very first visit, on the fact that the public library is always there to serve them as members of the community and will be throughout their lives—after school hours and school years are over for good.

The book talk, however, is probably the best and principal part of the visit. Styles of presentation vary, but the purpose of the book talk is to introduce children to wonderful and satisfying books—especially to those books that they might not pick up on their own, motivated by school needs or peer interests. The public librarian often consults beforehand with the class's teacher to find out about reading levels and interests of students. One or several books may be introduced, but the enthusiasm and knowledge of a librarian who has read the book and wants to share it is always contagious and is the measure of an effective book talk. With the availability of paperbacks, it is often possible and always desirable to have multiple copies of the title or titles for the children to borrow as the visit ends. Sometimes there are delayed responses to a book talk, and months may pass before one or two children will request a particular title which was introduced. During a class visit, it is well to present some variety but not an overwhelming array of titles.

A mixture of books and other media can be part of the book talk. Sometimes a short film or filmstrip is a good kickoff to a talk about related or spin-off books. Libraries which make especially good use of friends and volunteers can bring in a subject expert or traveller to introduce special books of fiction and nonfiction. A book talk can be blended with a book discussion when the book is presented by a child and others join in. Junior Great Books sessions are popular in many libraries.

Homework helpers or aides and homework hotlines are quite recent and very well used services of public libraries, especially where provision of school library services is uneven or poor. After-school programming for children who have no place to go after school is becoming more frequent.

Reading Aloud

Reading aloud is an art and children should be read to even after they can read for themselves. Eight- to twelve-year-olds enjoy it, too. Reading aloud develops the child's capacity to listen—an important element in learning to read confidently and a means to extend the child's acquaintance with language and to introduce words he cannot as yet read for himself. Opportunities for reading aloud should be scheduled in the children's room; a continuing story read a chapter at a time gives continuity to the reading and to the library experience. Reading aloud from a book by an author for whom the library has some spoken-word records or interviews is a vibrant experience in hearing the author's voice while thinking about his or her words and ideas. Older children who have enjoyed the reading aloud may be encouraged to take a book home to read aloud to younger siblings, or to continue the same book at home, sharing it with family members. Sometimes a children's librarian will read an exciting introductory chapter from a book and then make copies available for the children to take home and continue on their own.

Reading aloud gets high marks as a reading motivator. Reading aloud sessions at the library may be the only experience of book sharing for children whose home situation does not provide this experience.

Jim Trelease, an advocate of reading aloud to children, says in his *The Read Aloud Handbook* that "if all sectors of the community work together to bring the excitement of books into our homes early enough and to develop libraries that are truly 'delivery rooms for ideas,' then we need not fear an electronic Pied Piper stealing our children's minds and imaginations."[2]

Reading books to and with children is applauded also by educators, who attest to its value, particularly when it begins at home. Dr. Jeanne S. Chall, director of the Reading Laboratory at Harvard University Graduate School of Education cites research results which show that "reading to children can enhance their language development . . . expand their vocabularies and give them a more advanced understanding of grammatical forms. . . . It imparts the whole ritual of the book—of looking at it, puzzling it out and turning the pages."[3]

When reading does not take place at home, the school and the public library are in a position to provide effective ways of encouraging children to learn that reading is not only a skill but also a source of lifelong enjoyment. Hundreds of school principals have designated a fifteen minute period each day (generally referred to as a sustained silent reading period) when everyone—teachers as well as students—will stop to read a book. Children have learned from this that reading is an activity valued by their principal and teachers, and that a lot of reading can get done in a concentrated reading break each day. It is still true, however, that no amount of modeling of reading enjoyment by others can equal the day in, day out, motivating power of parents who are seen reading at home. Recognition of the parents' influence has sparked Parents as Partners in Reading and similar groups around the country.

Some basic consideration to ensure reading pleasure and to convince children that they can be and want to be readers must be kept in mind:

• Books should be made available which appeal to children *where they are* in terms of interests and ability;

• Children are more likely to read in an environment in which the adults around them are readers, be they parents, teachers, librarians, or coaches, counselors, or neighbors;

- Accessibility is the key, if reading as a habit is to be inculcated early; homes without books, magazines and newspapers are not likely to produce readers.

"I believe that *real* reading proceeds in the mind of the reader; that the reader is 'taken over' as it were . . . that, however valuable the book itself may be, the form it assumes in the mind of the reader is, for that person, the reality."[4] These words by Dorothy Butler were written in support of reading beginning at home, and they sum up the complexity and the very personal character of reading.

We will have more to say in a later chapter about kinds of books children are likely to be drawn to, and the importance of good selection criteria.

Storytelling

Storytelling is not just for little children, any more than is reading aloud. It is not even just for school-age children either, for it is an old art as old as history itself. The troubadours of the Middle Ages sang their stories to kings; the oral tradition of passing along knowledge and changing it to suit the audience and the teller long predates the written story. Storytelling is an excellent way to introduce school-age children to places, peoples, and ideas outside of their immediate experience as well as to introduce the literature of various heritages. Children in the public library program can also be given the opportunity to learn to tell stories themselves. Storytelling provides an opportunity to test oneself before an audience and to develop good diction and enunciation, memory, poise, and dramatic skills. Legends, myths, folklore, stories from history—many of the areas not well covered in today's crowded curriculum—can be brought to children through public library storytelling sessions. There are some excellent books (see the bibliography) which can be used to help children to prepare for this experience.

There has been a real renaissance of interest in storytelling for adults as well as for children. There is even an association called the National Association for the Preservation and Perpetuation of Storytelling. It has a membership of professional storytellers who hold an annual festival and it numbers among its members many who tell stories in public libraries. The organization's newsletter, *Yarnspinner*, gives profiles of storytellers and their styles, as well as storytelling activities in theatres, colleges, and libraries.

Puppetry

Pupperty, like storytelling, has a long tradition of theatre arts behind it, but library programming for children has certainly helped to popularize it in this country and in this century. The Muppets, who gained their fame as household familiars on the TV program "Sesame Street" and went on to their own TV shows and movies, follow other famous TV puppets such as Kukla, Fran and Ollie and the even older ventriloquist's dummies of radio era fame, such as Edgar Bergen's Charlie McCarthy. All of these have kept the art and practice of puppetry in the public eye. Many kinds of puppets, including simple finger puppets, are used regularly in public library storytelling and storyhours. At the Tredyffrin Public Library in Strafford-Wayne, Pennsylvania, puppets are used in impromptu shows with classes or day camp groups, and audience participation is encouraged. This library also has an active puppet-lending service.[5]

Puppets are a wonderful prop for shy or inarticulate children. From behind the scenes they can create the action by manipulating the puppets and can speak for them in roars or whispers. Puppets give a sense of power to the puppeteer, and they are a very good means of helping children to act out what they would like to do and say.

Other Programming

Most children's programming is produced on a slim budget and volunteers are always welcome, especially those with special talents to share. This is not the only reason, however, for involving other community agencies or local resources. The local zoo, the art or nature museum, collectors eager to talk about their collections—all are excellent sources. The library can sponsor contests or exhibits of local crafts and art work. Children's own drawings, perhaps through collaboration with an arts alliance, can be the focus for activities that will draw an audience. It is very beneficial to the library program and its image to be thought of as an enabler and facilitator and a center of creativity.

In one children's room a local orchestral group offered a brief concert and the conductor encouraged the children to draw their reactions to the music. The images, the shades of color the music evoked, were such interesting interpretations that the children's librarian held a "family night" party for all to view the drawings and paintings and to exchange ideas about future music programs that would enhance appreciation and awareness. As schools and all other organizations well know, people will turn out in droves to see their own children perform or admire their work, so children's participation in activities in the library will bring the community in. The library's collection of musical recordings can also be used to stimulate creative responses, drawn or written. Family nights are also often the occasion for pajama-clad preschoolers to visit the library with other family members to hear bedtime stories.

The most frequently found program for children is the book and author event. Many children would like to know more about the person who wrote the story or created the pictures in a book or group of books. If local authors or children's book illustrators are available, chalk talks or talks about how books are made, from conception to production, are often fascinating to young audiences. Birthdays of famous authors are often celebrated. When children in one library reading club designed a birthday card to send to E. B. White, his response to the children was memorable and added greatly to the excitement of reading his wonderful books.

Art and crafts, including recently origami workshops, have kept many a child busy and happy in a library setting. How-to books are rather easier than some for not-very-good readers to read, and there are experts who are willing to help with hands-on experiences in many communities. Activity sessions often accompany storytelling, puppet plays, or reading aloud in programs for older preschoolers and on up the age scale.

Film Programs

Film programs seem to capture the interest of the television generation more readily than most other kinds of programs. In our experience, attendance at film programs accounts for a high proportion of the attendance statistics in programming for children. Conscientious children's librarians have searched hard for quality films, and often tend to select those that are in some way book-related. A few abstract and concept films have been used successfully with younger children, but by and large films that are based on books are most often used. There are some problems in film selection, as Marilyn Berg Iarusso outlined in her article "Children's Films: Orphans of the Industry."[6] Martha Barnes, who surveyed the film situation six years later, in 1981, concurred with this view, citing the glut of films which are merely spin-offs from television, some of them problem-oriented films about young people and their growing up. Sometimes these films are well made and are good for generating after-viewing discussion and some follow-up reading. Although Barnes contends that there are not enough distinguished animated films for children, she mentions some of the better ones, such as those produced by the National Film Board of Canada and the Bully Budd films, for their ability to promote visual literacy.[7] The "iconographically animated" films based on books from the Weston Woods Studios are always popular with preschoolers, especially as introductions to the books themselves. The adaptations from picture books by Phoenix Films and Barr Films are also outstanding contributions to the field. The live-action presentations of traditional fairy tales produced by Tom Davenport often provoke discussion, particularly among adults. Children of all ages and adults both enjoy films, and they can keynote a fine program for family enjoyment.

Reference should be made here to Maureen Gaffney, who has done some research with young film audiences' reactions to films. Through her work in libraries and at the Media Center for Children, she has helped children's librarians to select good films for programming.[8] Other guides for film selection are the New York Library Association's *Films for Children: A Selected List*, and the annual Notable Children's Film List, produced by ALSC for ALA distribution.

Broadcasting Programming

Since radio and television are the most influential media in children's lives today, many libraries have used the media to promote the library. Simple spot announcements about library programs or invitations to use library resources have been used to communicate with the community. In 1983, a life-size, cartoon cutout cat, Cap'n O. G. Readmore, began to appear on ABC television's Saturday morning programs, brought to the screen with the collaboration of the Center for the Book in the Library of Congress.[9] As he appears on various prime-time specials, as well as on Saturday morning programs, this character extols books and the value of reading in thirty-second spots while making a tap-dancing exit! "Eye on Reading," a CBS contribution of public-service spots, featured one-minute, dramatized segments from children's books aimed at stimulating interest and selected by professionals from ALSC and the International Reading Association.[10]

Television programs produced by local libraries for children's viewing abound. There is, for example, "Humpty's Corner," a series of programs appearing on the local-access cable channel under the sponsorship of the Lancaster County Public Library in Pennsylvania. The programs include storytelling.[11] In New York state, "Summer Bookwatch" involves eight librarians in the Monroe County system in cooperation with a local Rochester station. This program features storytellers, book reviews, and reading aloud segments. The county system's children's consultant reported that its success could be gauged by requests for the book used on the air, and by enthusiastic reactions of inquiring parents.[12]

Linda Thomas, children's librarian at the Dover Public Library, gives interesting information on adapting a book for camera work and television viewing, and reports that a half-hour program may require as much as four hours of preparation time.[13] The Public Library of Columbus and Franklin County also initiated a cable TV program, "Discovery." The program emanates live from the main library's "Center for Discovery."[14] Volunteers perform as camera assistants and operate the video equipment owned by the library.

Every Thursday afternoon "Kids Alive" appears on a local cable channel in Bloomington and Monroe County, Indiana. The library trains children ages eight to fifteen to be camera crew members and operators, interviewers, special effects managers, and directors. The children, trained to take care of all aspects of the production, first serve in a production called "Kid Stuff," a nonscripted show which includes children as young as four years of age. Channel 3 counts among its viewers for this show nearly one hundred percent of the children in the viewing area, drawn without doubt not only by the content of the program but the fact that other children are responsible for it. The programs are jointly funded by the Monroe County Public

Library, the City of Bloomington Telecommunications, and the local cable operator, Horizon Communications Corporation.[15]

In a first in telecommunications, an interactive TV program produced by American children was linked via satellite with children in Australia. The teams of children participating in the venture included some who were responsible for "Kids Alive" and "Kids–4", both local origin cable TV programs. The "Kids–4" program is aired out of Sun Prairie, Wisconsin, on a channel that features programs solely for children. Supervised by volunteers, the two hours daily of programming is directed, planned, and produced by children. Participants are between the ages of nine and thirteen. They are auditioned and, if accepted, they may write scripts, direct, act as hosts, or work with the cameras. Each child spends a minimum of two hours a week working on the show. With this kind of talent then, the satellite transmission took place at a conference sponsored by the American Council for Better Broadcasts (ACBB) in Washington, D.C.[16]

Television which promotes reading directly includes reading aloud programs, picture story times for young children or preschoolers, and reading clubs. "Reading Rainbow," started in 1983, was co-produced by the Great Plains National Educational Network at the University of Nebraska and WNED-TV/Channel 17 of Buffalo. The half-hour segments introduce books to read; children read their own book reviews, and references to the library as a source of reading material are frequent. Again, ALSC has been involved in an advisory capacity.[17]

Enthusiastic librarians from the Porter Public Library in Westlake, Ohio, describe a program which involves a school-age child audience in the studio, a children's librarian, staff artist, and library clerk. The program, "Porter P. Mouse Tales," was launched on the local cable station three times a week. The second session of the program was directed to a preschool audience during an eight-week series which featured toys, crafts, and action that had visual appeal for the young child. In evaluating the program, librarians concluded that although there was a great amount of preparation time required, the rewards were worth it. The program, they found, opened a new channel to people in the community who were not library users.[18]

Using the telephone as a medium, a number of libraries have emulated the very successful San Francisco Public Library Dial-A-Story program as a model and found it to be most successful. The San Francisco program, which has been going on since the early

1970s, has been replicated from the Queens Borough Public Library in New York City to the Seattle Public Library, where as many as 27,000 callers have been counted as listening to the brief story program in one month.[19]

With television's promises—often wrested from stations by determined advocates—to devote more time to quality programming for children, children's librarians are finding, and should find, more time to devote to this medium, which can extend their reach in disseminating programming. The field is really wide open for advice on children's reading, consulting on productions, tie-ins of programming with books, in-library viewing of videotapes, follow-up discussion, and many other techniques. As more librarians become involved with TV and more knowledgable about cable and its potentials, television people are becoming more willing, even eager, to share their technical advice in exchange for assistance with quality content.

School-Age Children Not in School

What of the school-age children who are not in school at all? There are many of them: disabled and homebound, incarcerated or otherwise institutionalized in a variety of hospitals, homes, and other agencies. Children's librarians in public libraries have a primary responsibility for these children. Since the mainstreaming of disabled children into the public schools in the 1970s, many children have had access to school libraries, but there are still many who rely on the public library for at least some of the intellectual and recreational benefits that are available to other children. One effect is that children's librarians have seen more learning disabled and physically impaired children coming with their class from the schools. The need to tailor a book talk or story hour or other children's program presentation to this audience has required special awareness and sensitivity by library staffs. Many are learning to "sign", or to use local experts in work with the hearing impaired. Some librarians have been able to find suitable nonprint offerings for those who are designated as learning disabled and others have been through sensitivity sessions to enable them to better understand the needs and desires of these children.

For reaching out with service to children who are not in the schools and who cannot come into the library, children's librarians must rely in large part on good contacts with youth agencies and institutions. It is important for the children's library staff to think in terms of becoming part of a team of those who work with these children daily. Many children under the age of twelve are today at a crossroads in their young lives, suffering from addiction, depression, victimized by divorce, death, illness, separation, abuse, and other ills. Those who work with them often seek the bibliotherapeutic help they can get from librarians, who have the tools and materials that may help these children to find a reason for living and a way of life. Children's librarians may be an important link for youth workers with library resources that are not in the children's department, and they should be alert to opportunities to make connections for them with other staff members in the reference and other departments.

One aspect of "program" is hard to define exactly, but terribly real and important nevertheless. It can be summed up as library environment and librarian attitude, and it manifests itself as acceptance and respect from intelligent, educated people who are working at jobs they obviously like. It is a great builder of self-esteem in child patrons. It is part of the atmosphere of the library and the expectation of the librarians that you are a responsible and trustworthy person, a thinking person whose thoughts matter. There is something about a good library and its children's department that presents a pleasing sense of order, calm, and rationality, a sense of leisure and yes, of quiet and space, to children who may have little acquaintance with either. Fresh flowers or plants, art reproductions on the walls, may contribute much to a quality of life and open a window on a lifestyle unknown to many visitors. Very often early impressions remain through adulthood, and the library and its books have been recorded by many as having helped them to transmute certain of their negative life experiences into positive ones. An informal study conducted in New York revealed that many adults who now regularly use the public library had good experiences in libraries as children. Watching expectant young mothers—many of them barely teenage—delight in body movement exercises to the strains of Vivaldi before a session of looking at some picture books, gives a new vision of the library's potential role in cultivating appreciation of varied cultural experiences and widening horizons.

In some areas, living conditions in the home may be the determining factor in whether or not a child borrows library books. The family may be too large, the living quarters too cramped, to allow for enough privacy to read a book or listen to a tape or recording; the dog, or some animal less welcome, may gnaw a book; parents may fear accumulating overdue charges; or the children are part of a transient population, never certain when it will be necessary to move on with little notice. In libraries and branches in such neighborhoods the circulation figures may be low because the children do not borrow materials, while attendance figures may be high. Children are using the library to take advantage of after-school programming, or to sit and do homework or read quietly, or to have someone read to them. The library in such areas, usually urban, may be more precious and more needed by the children than those in parts of the city where many more books and other materials show high use in circulation.

Adult Users of the Children's Department

It is impossible, as we have seen, to think of the children's library program as being just for children. From the infant who first comes in in his parents' arms to the student, the children's librarian is aware of and often in touch with the various adults who relate to the child. To work with children in libraries is to encounter all the adults who are influential in their lives: parents and other child-caring adults; teachers; health care professionals; legal professionals; and many others. In the chapter that follows we will look closely at some of the kinds of parent education programs that libraries have been offering lately. Most of them relate to preschoolers, but there are some parents of older children, too, who continue to come to the library and to take a great interest in what their children are reading.

By the time the child has become an independent reader and library patron, parents may focus again on what the child is reading, and may sometimes have problems with it. A parent may be concerned that a boy reads only sports or science fiction, or that a girl reads only fiction—perhaps only horse stories or mysteries in a series. In the present climate of distrust and many would-be censors, many a concerned parent will be anxious about what values are being assimilated from the books the child is reading. Children's librarians must know what is in the books in the collection and be able to discuss them intelligently. It should go without saying that every public library should have a written book-selection policy and be prepared to stand by it. This is no less true for the materials in the children's room than it is for adult fiction and other adult materials, such as periodicals. Special programs for parents and other interested community members should be presented at which books and their positive values for children are discussed. This sort of programming raises the level of community awareness so that if censors strike the community cannot be as easily led by them as it otherwise might be.

The rise in interest in preschoolers and early learning, and concern at the national level and at all levels for family reinforcement of education and literacy has attracted a variety of professionals from other fields to the public library. The professionals from early childhood education are interested in seeing preschoolers in a library learning setting, and librarians are pleased to be able to ask them to share their expertise in seminars and workshops with parents who might not otherwise have an opportunity to learn about child development and rearing. The library has become, in many cases, an informal forum in which child advocates can share information among themselves and with parents, teachers, and other agency personnel.

In addition to the adults who use the services and materials of the children's department in their roles as parents, teachers, and other child caregivers, there are a number of adults who use the resources of the children's room for purposes that have no direct relationship with a given child or group of children. Children's literature is a branch of literature and as such is of interest to students, book critics or analysts, historians, those who study social trends, behaviorial psychologists, advertising agents, promotion people, television directors and filmmakers, and many others. Old and rare children's books are avidly collected, and their illustrations—and those of contemporary books as well—are constantly being studied by artists, designers, and others for reasons that have nothing to do with the use of these books by children. The children's book collection in many large libraries is in fact really a reference and, very often, a research collection.

In a final chapter, we will talk in great detail about literature for children and some of the problems and the opportunities that surround it. In the following chapter, however, we turn to library preschool programs, and some of the parenting programs libraries are increasingly engaged in organizing.

9

Early Childhood, Preschool,
and Parent Education Programs

Antipoverty activists of the 1960s used to good advantage the statistics showing that intelligence grows more rapidly in the first five years of life than it does in any later period. In order to combat the educational deficiencies and subsequent learning failures found so frequently among the poor, these advocates for better opportunities for the economically deprived were instrumental in the development of programs to build the child's educational foundation before school entry. Head Start was, of course, a major program in this field, and there were federally funded programs for early learning under Titles I, III, and VII of the Elementary and Secondary Education Act of 1965. The importance of early learning and preschool education received strong support from the government and from childhood development and reading specialists. Perhaps these concepts and concerns got their greatest visibility and reinforcement from the preschool television program launched with a combination of foundation and government funding: "Sesame Street." This highly successful and still continuing program, broadcast over educational (now "public") television stations, popularized the notion of basic learning and concept development for three to five-year-olds. Aimed primarily in the beginning at inner-city, minority children, it soon became clear that middle-class children were also benefiting tremendously from it. It should be noted that there was a reading and library component built into the program from its first planning stages in 1968 and for several years after it went on the air. The Reading Resources Committee for "Sesame Street" was organized, at the request of its producer,

Joan Ganz Cooney, by Virginia H. Mathews, of the National Book Committee, acting as consultant to the Children's Television Workshop, parent organization of "Sesame Street." Linkages were arranged with the then Children's Services Division of ALA (now ALSC), and members of the committee were, in addition to Miss Mathews, Augusta Baker, of The New York Public Library, Anne Izard, of the Westchester County Library, and Harriet Brown, then a supervisor in the elementary school libraries of New York City. This committee met with the creative people on the program—directors, script writers, and artists—as well as with research and promotion units. It recommended books to be incorporated into the shows and wrote a manual for parent follow-up, as well as promotion materials to encourage children's and school librarians to take full advantage of programs and materials. Public librarians were encouraged to beg, borrow, or buy television sets for in-library viewing of "Sesame Street" and to follow up with preschool activities related to books.[1]

At about this same time, Swiss psychologist Jean Piaget's theories about child development became a popular area of study. Particularly germane was his thesis that the success and rate of developmental growth in a child was dependent upon the child's environment. Exposure to a rich variety of stimuli and experience, he believed, increased the child's ability to cope and to develop in response to those stimuli. Experiments and research, all largely government funded, pursued the idea of preschool preparation for later success in learning. A few of these showed methods and results which were truly influential and carried over into ongoing programs. Far too many others, however, were stopped short of useful conclusions by cuts in education budgets and research funds.

Libraries, subject to the same economic upheavals as other educational agencies in the early 1970s, nonetheless stepped up their exploration of various kinds of programs for preschool children, despite minimal or nonexistent funding. Community interest and the sense of need, even urgency, has persisted since that time. The public library, in providing a stimulating yet nonjudgmental environment, became an increasingly important resource for parents and other caregivers who wanted to help small children learn. Without attempting to duplicate nursery school or day-care regimens or instruction, librarians devised more programs to attract parents and other adults concerned with preschool children, as well as the children themselves. These librarians were eager to work closely with other com-

munity agencies, and to enlist community resource people to conduct
library programs for parents who were interested in early childhood
development. From the early 1970s, when day-care became a more
widespread phenomenon, programs for the early childhood group,
distinct from the traditional preschool programs, flourished as federal
funding administered through the states became available. Parent
education components were built in to most proposals, even though
the content of many programs still emphasized preschool interests.
The many burgeoning programs for children five and under could be
categorized under their several areas of emphasis: Parent Education,
Toy Lending, Preschool/Parent Outreach/Toddler Programs, Bibliographies on Parenting, or Kits of Materials. The more ambitious
programs included a significant parent education emphasis.

In addition to concern for the toddler and preschool child there
developed awareness of the need to begin earlier to prepare teenagers
for parenthood. This was in part a response to the increase in the
number of unwed mothers, many of them in their early or middle
teens. In 1975, a federally funded project called "Exploring Childhood" was attempted in some junior and senior high schools in order
to acquaint seventh to twelfth graders with some theory and practice
in child development.[2] The growing teen-parent group was accompanied by the proliferation of foster care and foster homes, as well as
by a rapid growth in nursery schools and day-care. By 1970, one of
every five preschoolers was enrolled in some form of early learning
program, many of them funded programs for the poor. While the
1980 census has not as yet yielded all tabulations concerning children,
it is significant that figures revealed so far show that there is nationally a twenty-five percent increase in nursery school attendance and
about an eleven percent increase in kindergarten enrollment:
3,388,000 and 2,477,000 respectively.[3] In 1970, 2.5 million mothers of
children under age six were in the labor force; by 1980 this number
had increased to 5.1 million and on September 5, 1987, the *New York
Times* reported that there were 6.6 million mothers in the labor force
with children under six years of age, and 8.8 million with children
between the ages of six and seventeen.

In New York, in the early 1980s, the Institute for the Study of
Exceptional Children conducted tests to try to establish several
things: the onset of cognitive function and intellectual growth in the
development of the very young child; how the infant processes
information; and the length and depth of concentration required to

perform certain tasks which will foretell the child's later capacity to talk or learn to read. Interaction with parents early in the infant's life and the degree of the parents' reinforcement and encouragement were shown as most important. The Educational Testing Service and Roosevelt–St. Luke's Hospital, affiliates of the Institute, have been conducting studies that suggest that the newborn is equipped with more cognitive abilities than had previously been believed.[4]

Project EARLY (Early Assessment and Remediation Laboratory), under the auspices of the Chicago Board of Education, screened children with potential learning problems and also provided a method of predicting learning disabilities in children three to five years of age. The project's educational aids have been nationally distributed. Project EARLY tests learning disabilities which may affect a child's later ability to read, such as weaknesses in areas of gross or fine motor skills, language, memory, or visual discrimination. The director of Project EARLY, Dr. Nancy K. Naron, suggests to parents ways to improve perceived weaknesses in language and motor skills, including manipulation of such objects as balls, shoestring laces, or a bean bag. For memory tasks and language she suggests fingerplays, nursery rhymes, and word games.[5]

Public library preschool programs began in earnest about the middle of the 1970s. Ferne O. Johnson, one of the pioneers in the field, edited a book of suggestions and program ideas called *Start Early for an Early Start* which came out in 1976 and gave great impetus to preschool programming.[6] Frances A. Smardo of the Dallas Public Library was another early advocate of preschool programming. She prepared, for a speech at the 1978 ALA conference, an analytical study of recommendations made by early childhood education experts with regard to the role of the public library in serving young children from infancy to six years of age. The major recommendations included:

- Children's librarians should be specifically prepared for work with adults and young children;
- The children's librarians should have knowledge and expertise in children's literature, child development, and materials selection for very young children;
- Senior citizens may be used as volunteers;

- Use of an early childhood consultant was indicated;
- Parent education services and programs may be conducted by experts in the field;
- Child-care teachers and personnel should be trained in storytelling and materials' selection;
- Programs and services should be provided to permit parent-child interaction;
- Services, programs, facilities which are directly related to reading and language art activity should be made available;
- Make available materials, books, educational toys, and audiovisual materials, and realia for home and library use by young children;
- Greater coordination and integration of preschool services and programs, materials, personnel, and facilities to avoid duplication of effort within a community is indicated.

Dr. Smardo's recommendations for research call for a study of the degree to which public libraries meet or fall short of the recommendations; to compare these recommendations with those of parents, teachers, and children's media specialists in regard to their perception of the public library's role in serving the preschool or younger child; to determine the extent of duplication of effort in the area with other community agencies; and to explore the feasibility of an interdisciplinary program involving library schools and others in the education community in the preparation of students planning to work with young children in public libraries.

In 1980, Dr. Smardo raised the question, "Are Librarians Prepared to Serve Young Children?"[7] In her article she lists qualifications of personnel as the most important aspect in the success of this work. Never, since the early days of the pioneers in children's work (who also set great store on the personal characteristics of the person who was to work with children), have the qualifications of the children's librarians come under such close scrutiny. The consensus is that these specialists should possess knowledge and understanding of child development; knowledge of how to work effectively with both parents and other caregivers; ability to relate not only to children's literature but to the literature of child psychology; and awareness of childrens' rights and the variety of legal and socioeconomic questions related to the child as growing human being and citizen.

The last decade of intensive work with preschool children—most recently focusing on the two-year-old toddler stage—has demonstrated that the work proceeds most effectively if the staff understands the child's mental and emotional growth patterns and is prepared to work with them. In 1985, based on research for her doctorate at Columbia University, Ann D. Carlson codified an analysis of the information about child development from birth to three years of age, and linked it with implications for literature sharing in library programs. Dr. Carlson surveyed some 324 libraries thought to have programs for children under three, and analyzed the seventy-eight percent response returned to her. The indications for good programs based on research turned out to coincide to a remarkable degree with the "instinctive behaviors of the children's librarians, who were matching library activities to what they knew about very young children before there was much proof that they were doing the right things."[8]

The cognitive theories of Jean Piaget[9] played a very important role in the development of Ann Carlson's "schema" because as she says, they "so clearly and specifically define the intellectual development in young children." The psychoanalytical theories of Erik Erikson also play a role in the development of the profile of child development behaviors to which librarians can match their programming.[10]

The behaviorial theories of Robert Sears are also vital in their influence on this matter.[11] Arnold Gesell and his associates at Yale,[12] and Jerome Kagan[13] are among the many others who have thrown light on early childhood development. Jerome Bruner and his work with young children and language development;[14] Kenneth B. Clark and his studies of the effects of prejudice on black preschoolers—which influenced the U.S. Supreme Court decision to order desegregation of the public schools;[15] Urie Bronfenbrenner and his studies of the influence of family on the young child;[16] and Bruno Bettelheim's analysis of the meaning of reading and fantasy for young children:[17] all these and several others should at least be known to children's librarians who would work with preschoolers, and school-age children as well. Burton White's statement is a key for librarians: "Almost everyone who has studied young children agrees that one hallmark of early human development is variability. After all, children are not production line products."[18]

Citing earlier work in the field, Smardo points out deficiencies in the competencies of children's librarians who work in early childhood programs. Dr. Annette Phinazee, of the library school at North Carolina Central University, confronted this lack before initiating at the library school an early childhood specialist program with a model center, laboratory work with children and parents, and a carefully structured curriculum. The program is unique in the library education field in that it included study in early childhood materials, internships in the community, and study in the fields of psychology and education. The University of Pittsburgh Graduate School of Library and Information Science also offers one course that includes programming for preschoolers with emphasis on reading as a learning process.

The Dallas Public Library system has created a position of librarian for early childhood services, but librarians trained in child development as well as in librarianship are still few and far between. More continuing education and staff development programs are the answer—such as the one now being carried on by The New York Public Library, about which there are more details later in this chapter.

Although the library programs in question are aimed directly at the preschool child, mostly the three to five year olds, it soon became apparent that an important component of any such program was one addressed to parents and the parents' role as the child's first teacher. For many parents, the library program is an opportunity to become acquainted with community resources such as day-care services, family counseling, and health services that will be of help to them in rearing their children. Many libraries since the late 1970s have included parents in early childhood and preschool programs and many have also provided for information directed to parents. Many parents have learned in this way to use the library as a source of referral to other agencies which can be useful long after the children have outgrown the preschool programming. Since it is now widely recognized that learning begins long before a child starts school, children's librarians have become more active in reaching out to parents to help them to exert their most constructive influence on children in the home. We know now that the degree and scope of future social, linguistic, and creative skills are largely determined and acquired from birth through age five, before children enter the expanded school environment.

Ferne O. Johnson, an early proponent for programming aimed directly at parents, observed in 1978: "It is important that parents capitalize on all opportunities to help their children grow in all dimensions during these early years . . . . Parent support programs have great value. Mothers and fathers need to understand that the time to introduce pictures, books, selected toys and other forms of library media to their children and to start using them effectively is while they are yet infants."[19]

Confirmation based on further research and experimentation has continued in the 1980s. In 1983, *A Nation At Risk: The Imperative for Educational Reform, A Report to the Nation and the Secretary of Education* by the National Commission on Excellence in Education addressed this injunction directly to parents:

"As surely as you are your child's first and most influential teacher, your child's ideas about education and its significance must begin with you. You must be a living example of what you expect your children to honor and emulate. Moreover, you bear a responsibility to participate actively in your child's education. You should . . . nurture your child's curiosity, creativity and confidence . . . . Above all, exhibit a commitment to learning in your own life."[20]

In 1984, a task force on excellence in education was made responsible for preparing ALA's formal response to *A Nation At Risk*. Its report, entitled *Realities: Educational Reform in A Learning Society*, cited four realities of which the first was "learning begins before schooling." The report details what libraries can do about preschool learning:

"Libraries contribute to preschool learning in two ways: through the services, programs and materials that help parents increase their skills and capabilities, and through programs that serve children directly.

Library service to parents and day care staff supports preschool learning in a variety of ways. Libraries provide books for adults to read aloud to children. Groups of children in child care and day care centers and in public libraries listen to stories and act them out. Children borrow books and records from libraries. Toddler programs that bring very small children and their parents to the library together provide a basis for later, more independent use of libraries by children as they grow older.

All these experiences for young children require action by motivated, enthusiastic adults—adults who will instill a love of reading. Parents, volunteers, and day care center staff learn from librarians how to select and use materials with children. Librarians have the skills, experience, and desire to conduct workshops for parents, older children, babysitters, early childhood specialists, teachers, and volunteers. The library has information to help parents face problems which they face daily. In some communities, multilanguage collections for parents and preschoolers are essential. Through libraries, parents can learn how to use television and newer technology, such as computers, to nurture children's creativity and confidence.

Librarians also help create community coalitions of school personnel, public librarians, members of parent-teacher groups, and others concerned with preschool learning. Public library staff who provide information and referral services help parents develop effective partnerships with schools, preschools, day care centers, and other early childhood agencies.

Unfortunately, limited funds in many of our public libraries have caused cutbacks in children's services. Day-to-day realities of operating and staffing public libraries result in the lack of a full-time children's librarian in many libraries and branches. Because of limited library staff, parents and preschool children may wait months before being able to participate in a storyhour program.

To ensure that children and their parents have library services for effective preschool learning, public officials should:

- Appropriate funds for parent education and early childhood services in public libraries, particularly those which demonstrate outreach and which promote cooperation with other educational and community agencies.
- Establish state and federal regulations for preschool day care services which mandate book and library resources as part of the basic program requirements."[21]

A still more recent official document contains specific recommendations relating to young children and libraries, and also to parent education and parent support programs. In *First Lessons: A Report on*

Elementary Education in America, U.S. Secretary of Education, William J. Bennett writes as his general recommendation: "Parents have the central role in children's education and must be empowered to play it successfully."[22] He goes on to say, "Every school should have a library, and every child should have and use a public library card." Further: "Since we know, for example, that reading to young children helps them to learn to read, illiterate parents should have sources of help with this activity. Each community can find suitable ways of providing such assistance; parents are certainly not the only possible 'readers'. Many libraries organize excellent story hours, sometimes staffed by librarians, sometimes by senior citizens, sometimes by regular volunteers. Cousins, uncles, and neighbors can read aloud to other peoples' children. And there is no reason why a local radio station cannot produce and broadcast a story hour several evenings a week . . . . Children must have access to books."

Mr. Bennett sounds the same warning that has come from others: "many parents foster early interest in sounds and letters with alphabet books and magnetic letters on the refrigerator. The idea is not to rush children into reading but to enjoy all the preparatory steps that lead up to it." As Dr. Lillian G. Katz of the University of Illinois said in 1980, parents should not be pressured into tutorial and instructional roles per se. "Parent educators should help parents to think through their own goals for their own and their children's lives." Caution should be used in going "beyond strengthening the so-called parenting skills to include training in tutorial and instructional skills as well."[23] Children do not need to be actually taught to read at two or three or four or five, but they do need to be listened to, talked to, read to. Libraries can be the child's, and the parents', greatest sources of help and assistance.

Early childhood-preschool-parenting programs are coming in stronger in all parts of the country with this encouragement from the highest levels. Unfortunately, the encouragement has not yet been supported with funds to public libraries so that they can really expand this work without doing so at the expense of other program elements. Since the importance of play and talk and response is so widely recognized, toys, games, and songs have become an essential part of programming for children. Sometimes the electronic media— video, or even computers—are used. The responses to Ann Carlson's survey showed that most librarians included simple stories, finger plays and songs in their programs.[24] Others included musical activities, simple puppets, flannel or felt board stories, poems, creative dramatics, marching activity, and puppet shows. Additional activities mentioned were: short films or filmstrips, very simple arts and crafts, circle games, realia handling (for textures, shapes, etc.), puzzles, tell-and-draw stories, study prints and pictures, participation stories, tactile objects, dress-up activity, holiday celebrations, tasting, touching, smelling, among others. All of these were done by some librarians with children under three years of age, and with more complexity, with the three-to-five-year-olds. Storytime topics included pretend activities, animals, transportation by car, train, or plane.

Toddler Programs

As we have seen, programs for the under-threes are gaining greatly in importance in public libraries. Experiments in storytelling or book programs for two-year-olds and sometimes even younger children, are often called "toddler programs."

Juliet Markowsky, of the Westchester Library system in New York, identified toddlers as two-to-three-and-a-half-year-olds. "Why have a storytime for toddlers at all? . . . They are in a 'passive language' stage, absorbing language at a very rapid rate, and understand more than they can say."[25] She has seen great benefit from social exposure at the library storytime, and feels that it gives a great opportunity for the librarians to establish a positive relationship with parents.

A library volunteer in Summit, New Jersey helped the children's librarian with a program for two-and-a-half to three-and-a-half year old children. A series of four programs were planned, scheduled every other month. A film, a filmstrip, and books were used, as well as play with puzzles or manipulative toys. There was picture book reading, simple fingerplay, and easy craft work. Parents were encouraged to attend the child's first group experience and share their child's enthusiasm. The volunteer, who had been a nursery school teacher, felt that her early childhood education experience might be helpful in helping the librarians to plan storytimes in the library.[26]

Kathleen Englehart, children's librarian at the Shaker Heights, Ohio, public library, reported that her Toddler Story Hour offered eight programs weekly in twelve week sessions. Thirteen children were registered for each group, and programs were evaluated by parents. The program was judged successful not only in terms of the responses of children and parents, but because circulation figures increased in the library overall, and new adult faces were seen in the library as patrons.[27]

Toddlers in the Parent-Tot Time at the Racine Public Library in Wisconsin, were part of an experimental program conducted by the director of children's services. The toddlers were enrolled in a session for parents and children of eighteen months to three years of age. The children's librarian made a twenty-minute picture-story presentation and introduced finger plays that toddlers and parents could perform together. The strategy was to prepare an audience for the regular, more structured preschool picture book programs which these children would attend later. This preschool program in Racine was a very active and visible one; programs took place not only in library locations but also in local churches. Storytellers might well be trained librarians, but they might also be volunteer aides or "grandma helpers."

Part of the information kit distributed to parents and participating caregivers was a *Handbook for Parents* describing the purpose of the preschool programs: "Since pleasant experiences with books help to create the desire to read, this activity is designed to promote reading readiness in preschoolers. A first step in developing language skills is the ability to listen and absorb; storytime is therefore a step in the development of language skills." *Rock-a-Bye Baby,* an attractive booklet, starts with ideas for exposing the infant from birth to six months to sounds such as the parent's voice singing, chanting, or playing; to books on reading, directed to the parent. This information piece for caregivers was developed by the Racine library staff as far back as 1974.[28]

"Two's Company," held in the Westover Branch of the Arlington County, Virginia, library is a program for two-and-three-year-olds, and is essentially a picture book program which is made into a special celebration each month. Parents are included in the booksharing and puzzle activity after the formal reading portion of the program.[29]

The profile of an imaginative and wide-ranging program of services to young children comes from Virginia Richey, the children's librarian of the Monroe County Public Library in Bloomington, Indiana. She writes:

Although our services begin at birth, our programs begin at twelve months. The twelve-month to thirty-month age was selected because of language development. This early program is called "First Friends" in general, with specific programs having thematic names such as "Let's Celebrate" or "Noisy Day." These programs are designed to give the child and parent or caregiver the opportunity to explore a learning environment together, observing activities and techniques for learning language and expanding vocabulary, learning songs and rhymes, using materials that could easily be made at home. These aren't "sit and listen" programs, even though there is a ten-minute introduction for the parents, but rather self-directed interactions with the materials set up by the program presenter. Our board book collection, records, cassettes, "learning materials" and parents' shelf materials are highlighted.

At thirty months we begin a small group storytime, still with parents, that we call "Introduction to Storyhour." At this point, we begin to ask for listening and go on to develop listening skills along with language skills in small group storyhours for threes and young fours, five and older fours. We've separated age groups in the small groups so that storytelling and materials selection can be as appropriate as possible. Developmentally delayed children in the preschool years are included in the groups they will respond to best. Large group programs have broader age spans—the once-a-month storyhour "extravaganza" averages 150 in attendance each session. Workshops such as "Little House of Your Own" or "All Around the Town" will usually have a broader age range as well. In the summer, we present "Learning Through Play" in which children and adults explore three learning activities each week. Bedtime storyhours in the summer draw whole families. In the fall parents and preschool children drop in one day a week for "Back to the Library" activities. This program gives younger siblings something to show off and talk about at home when older siblings are starting school. In the spring, a series of experiential programs gives young children the opportunity to create concepts and vocabulary about things they have handled and touched—instruments of the orchestra, for example, or live rabbits. "Make-A-Book" sessions we try to present at least once each program season.

In addition to scheduled programs, we arrange special services or programs for preschoolers as well as for school-age children. Preschool groups come to the library for the "First Visit" program and then enjoy coming back regularly to borrow materials, play with blocks and puzzles, and to use the children's room. Parents with hospitalized or homebound children use a "Sick Kids Kit" to help entertain children in difficult circumstances. Children of all ages travel from Bloomington with "Travel Kits" from the library. Grandparents can request a special kit to help them entertain visiting grandchildren.

Since the Early Literary Skills Project was approved, we've begun special evening programs for parents and caregivers. The project both enhances services and materials already in place and pushes us to begin new services. Our focus this year is on the child from birth to age three who is at risk in learning to read due to the parents' lack of reading skills. The ELSP specialist is developing materials and programs for parents who are teens, are illiterate or have low reading skills, and are in low-income programs. The project itself is funded through the library's regular budget, but the specialist is funded through a LSCA grant for one year.

Most of our programs are funded by the Monroe County Public Library Foundation, a not-for-profit organization which raises money for the library through booksales and other activity, and which channels gifts of money to library programs and materials. The library budget covers only salaries and some materials.[30]

Toys for Learning

Toy lending, as well as toy manipulation in library programs, is often noted as a component linked with play for significant educational benefit to the preschooler. At the San Francisco Public Library, references to toys appear in their You, Your New Baby and the Library program, and toy catalogs are made available to new parents as part of the package prepared for them. In the Monroe County, New York, library at Rochester, "surprise boxes" for parents included manipulative toys to help parents to teach concepts leading to reading readiness for their preschoolers.[31] The Westchester County Library System's Parent Education Program, begun in the fall of 1978, included a noncirculating, educational toy collection for libraries in the system, and parts of its seminars and workshops for parents were devoted to the use of toys, discussed by teachers associated with local day-care centers or nursery schools.[32]

The Canadian Association of Toy Libraries has issued an interesting booklet in *Toy Libraries 2: The Many Uses of Toy Lending*.[33]

In it, reference is made to the first toy lending library, Toy Loan in Los Angeles, started in 1935. A most interesting part of its discussion of the many uses of toys is the extensive section on toys for the handicapped child. Toys for the learning disabled, the blind child, and several special categories of toys are covered. One of these comprises improvised toys devised from objects found or used in the home, including pots and pans, clothespins, spoons, and the like. Also discussed are representational toys, such as doll houses and furniture and mechanical toys such as cars, trucks, airplanes or boats, which represent real objects in miniature. These latter are described as great learning tools for blind children, for aiding them in the understanding of spatial concepts or arrangements. The third category is developmental toys, considered helpful in teaching concepts or developing motor skills and also in expanding the child's awareness from the concrete to the abstract. Such toys are believed to be particularly helpful for blind children, for whom they should be designed with recognizable shapes and textures. Pleasing to the touch, they should produce clear and satisfying sounds, and be crafted with more than usual care and attention to safety aspects in their use by children.

A section on toys is found in material which relates to an early and especially well-planned program for toddlers and infants in Connecticut. In *Materials for Adults to Use with Children from Birth To Three*, the authors note, "The young child's activities with toys and other play objects form a major part of the child's search for meaning."[34] In commenting on the selection of toys listed in the booklet, they describe types of interaction children experience in their play with toys: "investigation, impact, change and dramatic play."

At a time when unemployment was at its height in the state (around 1982) the Allen County, Indiana, Public Library introduced, among other new services for its patrons, a toy lending service which keeps the toy collection constantly off the shelves.[35] Project Little Kids in Greenville, South Carolina, also circulates toys along with other materials to its public.

It should be noted that child psychologists have differences of opinion about the effectiveness of toys as a developmental resource.

Dr. Burton White, for example, is extremely critical about many toys on the market today, observing that "when the child is crib-bound, between the ages of one to seven months, toys can be a means of entertaining and instructing." At this age, he notes, the baby is more or less stationary, and "going to stay where she is placed." When the child begins to crawl, however, "toys recede in their importance." He deplores the commercial competition in the toy field, especially for infants and toddlers, and his comments about specific toys are worth study. He believes that most toy designers currently lack the expertise and knowledge they should have about "the rapidly changing interests and abilities of infants and toddlers."[36]

Over five hundred toys are to be found in the collection of the Howard County, Maryland, library system children's department. All have been evaluated, says Karen Ponish, the early childhood specialist, for developmental as well as structural features.[37] The Babywise center is designed to meet the literacy or preliteracy needs of children, and is in fact a media center for the first three years of life. The toy library occupies an area of some twelve by fourteen feet in the middle of a well-stocked children's department which also houses books and nonprint materials. There is a photographic catalog of the toys which may be selected for circulation to parents, day-care providers, and family day-care homes where storytimes take place. There are workshops for parents on the use and value of toys and play, a parent-child learning center, which features speakers and various materials and activities suitable for very young children.

Funding for the Babywise program is through a two-year grant from the Maryland State Department of Education and through county funds to incorporate the program in the library's regular service for children and families.

An overview of preschool programs from around the country shows clearly that most programs tend to have particular areas of emphasis. We have already cited some which focus on the infant and under-three group and many of the examples which follow have this early childhood component. Concomitant growth has occurred in the so-called parent education library programs, as the following examples clearly demonstrate. Practice has indeed shown that the most effective preschool programs are in fact those which provide in-library activity for both parents and children and which also provide parents, and other adult caregivers, with the know-how to follow up the library beginnings on their own. Besides learning to share book

and book-related experiences with children, adults are presented
with bibliographies, hints on how to select books and other materials
(including toys, as we have seen) for children; provided with opportunities to meet experts on parenting topics; or provided with referrals to sources of help on child rearing, health, and other matters
relating to their preschoolers.

This concentration on parents and other adults associated with
preschoolers is certainly not new to children's departments, but the
rationale for it is now so strong as to be irresistible. Says Linda Silver,
head of children's services at the Cuyahoga County Library in Cleveland, "Service to adults has always been an important, although
often unrecognized, part of the children's librarian's job."[38] But it
looms ever larger as the realization grows that neither the library
alone, nor the library together with the schools and all of society's
other child development agencies, can make a significant positive
impact on children without the active involvement of parents, family
members, and all other adults who share responsibility for their
welfare.

A few examples of parent-child and parent education programs
follow.

- Child's Play, at the Middleburg Heights Branch of the Cuyahoga
  County, Ohio Public Library system, consisted of a series of three
  workshops designed for parents with their four and five year old
  children. These were hour-long sessions. For the first half hour
  parents attended a lecture by themselves, and then joined their
  children for the second half hour. Topics included Exploring Our
  World (the five senses), and There's No Place Like Home (featuring
  materials found at home suited to play and learning for children).
  In the same Ohio system at a different branch (Brookpark), Tot Talk
  introduced books, finger plays, and other games and crafts for
  parents to use with infants and toddlers. The second of two sessions featured a film, "What's So Great About Books?" and the
  distribution of a bibliography. A third session was held in a school
  under the auspices of the PTA.[39]
- In 1987–88, reports Priscilla L. Drach, children's services manager
  and project administrator for the Cuyahoga County Public Library
  system, Project LEAP was underway and in full swing. The acro-
  nym stands for "The Library's Educational Alternative for Pres-

choolers," funded by an LSCA Title I and III grant through the Ohio State Library, of $100,000 for one year, plus matching funds from local sources. The objectives are to "give children through five, who are in child care situations and unable to enjoy traditional preschool library services, the opportunity to experience quality literature and art by carefully selecting materials that will provide solid book-related reading-readiness and cognitive learning experiences." Branches participated in the selection of the fifty child care centers targeted for visits and special materials: five-hundred kits containing concept-related books, realia, lists and storytelling tips; forty puppet show packages ready for use. Workshops will be given for at least one-hundred child caregivers and one-hundred parents of preschool children, linking them to the library, which will provide continuing support and training through site visits by the staff. A newsletter published by the project contains activities and ideas for caregivers and parents. An advisory committee includes a variety of politically, socially, and educationally active organization concerned with families and early childhood.

The project is a significant response to a state law which became effective on March 11, 1986 establishing standards for the qualifications of day-care center staffs, and requiring every staff member to complete annually five hours of in-service training in child development or early childhood education until forty-five hours of such training have been completed.

- Children's literature classes for parents were held in the Bethlehem Public Library, a part of the Mohawk Valley Library system. Micki Nevett, children's and young adult consultant for the system, required registration for the four hour-and-a-half classes held weekly. Children's literature and its history was covered, and there was discussion of picture books, contemporary fiction, audiovisual presentations, and answers to parents questions, with time for participant discussion.[40] Such a formal course may be unusual, but children's librarians do a great deal of informal teaching about children's literature and its selection as parents watch while they work with children, and leave the sessions with books to read at home and lists of others.

- At the Farmington Village Library in Connecticut, Nancy De Salvo developed an "Infant-Parent Kit" designed to assist parents in influencing growth and learning patterns from the earliest stages.

The kit included books for parents to read, such as *Reading and Loving* by Leila Berg, *The First Three Years of Life* by Burton L. White, *The Baby Exercise Book* by Jamie Levy, and *Finger Plays* by Emilie Paulssen. The kit also included a cloth book, a toy for an infant, and lists of films, recordings, more books for parents, first books for young children. In listing recordings, a significant quote is included: "Music should be included daily for infants as well as for older children. The presence of music, whether through recordings . . . or parents' singing or playing, can awaken early responses to musical sound and can encourage infants to learn to listen."[41] Toys in the kit are listed by manufacturer. Most of the materials are for the child of under one year of age, but some may be used with older preschoolers. Parent programs are held several times a year in connection with the kit, and include the showing of a child development film.[42]

- The Surprise Boxes program, an imaginative invention of the Henrietta Library of the Monroe County, New York system, has already been briefly mentioned, but deserves a closer look. Each of five available boxes has a theme (circus, music, games) and each box contains materials for teaching concepts. Boxes are loaned for two week periods only to parents of preschoolers. The Rush Library, of the same system, loans some twenty-two concept-building toys to parents of preschoolers. The toys are characterized as teaching spatial relationships, seriation, concepts of left and right, and are circulated in plastic zippered bags.[43]

- The Orlando Public Library in Florida has had many good ideas for preschool programs, and pamphlet and bibliography titles it has coined have been widely picked up and used by others. Among these are *B is for Baby* bibliography and the pamphlet for parents of newborns distributed in maternity wards entitled *Catch 'em in the Cradle*. Eight hospitals were initially involved in distribution of the *Catch 'em* pamphlet and about 1,000 are distributed each month. The Orlando program provides workshops for parents on reading aloud, storytelling, and puppetry, as well as an information and sharing literature program. The library also produced a film, "What's So Great About Books?" which is used by many other libraries in their programs.[44]

- The Westchester County Library system received funding from the county's youth bureau for a pilot program in the fall of 1977 to be held in three library locations. This included a six-session program for parents, some held in the evening so that working parents could attend, and the topics discussed included: development of the child's self concept; developmental levels of preschoolers from two to three-and-a-half years of age; activities to be shared by parents and child at home; foundations for communication between parents and children, including a "parent effectiveness training" presentation; discipline and parent concerns on the topic; use of toys in the developmental process; and reading aloud and television and its influence. Books were introduced and discussed in relation to these topics. After being re-funded for one additional year in six additional libraries in the system, the project ended because funds from the regular (and diminished) library budget could not be found, but an attempt to continue, with an invited day-care coordinator from each community leading a session, was a response to public interest.[45]

- In the New York City Public Library an Early Childhood Resource and Information Center was set up in 1978, initiated by myself as coordinator of work with children and ably directed by Hannah Nuba Sheffler. It includes programs of about one hour, workshops and seminars, presented by early childhood specialists on a variety of topics related to children in their first five years: toy selection; books and toddlers; music and movement; discipline; detection of learning problems and other topics. Workshops require advance registration and many programs draw crowds of 150 to 200 persons. Significant features of the enterprise include the continuing interest of an advisory committee composed largely of leaders from the early childhood education community; a resource collection of materials including such subjects as prenatal care, day-care and headstart programs, adoption and foster care; and parent-child activities. There is also a family room where parent and preschooler interaction and spontaneous learning about many things—including each other—is made possible and actively encouraged.[46]

Starting a Parenting/Parent Education Program

With these examples before them, and new programs going forward daily, children's librarians are often inspired to begin a parent education program themselves. But how to start? Assuming the management concerns discussed in an earlier chapter have been considered, and that assessment of need and commitment to some reshuffling of resources by top management are in place, there are many possibilities for starting small and developing an exciting, useful, and successful program. The beginning may be simply a *regularly scheduled* series of preschool reading aloud or storytelling sessions for the very young. Since young children are generally accompanied by a parent or other caregiver, the next step of attracting the adult is relatively easy.

Some children's librarians hold separate programs for the parents while the children are listening and looking at picture books. The program may start initially with the parents being told what is happening in another room with the children, the titles of books being used, and the kinds of activities taking place. This can be upgraded into some discussion about the characteristics and interests of children of preschool ages, and the selection of books and activities that will aid the development processes. Later sessions may begin to feature resource people from the community: an early childhood specialist talking about learning and curriculum; a nurse talking about health and child care; a family counselor talking about behavior and parenting problems and how to solve them.

Just as the children's preschool library program may be most effective when it is limited to about fifteen or twenty children, a group of ten to fifteen parents allows for easy interchange among themselves or with the discussion leader. Sometimes parents have chosen to meet informally in the library, and the librarian may wish to set aside one day or session in the parents' program to promote this informal dialogue and encourage the "rap," share-and-listen sessions. Parents reinforce each other over coffee and cookies and learn to deal a little better with the common problems and joys of preschool children.

Promoting Parent-Child Activity

One thing that makes it very much easier to develop a related program for parents while their children are there enjoying a program of their own is, of course, that they constitute a captive audience. A small but practical matter is that having such a program minimizes the use of the children's library program as a baby-sitting service while mothers shop or visit. The dual programming puts the whole venture into the right perspective. The foundational necessity is to convince the parents that they have a genuine and very important role to play in shaping their child's future, first in school, and later in the workplace and in life itself. Once they understand that whatever their degree of education, and however much time they may have, they *can* exert tremendous influence on their child's future reading habits, learning ability, and success, they are ready to find out *how*. Then, it is vital that the librarian not make it sound sophisticated or beyond them, or surround the simple techniques with professional mystique or jargon. What they are going to practice doing is natural and easy, once it is understood. It is interaction between parent and child in which the parent is mindful that learning is taking place, but not to the extent of taking the enjoyment out of it! In talking with parents and showing them how, it must be stressed that instilling a feeling of joy and pleasure in learning, in talking, in playing, in listening, and eventually in reading, is the most important part of what they are trying to achieve.

Without snowing them with facts, theories, and impressive names, the librarian's job is to let them know that conclusions like the following have been drawn by child psychologists and educators who have studied parent early intervention and made many recent and significant findings. Dr. Urie Bronfenbrenner has stated, for example, that, "Parent-child intervention resulted in substantial gains in IQ which are still evident three to four years after termination of the [research] program. . . . Parent intervention influenced the attitudes and behavior of the mother not only toward the child but in relation to herself as a competent person capable of improving her own situation. . . . In the early years of life the key element was the involvement of parent and child in verbal interaction around a cognitively challenging task."[47] The early intervention study by this noted child psychologist from Cornell University provided, among other things, for frequent home visits in which parent and child were encouraged by examples and materials to engage in such verbal interaction around tasks that increased in complexity. If similar programs exist in the community, the professional visiting the homes should be or *could* be equipped with library materials for the preschoolers and parent. Bronfenbrenner underscores the need to "reinforce the parents' status as central in fostering the development of the child."

An important element is the joint parent-child aspect of the program so that activities such as finger plays, sing alongs, games and crafts may be shared, and parents may learn techniques for home use. Some librarians have reserved weekends for activity programs for preschool children and parents to participate in together. These may feature special activities such as finger painting, rubbings, body movement exercises, and many others. These programs are planned to provide opportunity also to show parents easy craft books which can suggest ways in which to spend time with their toddlers that will help the children develop skills and also demonstrate parent abilities during play time. These activity times may also afford parents a chance to observe their child's behavior and notice particular talents and abilities.

We mention here again the large and growing number of teenage parents, whose awareness of their role in stimulating thinking and conceptual skills, and eventually reading skills, in their young children may need to be awakened and encouraged. As a rule this group of mothers is equally as interested in helping the child develop as is a group of older mothers, but the teenagers are generally less well prepared for care and nurturing in either physical or intellectual aspects. Children's librarians may need to rely on other community agency staff to help them to approach and assist these young mothers. The children's department may begin to think of itself as a source of information and materials for making decisions and choices, and also as a coordinator of possibilities and a forum for exploration of these possibilities for the teen mothers, older parents, and other adults who affect the lives of preschool children.

Some libraries, like the Brooklyn Public Library in New York City, have set aside a small area for parents or a parents' bookshelf. In the Dayton and Montgomery County Public Library systems in Ohio, this shelf is called "Mother Hubbard's Cupboard" and features a handsome collection of books on parenting, and records for preschool play and activity, in a cupboard-like bookcase.

Selecting Books

Of course in addition to books on parenting, which are relatively few and which in any case will not be of interest to all parents, there are the old standby source books for adults to use with children. These "lap books" (because they are often used with the child on the lap) are books of nursery rhymes, singing rhymes, nursery tales, and

ABC books. Many of them have pictures which are graphically pleasing to the young child and enable him or her to follow along and "read" as the pages are turned. It is difficult without demonstration to model the reading aloud techniques, the importance of holding the book just right, and of allowing plenty of time for looking at and examining the pictures and responding to them. The aforementioned film, produced by the Orlando Public Library, called "What's So Great About Books?" may introduce or reinforce the concept.

Once parents are introduced to some of the fabulous books that constitute the literature for young children, they often become as enthusiastic as do their children about particular authors, illustrators, and titles. Books featuring familiar sights in the child's experience are compelling because they reflect, and perhaps shed a new light on, the child's everyday life. But ever since these pictures books have existed in their wonderful variety, young children have also been drawn to creatures and objects which they may never see: a rabbit in trousers and jacket escaping from a vegetable garden, a personified steamshovel, and more. Parents may like or not like certain artists or ideas expressed in a given book, but there is plenty of choice. Serious discussions about values promulgated or cultural aspects found wanting can keep a dialogue going between librarian and parent concerning books to be read and shared with a particular child. Since parents are interested in instilling values inherent in their particular backgrounds and culture, the library collection should display a range of ideas and viewpoints reflecting the diversity of opinion among people. Parents will grow tremendously in their expertise in choosing books for their own children if they are exposed to a large and varied collection of books and deftly assisted in establishing selection criteria. A mix of animal stories, realistic family-friends-and-neighborhood stories, and some simple fantasy to stir imagination can be tailored to satisfy the most demanding parent and child. Stories that feature rhythm and repetition and interesting sounds are delightful to the young listener of preschool ages. And many can be found that are even bearable to the parent who may be called upon to read and repeat a given story unceasingly when words and pictures have touched a responsive chord in the child and become comfortably familiar!

Nonprint Media

We have talked about the importance of toys and described several programs that make lavish use of them. Many libraries have produced bibliographies for parents that include them, usually identified by manufacturer, and selected from among those noted for safety. Among those listed for the youngest children are stacking toys, easy puzzles, ABC blocks, building blocks, and other educational games that can help a child learn to order, sequence, categorize, and recognize shapes and sizes and fits. Some toys may be based on storybook characters or on a character seen on "Sesame Street" or some other TV show, though the simplest toys are recommended for infants and toddlers. These would include nesting boxes, counting frames, animal-shaped puzzles, threading boards or lacing cards. Very simple musical toys or instruments may be used with older preschoolers, three- to five-year-olds, such as cymbals, bells, rhythm sticks, gourds, tambourines, and other instruments used in a small rhythm band.

Many parents may be interested in filmstrips of popular picture books and these may help them in selecting from a variety of picture books on the shelves when annotations are brief. In addition, recordings and cassettes of music are especially useful for the parent who needs help with singing, chanting a rhyme, or introducing art to a child. Is this just recreation or is it fun with a purpose? Listen to Dr. Brian Sutton-Smith: "The type of learning that occurs in play . . . is the learning of variability. As the player builds up a rich pattern of associations with his materials (and his people), he enhances his ability to give birth to more novel suggestions when they are called for."[48] Imagination, image building, extrapolation, relating one idea to another—all of these skills used in problem solving, decision making, and entrepreneurship—*begin* here.

Reaching Out to Parent and Caregiver Groups

Finding parents who don't come to the library but who use other community agencies is not now as difficult a task as it might once have seemed. There are more agencies, often better organized and with more professional personnel, whose staffs are more aware than they may have been formerly of their own and their clients' need for reliable information and assistance in all aspects of parenting. They are also apt to know more about libraries and the variety of services and expertise they offer. So all in all, there is likely to be better cooperation between librarians and other professional personnel. Many libraries have taken their preschool and parenting bibliographies, and sometimes their programs, to hospitals; films, books, and programs to day-care centers; seminars and workshops to Head Start teachers. The interest is vast and the field wide open where preschoolers are involved. The only deterrent may be the lack of sufficient staff in the children's department of the library to act upon all of the opportunities (or even most of them) to speak to adult groups, make special lists, and organize programs and projects.

Of special and primary importance is the organization of a continuously updated community resource file for referral purposes. With the breakdown of traditional family units, or in the absence of the extended family, there are virtually no reliable family resources through which to channel complaints or get advice. The library's community information file can only be properly constructed and maintained with the full cooperation of all childcaring agencies and sources of professional counseling services for families. Experienced community referral file developers have found that peoples' needs are so varied and so specialized that an age-specific file is limited in its usefulness. A recommendation might be, therefore, that the children's department examine carefully and help maintain that portion of the library's overall community information file that relates particularly to children, families, and parental concerns, continuously checking subject headings and entries. If the file is in the computer, as many now are, access in the children's department could be easily arranged. If it is in card form, a copy might be made for ready reference in the department.

Once the preschool-parenting program is begun, the potential for involving special groups of parents and caregivers is almost unlimited. In the changing family structure there are many single parents, both mothers and fathers; foster day-care mothers; working mothers; grandparents; teenage parents, many of them unwed and with little or no family support, who may not have completed high school; baby-sitters; parents for whom English is a second language; or the parents of disabled children. In an urban, and increasingly in suburban or rural settings, the librarian may encounter representatives of any and all of these groups, and the parenting program may be adjusted to accommodate their special interests and needs.

While mothers attend an English-as-a-second-language class at the Biblioteca del Pueblo de Lincoln Heights (a branch of the Los Angeles Public Library) their preschoolers may be registered to attend a preschool class. A minimal fee of three dollars a month is collected and earmarked for use for "mother and child" activities at the library. Only parents attending the English classes are invited to enroll their preschoolers in this particular program.[49] Also in California, bilingual programs and bibliographies were created for parents, in both Spanish and Chinese.

In Chicago, the public library system initiated a proposal for a Head Start Multicultural/Multilingual Resource Center Demonstration Project,[50] started in 1981. It was based on the fact that Chicago serves about 11,000 children in its large Head Start program, of which the majority are Hispanic. The program was launched in cooperation with the Chicago Department of Human Services. It was planned that the resource center would encompass a library and a classroom demonstration, with the library serving as reference resource and lending facility with a depository collection of materials with "multicultural and multilingual perspective." The collection of books, films, recordings, and other materials and realia would serve other Head Start programs in the state and the regional area, and would be available to other childcare programs as well. The groups to be served included, in addition to the Hispanic, other major ethnic elements of the Chicago area: American Indian, Polish, Greek, Italian, and Afro-American. The first fifteen months of the program was budgeted for $398,770.

Once staff training took place, the materials supported the concept in early childhood development and covered such areas as education, child abuse, cultural enrichment, parent involvement, and the health-medical field. Lectures, a bilingual newsletter, a reference bank, and cultural/ethnic holiday celebrations and events were planned as part of the program.

One area which should be of growing significance is that of intergenerational programs which utilize the experiences of grandparents and other seniors who find themselves as surrogate parents to preschoolers. There are already a few examples of storytelling and other preschool programs using "grandma helpers" but a great many more are needed. There are still few programs, however, geared to attracting the growing body of older women who have become responsible for small children, and this could be an innovative and worthy "first."

Librarians who undertake preschool-parenting programs have an opportunity to extend library walls, and create community wide networks and exchanges. The parent population—with all the special cases mentioned above—may be reached not only through schools, churches, and hospitals, but through all of the other childcare and child advocacy agencies. Professionals in nursery schools, Head Start programs, and day-care centers are in a good position to supplement and reinforce library expertise in books and other media, with knowledge in such areas as child development, child psychology, and intellectual and emotional growth. Doctors, nurses, and child welfare professionals are human resources of information, about children in general and about particular children, who are very nearly as valuable as the parents in assessing interests and needs. The library may be the chief coordinator and channel for all of these resources.

Worthy of note here is the comment by Faith Hektoen, for many years the consultant in children's and young adult services for the state of Connecticut's library services, a pioneer in inspiring work with preschoolers by libraries with a network of child-serving agencies. She observed that "By undertaking cooperative agency programs for parents that utilize existing library resources and becoming responsive to community needs, we are establishing a new working system that can create meaningful patterns of public library service to children through their parents."[51]

There are some sample library programs on which would-be programmers could model their outreach efforts to some degree. For one, the Seattle Public Library runs a van service to licensed day-care centers. A similar mobile service operates in Little Rock, Arkansas, and doubtless in a number of other cities and rural areas.[52]

For another, the children's department of the Monroe County Public Library in Bloomington, Indiana advertises, by flyer, "Arrange-A-Program." Their offer: "Invite us to bring a program to you. Arrange a program for your children's class, club or group. Your group must be a regularly scheduled group with adult support and opportunities for follow-up. The minimum size of a group must be ten children. Programs are available on a limited, first come, first served, basis. Programs will be available beginning September 21st, 1987. Call now to schedule programs." The programs below are among those listed as available, preplanned, for fall 1987: "Just for Kids! What a Librarian Does" for kindergarten through grade 8; "A Zoo for You" for kindergarten through grade 2. Granted, these offerings are a bit above preschool age groups, as advertised, but the latter one might be adapted and there are many other possibilities. In any case, the idea is a great one![53]

And another: starting in July 1983, a grant administered through the California State Library funded a project connecting libraries in the South Bay Cooperative Library system in Santa Clara with community-based childcare centers and other early childhood programs in the area. Aimed at the untapped library audience of three- to five-year-olds in day-care centers, the project was conceived as a way for the system's children's librarians to take book programs to the centers.[54] Judith Eisenger, head of children's services for the Santa Clara City Library, helped to develop the proposal for "Library-Child-Care-Link." Consultation with community college faculty, parents and center personnel, and a task force of librarians from the South Bay system evolved a plan for librarians to introduce literature for three- to 5-year-olds; develop a training kit for center staff and parents; and increase awareness of children's literature in community college's early childhood programs. Book collections were placed in the centers, and a monthly newsletter, a visiting storyteller for center visits, and a project coordinator were projected. Children's literature courses for working parents were to be offered on weekends, if possible, through the eight library sites in the system.

Staff Development for Preschool Programs

So now, here we have the merest beginning, in the majority of libraries, of a program with *huge* potential for public libraries. It is a program with big public (and public relations/political) appeal; a need with enormously important social, political, economic, and personal overtones; a ready market; experience, materials, and know-how modeled in the field. What more could we ask for? Yes, *money*—but money is not impossible to get with all the factors listed above. What is stopping us, then? Much the most serious barrier to action is lack of trained personnel. These programs are labor intensive in the extreme. Despite the great proliferation of preschool programs, little attention has been given to the staff development needs of children's librarians, who are finding themselves with more and more preschool children and parents to serve. Except for the program at North Carolina Central University, mentioned earlier, library education has largely neglected courses in early childhood or parent education—not surprising considering the sorry plight of education for children's librarians as a whole. Children's librarians and others who will serve preschool children under their supervision, will find it necessary to explore not only literature for preschoolers and their parents, but child development literature on their own account. Much of the responsibility for continuing education and staff development efforts will necessarily fall upon the employing libraries. It is to be hoped that they will have the assistance in this enterprise of early childhood educators in local institutions and of childcare agency staffs.

Continuing education opportunities for librarians are now focused, largely to make up for deficiencies in the area in the past, on the development of management capabilities. As we have seen, the most effective existing programs for developing preschool expertise often pair the librarian's knowledge of materials, and dramatic, play and story techniques with the expertise of professionals in the field of early childhood education. Volunteers and paraprofessional staff members with early childhood education backgrounds help to extend library programs for the youngest patrons and achieve linkages with community agencies. Their utilization to the fullest degree possible is recommended. Only in this way can the library initiate a community-wide network, an integrated approach to the prereading activities and needs of the young child.

Mention was made above of attempts at intergenerational programming. Older adults also represent a growing clientele in libraries and should be sought as resource people and aides in the work with preschoolers. This is especially appropriate if their life experiences include caregiving for small children. They can be surrogates for missing grandparent figures for the children, and good models and informal advisors for the young mothers especially.

We conclude this chapter with a new project now underway in The New York Public Library which will, we hope, pave the way for other public library systems to upgrade the capabilities of children's department staff in work with preschool children. This is the Early Childhood Project, funded by the Carnegie Corporation of New York, and growing out of the success of the library system's Early Childhood Resource and Information Center, described above. The new project will expand attention to early childhood services into its branches in three boroughs of New York City: The Bronx, Staten Island, and Manhattan. It is planned as a three-year project. The first year involved children's librarians from each of the three boroughs in an eight-week course, offered at New York University, in the theory and practice of early childhood education and child development through library service. The second year's activity was comprised of training for the entire children's services staff through workshops on early childhood educational principles. Special programs implementing these principles will be carried out in sixteen neighborhood branches with materials and services for preschool children, their parents, and other caregivers. In the third year, there will be a national "Sharing" conference, and evaluative material and other information will be developed for wide distribution.[55]

No two preschool-parenting programs will be just alike, just as no two communities are ever just alike in their needs and resources. All children's librarians can, however, share a common purpose with these programs: to try to ensure that all children from all types of families and all kinds of neighborhoods and backgrounds have the best possible chance to grow into the love that will stand by them all their lives if it is nurtured properly at the very beginning: the love of reading and of books.

10

Some Other Matters in Summary

Selection

There has been little said in this book thus far about the two aspects of children's librarianship that have always been perceived to be of paramount importance both by the librarians and those who perceived them: children's literature and the criteria for selection of books to be used with children in library programs. The already perceived importance is exactly the reason why they have not been stressed here—because although librarianship for children *is* about those things, there is much more to it than that. This book has endeavored to give a balanced and up-to-date profile of the professional and of the job to be done. Also, there are many, many fine books about books for children: analyzing text and art; categorizing books in terms of the values they espouse; describing the interest children might have in them; and telling how to motivate children to read them. There are journals devoted to this literature and its authors, artists, and editors; countless prizes—probably over a hundred of them—given for various aspects of excellence, some of them even judged by children themselves. There is a continuous flow of reviews and articles on children's literature, new titles, and recently, reissues of older books, many of them still as good and as appealing to children as they were the day they were first published, twenty, thirty, forty or more years ago.

Many of these books and journals will be found listed in the bibliography, but a few should have special mention. *The Horn Book,* with a long history of critical literary evaluation of books for children, is perhaps the best known and most widely respected source of critical opinion. Also, geared primarily to the interest of librarians, is the recently renamed *Top of the News,* now the *Journal of Youth Services,* the journal of two of ALA's youth divisions: ALSC and YASD. The third youth-serving division is AASL, which publishes its own journal, geared primarily to the interests of school library media specialists, *School Library Media Quarterly,* which also has reviews and articles. There is also the biweekly *School Library Journal* with reviews from librarians working with children on the front lines in both school and public libraries; *Wilson Library Bulletin, Booklist* (an ALA review journal) and the *Kirkus Reviews* which specializes in advance notice of books not yet published. There is a compilation called *Children's Choices,* by a joint committee of the Children's Book Council and the International Reading Association, in which children vote for their best-liked books.

Although all of the above are related to the library field they are avidly read by children's literature teachers, reading, English, and classroom teachers. There are many reviews and journals about children's literature and its selection outside of the library field, as well. They include: *Children's Literature Journal,* published by Yale University Press as an outgrowth of the Children's Literature Division of the Modern Language Association; *The Reading Teacher,* journal of the International Reading Association; and *Language Arts,* from the National Council of Teachers of English. Classroom teacher periodicals such as *The Instructor* are vitally interested in children's literature and how to integrate it into the instructional program. There are, in addition, many consumer publications, especially those addressed to young parents, which carry reviews on a fairly regular basis, as do the major newspapers, such as the *New York Times* and the *Chicago Tribune.* On the international scene, about which we will say more a bit later, there is also *Book Bird,* a periodical covering news and reviews of children's literature internationally.

A brief word about the prizes should be sufficient, too, as they are well documented in a number of places. The annual Newbery and Caldecott Awards for excellence in literature for children—the first given primarily for the writing, the latter for the illustrations— are the oldest (now more than fifty years old each) and the most prestigious; the Laura Ingalls Wilder Award, given only every three years and established in 1954, fills a gap by recognizing an author's entire body of writing over time. The Wilder Award has been presented to such all-time favorites as E. B. White, Dr. Seuss, Maurice Sendak, and Beverly Clearly. These three awards, more than any of the others, share a real influence in establishing and maintaining standards for style and criteria in book selection for children. The Wilder award, more than the others, focuses on child appeal and readability, as well as on literary quality.

There are too many other awards to name, but suffice it to say that they all have an important affect on promoting good writing and good reading for children. Some are sponsored by organizations which highlight books that address contemporary problems or special needs such as world peace or good human relations. These include the Coretta Scott King Awards, now sponsored by the Social Responsibilities Round Table of the ALA, which honor a black author and artist for their contributions. There are awards given to authors living in particular regions of the country or in a particular state. Finally, there are numerous international awards, some of which have been won, on occasion, by Americans.

The controversy over children's book awards and prizes rages continuously and will never be settled. Some inevitably agree with the choices, and some do not. Some believe that literary quality weighs too heavily in the judges decisions; others that it does not weigh heavily enough. There are those who contend that criteria for evaluation of books are simply not relevant in terms of whether or not children will like them. It is true that some of the Newbery and Caldecott winners have never caught on with children. John Rowe Townsend, a contemporary British author, wrote: "It seems to me that it is perfectly possible to judge books for children by non-literary standards. It is legitimate to consider the social or moral or psychological or educational impact of a book; to consider how many children and what kind of children, will like it."[1] Another point made by Townsend that must be always kept in mind by book evaluators and selectors is that "children are individuals."[2] Each child brings to each book a unique set of experiences, sensibilities, skills, insights, dreams, fears, and realities.

In his acceptance speech for the 1978 Nobel Prize for Literature, Isaac Bashevis Singer listed among the ten reasons why he chose to write for children the fact that children love a good story and will readily abandon a "boring" one. However, there are many gatekeepers in the path of a book on its way to the child who will find it a memorable influence in his life. Most children find their books through adults, who provide for a book's presence either at home or in a library or school. The majority of books which children "find" are those placed within their reach by some adult's purchase, selection, and formal or informal introduction. Later, books may be discovered by the child on his or her own, but this usually happens only after a love of reading has been developed in the early years and personal discovery is made possible by exposure and access to a variety of books and reading experiences. This is why parents have such a major responsibility to surround children with books and to provide motivation and a setting conducive to reading.

It is worth noting in this brief summary of selection considerations and criteria in choosing books for children that across the years the very best books for children, those that have endured because children truly loved them, have been marked by at least three characteristics: they are often not age-specific in their appeal, as adults may like them almost as much as children; they are written with flair by authors who are unafraid to use "juicy" words, subtle analogies, and quirky, complex characters; and they often have the classic combination of humor mixed with great sadness. Such books can be enjoyed on various levels, appreciated for their surface qualities, or for their deeper meaning. Librarians, parents, and other adults who are engaged in putting books in the way of children, should be aware of the characteristics and values which help to make a book creative and deepen its appeal so that it becomes influential and often unforgettable for a lifetime. It is these "good" books that help a child to grow. As Alice Brooks said many years ago, while she was still at the Center for Instructional Materials at the University of Chicago (still another important reviewing and critical resource not mentioned earlier): "[They] provide stimulus situations for new behavior patterns . . . or influence and reinforce desirable valuations and attitudes."[3] There will always be differences of opinion about what constitutes desirable valuations and attitudes but there is a substantial agreement on the characteristics and values of a positive lifestyle. Even so, some espouse teaching children how to form values without any hint of which ones are generally considered to be good ones, and which bad. In any case, it is important for adults concerned with children's literature to consider those characteristics that make a book creative, enduring, and useful to children, and compelling and fascinating as well. The chart Brooks suggested for analyzing children's literature lists values such as those she assigns to the development of the "inner life": self expression, interpersonal relations, adjustments in behavior, ideologies, and self-reliance. Librarians and others who make appraisals and share them, should point out these developmental values for children in the books under discussion.

More than two thousand titles a year are published for children in this country and many more thousands abroad, a few of which find their way here in translation or otherwise. How many of these books are good enough for children or even passable? What happens to all of them?

Briefly, the publishing business has changed exponentially over the past two decades, and not, many believe, for the better. Many old-line publishers with outstanding children's book departments and dependable back lists were acquired by conglomerates or other large companies. Many of them have nothing whatever to do with books and the "bottom line" became the first, and often the only, consideration as to whether or not a book would be published, how a book would be produced, and how long it would stay in print. Editors of children's books moved from job to job more often than was formerly the case, and heads rolled when bottom line projections were not met. As the budget picture for libraries worsened in the middle 1970s, book budgets were usually the first to be slashed, and juvenile publishing, which traditionally has sold seventy-five to eighty percent of its product to libraries, began to reflect the drop in sales. Acquisitions were curtailed, and books began to go out of print more quickly and to stay out of print—often within a year of publication. Added to this were the rising costs: sharp rises in paper, printing—especially color printing—and labor costs. A crowning blow was the 1979 Thor Tool Decision, a tax law meant for industry which turned out identical machine parts and warehoused them with tax write-offs. Applied to the book industry, this had dire consequences, because each product is unique, and it meant that publishers must pay taxes on unsold inventory. Inventory was slashed, and backlist titles, so depended upon by children's librarians because books wear out and must be replaced, and are new to each generation of children, went out of print for good. Slow but regular sales had always been the nature of the business, but now initial printings of new titles, except for a handful of best-selling authors and illustrators, are severely limited.

Other factors affecting the cost of books included discounts available from publisher or jobber, preprocessing costs, library bindings, and the ratio of paperbacks to clothbound books for the collection. New "FPT" systems, freight pass-through taxes that publishers pass on to buyers, depend on vendor or publisher. It has become difficult to identify the true price of a book from the invoice, although jobbers still claim that discounts are favorable to the juvenile library market.

Another major problem of selection is censorship. Librarians are specifically anti-censorship as a profession. ALA's Office for Intellectual Freedom wages a continuing war on would-be censors of everything from Mother Goose (attacked on grounds of anti-Semitic bias) to the books of Judy Blume and hundreds of others. ALA has its Library Bill of Rights and its statement on Free Access to Libraries for Minors, and there is also a School Library Bill of Rights, and other statements librarians subscribe to propounded by other groups. In the early 1970s, the Children's Services Division (now ALSC), devised what it believed was a clear statement of guidelines for re-evaluation of children's materials. It suggested that, since times have changed certain negative social attitudes, collections should be weeded and developed along more positive lines. The statement came head to head with the ALA Intellectual Freedom forces, which accused children's librarians of fostering censorship, and the statement was rescinded.

Concern about the appropriateness of certain books for children has preoccupied adults ever since a body of literature intended for children began to develop. In earlier times, even in the early days of this century, literature for children was heavy-handedly laden with morals and dictums about good behavior, but it was often filled with negative racial stereotypes and slurs. Books pictured a life that was serene and beautiful for white, Anglo-Saxon, Protestant children, whose good deeds, and obedience were rewarded with a happy death. Since the 1960s, not only have most of the stereotypes and racial and ethnic slurs been eliminated, but books have been made to reflect "positive" social values. Now, with the national swing to conservatism, and a large and growing population of rigid religionists, a whole new group of censors has descended on libraries and schools.

Good selection practice dictates a degree of objectivity and a high sense of social awareness and sensitivity, but since each selector brings a particular body of experience and subjectivity to the process, there is no absolute neutrality or "purity" in the process. The line between selection and censorship is admittedly a fine one, but librarians have developed guidelines and norms which can bear defending as part of the overall goals of library services to children. Striving for reasonable balance in the collection of materials offered to the public is an important objective. The concepts of "community standards" and "redeeming social value" of a work overall must also enter into judgments. These were criteria enunciated by the court, primarily in terms of adult books in which sexuality and possible pornography were the issue, but they must be considered even when the books are for children and sex is not the issue. Librarians must weigh whether an image or characterization in a book is only slightly out of balance, but that this fault is outweighed by other good aspects, or whether it has the potential to be actively painful or harmful to the self-image of any group of children or to the perception of them by others. Several studies have documented the fact that negative images in books can have considerable and harmful impact on self-image because they are in learning tools, in print, and are expected to convey valid value messages.

By the 1960s, the civil rights movement had spawned a generalized human rights consciousness which brought to the fore a score of social ills which found their way into books for children. Not only racial problems, but the less than safe and perfect lives of many children became subjects for children's reading: the nontraditional family structure, divorce, single parent families, complex and difficult family relationships, awakening sexual desires, the horrors of war, and many other problems. The conservative censors of the Right espoused the "right" values in books for children, traditional gender and family roles, and a "what's right with America" point of view. Those on the socially-conscious Left wanted children to know that all was *not* right with prejudices against minorities and ethnics, stereotypical treatment of women and the elderly, and neglect of the poor and helpless. Textbooks, which children are obliged to study in school, were shown to be more likely than trade or library books to stereotype racial or ethnic characteristics and age and sex roles. It became evident that extremists on both sides viewed books as powerful ideological weapons.

It was, in fact, the school and school library media centers which felt the greatest heat from attacks by censors, probably because the school setting carried the connotation of all the children being assigned a given book, whereas the public library, free of grades or homework compulsions, carries a sense of free choice for children. The Island Trees case from Long Island, New York, concerned a school library and finally reached the U.S. Supreme Court, brought

there by a student on the grounds that the would-be censors on the
school board were limiting his choices of intellectual fare.[4] The Court
agreed with the student, and the case not only dramatized the
frequent attacks on schools by parents or local lawmakers seeking to
remove books from the shelves but put an effective halt to many of
these activities.

The question of what to select with limited funds and how to
justify choices in case of attack is an ongoing dilemma for public
libraries, too. It is exacerbated by the fact that all too many still
operate without an official written selection and collection development policy approved by the highest level of governance. One recent
survey of public library selectors revealed that one-fifth of them
avoided buying anything thought to be controversial. Another forty
percent, considering a book possibly controversial, opted to reject it
by giving a more readily acceptable and professional reason for not
purchasing it. Selection decisions are probably easier to defend in
public library situations because of the voluntary and elective nature
of their programs and activities. A prime tenet of all policies is that
each parent or set of parents bears responsibility for their own child's
reading, and may request that any book or type of book be forbidden
to that child. However, this does not give the right to prohibit other
children from reading what they choose if their parents have no
objections. This philosophy in no way precludes the right of the
children's librarian to exercise judgment in selection of books for an
individual or for group programming. This right and professional
responsibility should be clearly stated in the written materials selection policy. Knowledge of the collection overall is extremely important so that every book selected can be defended in terms of others
already in the collection and in keeping with the stated policy.

The question is often asked as to whose values are the ones to
which children should be exposed. There is little doubt that while
books can have a significant influence on personal development, it is
the child's whole life experience in the world of family, school, and
community that largely determines the effect of what is read. There
is ample evidence that a wide selection of reading materials helps in
creating discriminating judgments. Even for young children, reading
guidance can result in their discovery that there are many points of
view and that not all books present absolute truths. A parent or other
adult who challenges a title in the children's book collection should
be commended for showing an interest and awareness of his child's

reading, but should be carefully made aware that the objection is valid solely for that child and not for other peoples'. Specific standards or values may not be the same for all of the diverse groups that use the library.

Perhaps the most difficult matters to settle are those involving racial portrayals in books for children. Consciousness-raising has made us more sensitive to the way in which all groups are represented in literature and in the media. A poignant story was told at the White House Conference on Children in 1970, about a parent who came home to discover her daughter crying while watching a popular television show about cowboys and Indians. She explained that she was rooting for the cowboys to win, because she couldn't bear to be always on the losing side. She was American Indian.

After World War II, some librarians did call attention to the negative images transmitted in some children's books. The low self-image of black children was attributed not only to the absence of positive characters who were black (successful, responsible leaders) but the perpetuation of misconceptions and misinformation in books that were widely available. Charlemae Rollins and Augusta Baker were pioneers in the children's library field who suggested guidelines for racial portrayals in books for children. Few black authors were published, although the books of Jesse Jackson and Lorenz Graham began to explore racial tensions and the problems of segregation in some novels for children. White writers such as John Tunis, who wrote widely read sports stories, Florence Crannell Means, and Lorraine Beim, also found publishers for books which presented the problems of race hatred and sought to promote racial understanding and harmony. These authors were all writing and being published in the 1940s.

Children's books are very apt to reflect the concerns and attitudes of the times in which they are published, so it is not surprising that the focus on racial and ethnic differences in the 1960s resulted in the publication of many more books for children which presented the pluralistic nature of American society. The books by Ezra Jack Keats showing black protagonists engaged in universally childlike experiences like playing in the snow (*The Snowy Day*), trying to whistle (*Whistle for Willie*), or in the throes of sibling rivalry (*Peter's Chair*) paved the way for many more books about children and families from nonwhite groups. *The Snowy Day* won the Caldecott Award, which helped a great deal to popularize it. In 1965, an article by Dr. Nancy

Larrick appeared in *Saturday Review* which jogged the awareness of many editors and made them more conscientious about looking for black and other minority writers.[5] It was called "The All-White World of Children's Books" and was based on research she had done from 1962 to 1964. In 1978, Dr. Jeanne Chall and three of her students in the Graduate School of Education at Harvard conducted a study of children's books published between 1973 and 1975. They concluded that while the portrayals of blacks in books for children had doubled in quantity within the decade between 1965 and 1975, the all-white world Dr. Larrick described still prevailed in at least eighty-six percent of trade books published in this country for children. Dr. Chall noted the increase in biographies about blacks, most of whom, however, were sports figures. Photographs of these athletes pictured them at play, but never initiating strategy or demonstrating the management skills of the game.

In 1969, Augusta Baker had written an open letter to publishers outlining criteria for depiction of blacks in children's books.[6] These criteria were in fact easily adaptable to portrayals of other minority groups. Reacting to the omissions and to the lack of opportunity for minority writers and artists to present their work to children even during a period of heightened awareness, the Council on Interracial Books for Children instituted awards for manuscripts by minority writers and illustrators. Winning manuscripts were offered to publishers. The council strongly expressed the conviction that the best representation of a group comes from members of that particular group, who not only know the culture from the outside, but feel it from the inside. Also in 1969, Glyndon Flynt Greer, a school librarian, initiated with friends and colleagues the Coretta Scott King Award, to honor the contributions of black authors and illustrators whose work reflected the ideals of Dr. Martin Luther King, Jr. and the black experience in books for children.

The 1960s and 1970s brought forward a number of talented black writers and illustrators, among them Eloise Greenfield, Julius Lester, Tom Feelings, John Steptoe, Ashley Bryan, June Jordan, Nikki Giovanni, Sharon Bell Mathis, Lucille Clifton, and two Newbery Award winners, Virginia Hamilton and Mildred Taylor. However, far less effort has been made in the 1980s to find new and talented minority authors or to keep good older books in print. In the 1970s some writers of American Indian heritage began to be heard from in books for children, including Driving Hawk Sneve, Rosebud Yellow Robe, and Jamake Highwater. Asian-American authors and illustrators also contributed to the awareness of the conflict that rages within young people of mixed races and cultures as they try to reconcile their feeling of "differentness" with mainstream white society. Lawrence Yep, Yoshiko Uchida, and Taro Yashimo are among these, as well as Shigeo Watanabe.

However, the fastest growing non-English-speaking group in the United States, Hispanics, Spanish-speaking people from several different cultural backgrounds, are still largely underrepresented in the literature for children. Pura Belpré, with her lovely Puerto Rican folk tales, *Perez and Martina* and stories from *The Tiger and the Rabbit*, has long been very popular in New York as well as in places without such a large Puerto Rican community.

The scarcity of bilingual materials continues to be an area of concern. Some progress along these lines has been made for Spanish-speaking learners in terms of dictionaries and some easy readers, but much more needs to be developed for this fast-growing population.

Several bibliographies include materials in Spanish and Spanish-English materials as well. One is the New York Public Library's *Libros en Espanol: An Annotated List of Children's Books in Spanish. Latino Materials: A Multimedia Guide for Children and Young Adults* by Daniel Flores Duran includes thirty bilingual titles. Isabel Schon's commentary on Spanish and bilingual books (*School Library Journal*, March 1983) contains evaluations of bilingual books worth noting including poetry books. In a review of current books on Hispanics in another article, Schon is highly critical of some common misrepresentations of Hispanics in children's books and cites authors who interpret the Hispanic experience from brief observations or after short visits to Spanish-speaking countries.[7]

In a study of the Jewish-American experience by Gloria Blatt, she suggests that recent books on Jewish life in America are quite representative of the group, contrary to objections raised by Myra and David Sadker in their book *Now Upon a Time: A Contemporary View of Children's Literature* or Eric Kimmel's article on "Jewish Identity in Jewish Fiction." Citing E. L. Konigsburg's *About the B'nai Bagels*, Judy Blume's *Are You There God? It's Me Margaret*, Emily Neville's *Berrie's Goodman*, and Bette Greene's *Summer of My German Soldier*, among others, she agrees with the varied presentations these authors have made of family alienation, struggles to assimilate, or the abandonment of strict religious observation in some Jewish families. Surpris-

ingly, Blatt feels one of the least realistic presentations exists in the
All-of-a-Kind Family series, citing them as romanticizing a critical and
difficult period of the Jewish immigration in America. None could
argue with her assessment of the contribution that Isaac Bashevis
Singer and the award-winning illustrator, Uri Shulevitz, have made
in the introduction of the rich heritage of the Jewish people through
their children's books.[8]

As budgets have decreased, multicultural and multilingual offerings have seemed to decrease also, but the demands of the influx of
immigrants dictates new attention to developing collections in non-
English language areas. Availability, quantity, and quality of materials pose a problem for librarians trying to meet the needs of Hispanic,
Korean, Vietnamese, Haitian, and other newcomers. Many libraries
in the past have, when budgets permitted, obtained not only transla-
tions of foreign language books but the books in the original language. However, books for children in foreign languages differ in
standards of production and are rarely available in multiple copies.
Problems of acquisition and cataloging need to be continually explored. Whenever possible, though, the children's room collection
should represent a broad range of cultures and languages in materials
for children. Books by people who belong to or spring from the
various cultures should be sought, as should books that portray
members of the cultures as individuals. Books carrying the overtone
that "different" from the mainstream white American culture equates
with "not as good" should be rejected.

When questioned, many authors say that they write for themselves, or for the child in them, but almost inevitably a book conveys
a message from their adult selves. The selector must be aware of
distortions, inaccuracies, or biases, even though the author may not
have consciously allowed them into the message. So obtrusive, or at
least evident, are some of the messages today that some recent fiction
for children has been dubbed as laden with "the new didacticism."
In most book controversies, treatment of sexual matters ranks second
only to matters of race as an item for special censure. Curiously,
incidents of violence in books for children arouse less controversy
than either one. Recently, with the rise of the New Right and the
religious reconstructionists, religious conviction runs stronger as a
source of conflict. Those views which seem most to conflict with
individual mores, or to represent the less traditional view in a
community dedicated to more traditional ones, are most likely to be

attacked by adults who wish to protect children from opposing viewpoints. Almost any book today may present a new and different type of selection dilemma. There was a controversy which made newspaper headlines in 1983 over a book called *Jake and Honeybunch* by Zemach, which posed an outright challenge to librarians' rights to selection. In this case, several influential children's librarians chose not to buy this title because they saw it as perpetuating old and negative racial stereotypes. Thereupon, the publisher went public with the allegation that they had censored the book.[9]

Librarians are usually the first to admit that, being human after all, their judgments and decisions in matters of selection cannot always be perfect or correct in all eyes. It must, however, be made increasingly clear, as special interests and points of view multiply, that librarians operate with an official mandate and professional training to meet individual need and to serve social interest by providing the best books they can find among the thousands published each year.

The "Classics"

One would think, on the face of it, that the "classics" of children's literature would be a safe choice with which no would-be censors would quarrel, but this is not the case. There is, of course, an eternally insoluble question as to what exactly is a classic. Almost all could agree that *Alice in Wonderland, Pinocchio*, and the adventure stories of Robert Louis Stevenson fill the bill. Children still read these today and find them satisfying for, respectively, their upside down logic and nonsense, personifications, and blood and guts. Reaching further back however, what of the *Odyssey, Pilgrim's Progress*, or even *Gulliver's Travels*? Few children encounter them until high school or college, and then only on required reading lists. There is Mark Twain, of course, as an example of a vintage American writer, but some of his work has come under fire for representation of racial stereotypes and attitudes which are recognized as hurtful and harmful to today's readers. His work may argue against the characteristic of "timelessness" as a major criterion for judging a classic, and is a strong indicator that all classics are not above scrutiny or criticism for use with today's children. There are such stories as *Mary Poppins*, the Milne books, and *Peter Pan* which maintain their popularity with many American children, although their British upper-class backgrounds—complete with nannies—may seem far removed from most of today's American children. Also, one of the latter day "classic" writers for children was, in the late 1980s, enjoying an explosive revival: Frances Hodgson Burnett's *The Secret Garden* was, at one count in 1987, to be represented by no less than seventeen reprint editions despite its turn-of-the-century quaintness and its high degree of old style didacticism. It does, however, hold great interest for some readers, who identify with the willful and independent characters of the hero and heroine.

The classics, then, are a mixed bag. Yet, many parents and grandparents read them, remembered them with pleasure, and want their children to experience them. Many more, perhaps, recall and cherish such librarian-scorned series books as the Nancy Drew stories, despite their formula-written sameness of plot and character; to many adults who enjoyed them, they might be considered childhood classics as well! Also, many books do not hold up well: *Black Beauty*, a favorite horse story of a couple of generations back, is a case in point. In all, librarians must be careful to examine pressures to "get back to the classics" and be able to explain that there are classics and classics!

There are many newer books which can be recommended for children with the confidence that most will enjoy them. These books are often called "standards" or "contemporary classics." Everyone's list of "musts" for inclusion in this company would differ slightly, but most would agree on FitzHugh's *Harriet the Spy*; some of the books of Beverly Cleary; *Charlotte's Web*; and many others. These books provide children with mind-expanding experiences that are rooted in the common human experience and which stretch their imaginations in a satisfying and unforgettable way. Although they are books for children and were written for them, they may speak also to the adult reader. They bring to childhood an added dimension of which no child should be deprived. They are books which can grow in memory, and with reading, and to which maturity brings new understanding. Rereading such books brings increased enjoyment for both children and adults.

Language plays an important role in the appeal and durability of a classic or a standard book that no child should miss having the chance to read. Be they descriptive or lyrical in quality, the words help to enliven the action and make the characters believable. Often they bear repetition and savoring on the tongue or in memory. There is something unforgettable about the tongue-twisting humor in Sandburg's *Rootabaga Stories*, the direct simplicity of *Charlotte's Web*. Children recognize the language in these books as expressing thoughts they themselves have had; the characters relate, in whole or in part, to themselves.

No serious consideration of books for children or the extent and difficulty of the selector's task can omit the place of picture books in children's lives. Who can forget the precise rightness of the words to fit the actions or the rightness of the actions themselves in Sendak's *Where the Wild Things Are?* Picture books are among the most ambitious, expensive, and complex of all book productions and they are among the most significant books because they may be remembered for a lifetime. There are many classics or standards among them now, some of them in print for forty years or more. Almost all of them are a product of this century and the recent past. Consider the long life and enduring popularity of such books as McCloskey's *Make Way for Ducklings;* Gag's *Millions of Cats;* and Margaret Wise Brown's *Goodnight Moon.* Arnold Lobel, Uri Shulevitz, Dr. Seuss, Eric Carle, Ezra Jack Keats, Peter Spier, Steven Kellogg, and Marcia Brown, among others, have brought a visual interpretation of the world combined with texts that have an appeal for a range of ages. The variety of these books and others, such as those of Gerald McDermott, Mitsumasa Anno, Brian Wildsmith, Donald Crews, Tom Feelings, John Steptoe, or Janina Domanska present a panorama of art styles to whet the artistic appetite, develop the creative concept and the visual perception. Picture books were once considered the province only of young children, but many are now published with the intent of reaching preschoolers to upper elementary-age children. The wordless picture book, so graphically splendid, and the photographic picture book, can be evaluated in terms of either or both text and art work. Picture books for older children may serve to heighten both verbal and visual literacy.

For picture book creators, the text is the important core upon which the picture is built. Sendak writes, for example, that for him, his illustrations give fantasy physical form; he sees illustrations as enhancing and enlarging upon the text. Photographer Tana Hoban sees pictures in her everyday surroundings, and translates them into the art forms that represent and present various verbal and visual concepts. For many children, the text and the pictures are equally exciting, and may be their introduction to art. They will busily "read" the pictures long before they can read the words, and these may ignite an appreciation of art. Book selection, then, in this area is fully as important as in any other, and picture books are not just "kiddie lit"—an odious term of contempt sometimes heard from the uninitiated! The increasing demand to meet the needs of the preschool child is bringing picture books into ever sharper focus.

Very often, the natural interest of children in language becomes even keener when they are introduced to poetry. Poet Kornei Chukovsky referred to the small child as a "linguistic genius,"[10] not only because the child can, and must, in the early years master a vocabulary in order to communicate, but also because he or she develops the capability of making distinctive, logical, and meaningful word associations. The spare framework for expression that is possible in poetry interests children, especially when it is shared in read-aloud situations. Many poets may be introduced after the familiar nursery rhymes have paved the way. These include not only the well-known "poets of childhood" such as Longfellow, Lear, Eugene Field, Milne, and Carroll, but Emily Dickinson, Christina Rosetti, Robert Frost, John Ciardi, and many more. Moments of delight come with the use of words and rhymes. Many contemporary poets are more understandable to children than they are to adults.

The popularity of Shel Silverstein's *Light in the Attic,* or *Where the Sidewalk Ends* attests to children's enjoyment of humorous poems. There are also the nonsense verses of Canadian poet, Dennis Lee, in *Garbage Delight;* the scary poems of Jack Prelutsky, rhythm in poetry by David McCord. Karla Kuskin and Myra Cohn Livingston are poets whose works have children and childhood in mind. Lee Bennett Hopkins and Arnold Adoff are well known for their topical anthologies, as is William Cole, who has many volumes of humorous and child-appealing poems to his credit. Nancy Larrick and Helen Plotz have compiled poems on subjects of contemporary interest. These anthologists have introduced works by Ogden Nash, Theodore Roethke, T. S. Eliot, e. e. cummings, Langston Hughes, Gwendolyn Brooks and Robert Frost, among others. Children should also meet the special poetry in the works of John Bierhorst based on the Native American culture, and other cultures reflected in books by Richard Lewis, and in the poetry of Harry Behn.

Informational books are perhaps the most plentiful of all types because they are used for school assignments. They are also generally the least critically analyzed because they are not "literary" in the narrowest sense. These books range from picture books about baby farm animals to discussions of nuclear fission. While many children do use these books of information to satisfy homework assignments, many others seek them to increase personal expertise in pursuit of a hobby such as model-making, cooking, repairing a bicycle or flying a kite. The range and depth of a child's curiosity does not necessarily correspond with chronological age. Accuracy and currency of information are especially important in selecting these books.

Biographies are popular for school assignments, and thanks to authors like Jean Fritz, there are lively and readable books about historical figures which present them with humor and personality. Books on science, travel, and history are frequently used to supplement school texts in these areas. Criteria for their selection are extremely important here, and accuracy and recency should be primary considerations. A book on space travel written five years ago is out of date now, and information on the emerging and developing nations of the Third World becomes quickly obsolete in light of their mercurial political situations. There is no reason why informational books for children should be less well written than fiction, but there are times when the demand for certain subjects results in less than thorough attention to literary quality.

Motivating Reading

Librarians devote a good deal of time to trying to select books that will appeal to the so-called reluctant reader. The child who is two grades or more below grade level in reading is considered to be having difficulty in mastering skills that will render him literate in school and adult life. There are some who have problems resulting from physical or mental impairments, such as dyslexia and other learning disabilities. But librarians are most concerned as a rule with the problems they feel they can do something about: those of the children who lack motivation and the desire to read. Librarians regard this child as a potential reader and a challenge, and look for slim or "skinny" books to try to make the experience of reading a whole book reasonably quick and satisfying. It becomes increasingly difficult to intervene and help a child to solve the reading problems that will affect him more the older he gets, and the longer the sense of reading failure goes on.

All too many teachers and parents equate reading with the decoding activity that constitutes the technical aspect of learning to read. But readers do not develop if they lack the thinking and inquiry skills that help them to make sense of what they read and so become interested in it. We have stated previously that lifetime reading habits depend in great part on the degree of *enjoyment* derived from reading. Motivation is the key, and most librarians, faced with reluctant readers, work on seeding and developing interests that will result in a self-propelled reader—the only kind that becomes ultimately, a fully literate adult. Sam Sebasta, in an article in *Language Arts* says it well: "Learning to read requires a little risk-taking and a lot of inquiring from the learner."[11]

The thrill of getting meaning from interesting words is an important factor often overlooked in a child's introduction to books. Bruno Bettelheim and Karen Zelan discuss this in *On Learning to Read: The Child's Fascination with Meaning*. Adults should not hesitate to use interesting sounding words with even very young children. Most children like to hear such words, try to repeat them and grasp their meaning in the context of a story or song. Bettelheim criticizes "the blandness of . . . text" in many beginning books for the very young.[12]

Accessibility is another important factor in promoting motivation to read. It has been shown over and over again that homes with few books, classrooms without books, and little or no access to school and public libraries, are all characteristic of unmotivated, unable readers. It is known, too, that as important as is physical access to books themselves, the presence of a *person* to serve as bridge between child and book is a vital part of the equation.

The children's library staff can play a unique role in this motivational aspect of reading. Unfortunately, most librarians meet failing and unmotivated readers when they are in the third or fourth grade, when damage to the self-image and bad habits are hard to undo. Happily the burgeoning interest in early childhood library programs is pointing in a direction which could prevent many reading casualties among children when they are older.

The first step, whatever the age of the child, involves working closely with the adults with whom the children spend most of their lives every day. Since parents and caregivers are usually the first concerned adults the child knows, they need to understand something of the why, the how and what the child reads. Librarians should share their experiences in reading with parents and other caregivers, and should encourage these adults to share, in their turn, information about the child. Parents can become partners in the motivation-to-read process, and can share enthusiasm for the aesthetic as well as for the practical benefits of reading. Help parents to think about the use of books to develop the imagination, the "mind's eye," and delight in language and in being able to express ideas. The popularity of Jim Trelease's *Read Aloud Handbook* (see bibliography) is indicative of the growing recognition of the rewards of this activity in a family setting which can be reinforced by and through the library.

Teachers are important adults in the lives of school children, and children's librarians can learn much from them. They can learn about reading levels, cognitive developmental skills, and various methods of teaching reading skills. Although children's librarians cannot be involved in teaching technical skills, they are in a very real sense involved deeply in developing readers. They should know something about the learning techniques and methods in order to relate their knowledge of books to different stages of learning development. The nursery school teacher, the kindergarten teacher, the classroom teacher, the reading teacher, and the subject teacher are all allies with whom the librarian should have constant interchange.

There are many reasons why children find books difficult and may never come to feel on familiar and comfortable terms with them. Psychological and environmental factors play a large part in the total picture as does a child's daily life, ability to communicate thoughts and feelings to an interested adult, and encouragement and realistic expectation of himself as a reader.

Before the child becomes a teenaged candidate for high-interest, low-reading level books, there are some known factors for providing stimulus to some reluctant readers. The outward appearance of the book is important in catching interest: an attractive cover; simple, interesting but not childish pictures; good graphic design. Children in this society are surrounded by professional packaging efforts from birth and expect to be enticed. This may explain the popularity of paperbacks; unless they are obvious reproductions of picture books, the paperback format often disguises the difficulty or easiness of the text.

Above all, children are drawn to a good story—the readability factor. Whether they are going to read it purely for fun, or for information, it must be written to sustain the reader's interest. It must have the ring of truth, of genuineness, to it, even if it is a form of fantasy. Being involved in a common human experience in a book appeals to children, because they can often relate to some element, at least, of the experience. Anne Carroll Moore has quoted Kenneth Grahame as saying that, "[children] have just as much 'sense' [as grown-ups] . . . it is only experience that they lack. In the matter of their reading, I think they have more sense since they are entirely unconcerned with other peoples' opinions of books. When they are bored, they stop reading the book. 'I don't like that book' is reason enough and it admits of no arguments."[13]

Penelope Lively considered the reluctant reader when she wrote, "I rather like the idea of the hostile reader, especially the hostile child reader—a scolding, restless figure who would rather be doing something else . . . resisting stubbornly, and yet up to a point unavailingly because whatever the book and however ineffectual its impact, the imagination is forced into a response of some kind."[14] It is this interaction—which must be the precursor to any degree of enjoyment—which librarians hope will take place.

International Interest

It is worth taking a moment to look briefly at the extensive and growing interest in children's literature and in library services to children internationally. This manifests itself in the plethora of awards and prizes in various countries and internationally. The best known of these is the Hans Christian Andersen Award, for which the International Board on Books for Young People (IBBY) nominates one American author and one illustrator biennially to compete with those nominated from other countries. The award is given for a body of published works by the winners, and so far the Americans who have received the award include Meindert de Jong, Scott O'Dell, Paula Fox, and Maurice Sendak. The International Relations Committee of the Association for Library Service to Children acts as liaison with international organizations, including IBBY, and serves as its American secretariat.

In 1979, the International Year of the Child, IBBY issued a statement which described the kinds of books which should be made available for children. The statement endorsed textbooks and library books that promote intercultural understanding and harmony among different people; books of fantasy to stretch imaginations or extend the mind to independent and creative thought; books that present nonstereotyped images; books that explore a heritage through the lore and legends of a people; books indigenous to a culture to encourage a sense of identity and pride in heritage. Books that show differences as human experiences common to all, explore human rights, and have concern for and appreciation of the planet which we share were also prescribed as desirable for children to read; along with books that "encourage literacy," lead to a healthy curiosity, and foster sensitivity, understanding; beautifully illustrated books, books of humor, books that inspire wonder and deep feeling for humankind.[15]

Virginia Haviland, Director of the Childrens Literature Center in The Library of Congress, was the first chairperson of the IBBY Round Table of Librarians Representing Documenting Centers Serving Research on Children's Literature. Children's literature research collections in many countries are viewed as central to the professional literature of a country as they bring together The Library of Congress, indigenous works of that country and the literature from others. Alice Geradts of the Netherlands described reasons for the existence of a children's literature research documentation center with national scope to promote children's books collection and production.[16] The centers maintain representative collections of the country's children's book output, and provide access to information for serious researchers and students of children's literature. Old and contemporary fiction, toy books, and original works are collected in a national center. Periodicals and professional literature are also desirable components of the children's collection in the centers. Geradts recommended detailed cataloging of historical materials to aid researchers.

In 1980, Geradts notes there were no children's literature research centers exclusively related to children's libraries, but cited five centers with special connections to children's libraries: in Brazil, the Fundacao Nacional do Libro Infantil e Juvenil, based in Rio de Janeiro, formed as a nonprofit organization to promote better books and libraries for children and young people; the Children's Literature Service, Public Services Branch, National Library of Canada in Wellington, Canada, which offered assistance to children's librarians and whose bilingual service was available to librarians as well; the Osborne and Lillian H. Smith collections in the Boys and Girls House, which functions as an independent branch of the Toronto Public Library and is well known for the special old collections and current children's books; La Joie par Les Livres in Paris, France, which links all French public libraries and is a department of the Ecole Nationale

Superieure des Bibliothèques; and Dienst Boek en Jeugd NBLC in the Hague, Netherlands, all of which have services for their children's librarians and libraries.

These national centers have the potential for coordinating research on children's literature or children's library work, for documenting and preserving national information in the field, for serving as the basis for an international network in matters pertaining to children's literature and research, for initiating conferences, and for providing literature for national and international journals about children's work and literature.

The *Children's Books International Exposition*[17] has become an annual event in the Boston Public Library since 1976 when director Philip McNiff planned it. The focus is not only on the creators of children's books or luminaries in the foreign book world of children's books, but on the exhibit of books from many countries representing children's book production from around the world. Worthy of note, too, is the Center for Children's Cultures of the U.S. for UNICEF in New York City, which is a good but small reference resource about literature for children in the developing and some of the newer Caribbean nations. The International Youth Library (IYL) in Munich, Germany should also be mentioned. The head of its English language section also has responsibility for the administration of the American, Canadian, Australian, and Scandinavian collections. The IYL also compiles *The Best of the Best* bibliography and *Children's Prize Books*.

Research Needs

Very few studies have been done about children's services in public libraries. Most of the research about children's use of library services has been done in school library settings. One study evaluating thirty public libraries verified that regular attendance at a public library program was effective in improving reading interest.[18] Another study in the early 1970s showed that storytelling was more effective in creating reading interest and positive self-image than a creative dramatics approach.[19] The relationship between the library habits of mothers and their first grade children resulted in the not-surprising discovery that the children tended to use the library in proportion to their mothers' use. The family's geographic proximity to the library was found to be a factor also. This study was undertaken in an economically disadvantaged area of Chicago. Another researcher studied the language differences between children's TV and picture books, and found that although vocabularies were the same, TV used shorter sentences as compared with the more complex sentence structures in the books used for comparison. She suggested the apparent ineffectiveness of TV in the development of language as compared to reading aloud to children at home. A demonstration project in the Public Library of Cincinnati and Hamilton County involved weekly visits by the children's librarians to special education classes and to children in correctional school settings. The introduction of books helped, over a period of time, in improving behavior and feelings of self-worth among the children.[20]

The reluctance among children's specialists to undertake research or even the documentation of children's service effectiveness for evaluation purposes, was discussed by the North Carolina children's services coordinators. Most concluded that children's librarians felt that they lacked research skills, but admitted that they could attempt simple sampling and surveys. First-time participants in summer reading programs from five libraries were followed up and interviewed in November. It was found, on the basis of the eighty percent interviewed, that more than half the children had used the library since the summer program, and almost all reported increased use of their school libraries. The individual libraries reporting on their own results noted that children's use was dependent on the degree of parental use and interest either in borrowing materials or program attendance. If distances were involved and no transportation provided, children could not come to the library. The librarians in this study learned some basic lessons about effective research methods: the need to standardize information-gathering procedures in group research; the careful wording of questions; and the desirability of training and background in research. These librarians felt that research could be a very valuable tool for them.[21]

Children's librarians need to seek formal training and experience in doing research, not only for evaluative purposes and in line with management responsibility, but as professionals in a field in which more knowledge would facilitate the work. There is very little research in building interests, turning negative experiences into positive building blocks toward learning, the possible role of child advocates or counselors who could work one-on-one with children. Materials, delivery systems—both need looking at more carefully, as does the way in which librarians can learn to work more effectively with other adults who influence children's attitudes and habits.

Several recent studies have centered about service to preschool children. The Learning Institute of North Carolina at Durham, in its three-part project, had as its primary objective improving public library services to preschool children in the state.[22] This study resulted in the development of a curriculum for training children's librarians in early childhood education concepts. A study of the effects of programs for preschoolers in the public library explored their mothers' borrowing patterns. It was shown that parents of children attending the library's preschool program borrowed more easy books for their children. In 1975, investigation was made into the possible contribution the public library could make to preschool children who were for some reason excluded from other preschool programs.

The 1924 Geneva Declaration of the Rights of the Child, and the 1948 United Nations' A Universal Declaration of Human Rights (which was fought through to acceptance through the efforts of Mrs. Franklin Delano Roosevelt) recognized the special needs of children. In 1959, the more specific Declaration of the Rights of the Child was added by the United Nations Assembly. The entitlement of children to special protection, love, a name and nationality, education, and freedom from religious, racial, and other forms of discrimination; the right to care if disabled, to recreation, and to "relief in times of disaster" were all clearly delineated in that document. One principle from the declaration stated that "services must be equal—in access, control and quality—without regard to the financial circumstances of the family. They must be tailored to the needs of the individual and delivered by persons and institutions fully and directly accountable to the individual recipient and the community of which he is a part."[23]

And there it is—an internationally endorsed principle which will only come to life and be implemented if every member of every profession which has responsibility for children wills it to, and actively does something about it. There is much to ponder in these entitlements, and much indeed that relates to the work of children's librarians. There are many implications here also for research, for instance: Are we directly accountable to the individual recipient of our services and how do we become more so? That entitlement to education: What are its many implications for children's librarians?

Are our services truly free of discrimination, as well as equal without regard to the financial circumstances of the family? What differences does the fulfillment or the lack of these entitlements make in the child's future. Do we know? Do we care? Is it really too much trouble to try to find out, and if we decide that it is not, how quickly can we get on with devising the research plan that will give us some of the answers?

Legislation, Rights, and Responsibilities

And so we have come full circle, back to the subject of the setting, the circumstances in which librarians must fight an uphill battle to do the best they can to ameliorate the lot and the lives of children, and the adults they are to become. Children are dependent on adults, and it is adults who must alter the circumstances of their lives.

In June 1970, the White House Conference on Children was held and a significant section of the conference report to the president addressed the issue of children's rights. One firm recommendation was that "a system of child advocacy" be developed to ensure adherence to the principles and laws governing the best interests of children.[24] But after decades of attention and statements about these matters, commitment to and implementation of the rights of children are still subject to shifting social and economic priorities.

In June 1980, a decade later, a substitute White House conference was introduced to replace the White House Conference on Children and Youth, which had been held every decade for more than half a century. The White House Conference on Families proposed recommendations that recognized the central role which families must play in a child's interests and well being. The New York delegation, which was among the most vocal, went prepared with the following proposals:

- Provision of a variety of childcare options by government and business
- Alternatives to institutional care
- Upgrading of personnel in childcare programs
- Elimination of transportation barriers to access
- Development of programs in family-life education in schools and elsewhere for children, youth, and adults

- Early detection and crisis intervention services including Headstart, family day-care, preschool and after-school programs, counseling and medical services, supportive services and assistance for parents
- Attention to the needs of adolescents and their families
- Attention to families (and family members) with special needs
- Linking community resources to schools

"The role of parents in the education of their children is primary and absolutely essential. Where federal funds are received for compensatory education programs, the federal government should make provision for programs for parents which involve outreach, advocacy and training in reinforcing the educational process at home."

- Federal and State regulations should encourage the study of cultural, racial and ethnic diversity and should "encourage study of persons with special needs to promote sensitivity and understanding"
- Require bilingual and bicultural education for nonEnglish-speaking groups
- Be responsive to media abuses of special groups and women
- Encourage affirmative action in public and private sectors
- Respect the diversity of American life
- Establish a National Council on Children's Rights
- Accord high priority to preventive services to avoid stress, violence, and crisis
- The Federal Communications Commission should establish standards for presentation of violence, sex, and racial stereotypes[25]

The unfortunate fact is that no recommendations about access to quality library services for children came out of the conference.

When the White House Conference on Library and Information Services (WHCLIS) was held in November 1979, it was the first one of its kind. Librarians had a ready-made opportunity to talk with government officials and community leaders about their concerns for library services to children and to the adults who rear them. A few of the resolutions passed by the delegates, who had been elected to represent their states at the national conference, touched on the improvement needed in delivery of library service to youth. Children were, for example, mentioned under the broad subject heading "Access," as part of a special population which required special services and equal access. It was clear from the low-key, vague and nebulous references to services for children, however, that advocates had not done their homework well enough.[26]

Groups with special interests which prevailed in terms of strong resolutions coming out of the White House conference were those which 1) lobbied state delegations in advance of the Washington conference; 2) had a strategy planned for "working" the conference—visiting state delegations to make their case, buttonholing influential and articulate delegates in the corridors, speaking up forcefully in small-group and intermediate-group sessions; and 3) came to the conference prepared with a draft resolution which was continually circulated, discussed, and worked on throughout the conference. Advocates in particular areas forged coalitions, and offered exchanges of support of objectives with other groups. Two groups which stand out as having been especially good at this political gamesmanship were the disabled, especially the deaf, and the American Indians. The American Indian delegates came away from the White House conference having had passed by the delegates a multifaceted resolution which was one of only twenty-five passed by floor vote. This resolution provided the basis for the addition of Title IV, Library Services for Indian Tribes and Hawaiian Natives, to the 1984 revision of the Library Services and Construction Act, and the first funding ever for Indian libraries.[27]

Make no mistake: a White House conference is a political exercise and opportunity of the highest order. Another, the second White House Conference on Libraries and Information Services is expected to take place early in the 1990s—possibly in 1991. This time, children's and youth librarians should plan and carry out the most forceful campaign they can muster with an eye to gaining, at last, some legislation at the national level which will allocate a small fraction of the nation's wealth to library services for its children.

Children's librarians share, in a large degree, the skills developed by all those who work with children, as outlined by Lana Hostetler. She suggests that we can "influence the policy-making process" with skills derived from working with children and their families:

1. We have experience in assessing an individual's grasp of an idea.

2. We know how to "break information into manageable pieces" and we can use this same process in presenting information to policy makers.

3. We have planning and goal-setting skills which could help us to plan agendas for presentation.

4. We have experience in using words or "vocabulary appropriate to an individual's level of understanding."

5. We know how to get information across in a limited time period—a plus when dealing with busy politicians.

6. We know about dealing with individuals who demand special attention.

7. We have learned to "listen and respond while guiding learning."

8. We are accustomed to applauding positive behavior and trying to ignore negative acts.

9. We often demonstrate a point by giving concrete examples.

10. We have used "creative approaches to capture interest."

11. We know how to mediate, negotiate and compromise."

12. We have learned the value of cooperative efforts.

13. We have worked creatively with limited resources.

14. We have at times had to make difficult decisions in a short time.

15. We can speak to the value of preparedness.[28]

These are all interpersonal skills; they are in fact, by definition, political skills. Above and beyond all this, we know the value of what we do and can do for children, for families, for communities, for the nation. To conviction and commitment we must add courage for the ambitious agenda we are bound to undertake.

Library services for children have a glorious potential. But nothing "just happens" no matter how right it seems. We must forge coalitions and attract allies who will help us to state our issues and concerns in every available public forum. Only in this way will we gain public support for improved library services for children. These issues must be put in a context of everything that affects the lives of children, both directly and indirectly. We must make it clear that not only do matters of direct consequence such as child abuse, welfare practice, health provisions, day-care and education matter to us and relate to what we do, but so do the economy and jobs and housing and the environment. Our concern that children shall have quality library services is nothing less than our concern, and our responsibility, for our society and its future.

Appendix A

Declaration of the Rights of the Child (1959) (from A
Universal Declaration of Human Rights—United Nations)

1. The enjoyment of the rights mentioned, without any exception
   whatsoever, regardless of race, color, sex, religion or nationality;
2. Special protection, opportunities and facilities to enable them to
   develop in a healthy and normal manner, in freedom and dignity;
3. A name and nationality;
4. Social security, including adequate nutrition, housing, recreation
   and medical services;
5. Special treatment, education and care of handicapped;
6. Love and understanding and an atmosphere of affection and
   security, in the care and under the responsibility of their parents
   whenever possible;
7. Free education and recreation and equal opportunity to develop
   their individual abilities;
8. Prompt protection and relief in times of disaster;
9. Protection against all forms of neglect, cruelty and exploitation;
10. Protection from any form of racial, religious or other discrimina-
    tion, and an upbringing in a spirit of peace and universal broth-
    erhood.

Appendix B

Selected Organizations with Children's Concerns

Advocacy and Legislation

Action for Children's Television
46 Austin Street
Newtonville, MA 02160
Publication(s): *Re:act*
  (semiannual)

Children's Defense Fund
152 New Hampshire Avenue,
  N.W.
Washington, DC 20036

National Association for the
  Education of Young Children
1834 Connecticut Avenue, N.W.
Washington, DC 20009
Publication(s): *Young Children* (bi-
  monthly)

National Foster Parent
  Association
P.O. Box 257
King George, VA 22485
Publication(s): *National Advocate*
  (bi-monthly newsletter)

National PTA (National Congress
  of Parents and Teachers)
700 N. Rush Street
Chicago, IL 60611
Publication(s): *PTA Today* (7 per
  year)

Books and Other Media

American Reading Council
45 John Street
New York, NY 10012

American Association for
  Library Service to Children
Division of ALA
50 East Huron Street
Chicago, IL 60611
Awards:
Newbery Medal—for literature
Caldecott Medal—for picture
  books
Laura Ingalls Wilder Award—for
  body of children's literature
Publication(s): *Journal of Youth
  Services* (4 per year)

American Association of School
Librarians
50 East Huron Street
Chicago, IL 60611
Publication: *School Library Media
Quarterly* (Quarterly)

American Center of Films for
Children
Division of Cinema
University of Southern California
University Park
Los Angeles, California 90009
Awards: Ruby Slipper—for
excellence in children's
filmmaking

Association for Children with
Learning Disabilities
4156 Library Road
Pittsburgh, PA 15234
Publication: *ACLD News Briefs* (6
per year)

Association for Educational
Communications Technology
(AECT)
1126 16th Street, N.W.
Washington, DC 20036
Publication(s): *Instructional
Innovator* (8 per year)
ECT Network (8 per year—free to
members)

Council on Interracial Books for
Children
1841 Broadway
New York, NY 10023
Publication(s): *Interracial Books for
Children Bulletin* (8 per year)

Catholic Library Association
461 West Lancaster Avenue
Haverford, PA 19044
Publication(s): *Catholic Library
World* (10 per year)
ABC Bulletin (newsletter of the
children's section)
Awards: Regina Medal—for
dedication to children's
literature

The Children's Book Council
67 Irving Place
New York, NY 10003
Publication(s): CBC *Features*
(three times yearly)

Children's Television Workshop
One Lincoln Plaza
New York, NY 10023
Publication(s):
Sesame Street Magazine (10 per
year)
The Electric Company Magazine (10
per year)
Contact Magazine

Information Center on
Children's Cultures
U.S. Committee for UNICEF
331 East 38th Street
New York, NY 10016

International Reading
Association
800 Barksdale Road
Box 8139
Newark, DE 19711
Publication(s):
The Reading Teacher (8 per year)
Journal of Reading (monthly)
Reading Today Newsletter

Media Center for Children, Inc.
3 West 29th Street
New York, NY 10001

Child Development

Association for Childhood
Education International (ACEI)
3615 Wisconsin Avenue, N.W.
Washington, DC 20016
Publication(s): *Childhood
Education* (6 per year)

Administration for Children,
Youth & Families
Office of Human Development
Services
U.S. Dept of Health & Human
Services
Washington, DC 20201
Publication(s): *Children Today*
(bimonthly)

Day Care Council of America
711 14th Street, N.W., Suite 507
Washington, DC 20005
Publication(s): *Day Care and Early
Education* (4 per year)

Children With Special Needs

American Association for Gifted
Children
15 Gramercy Park
New York, NY 10003

Association for Retarded
Citizens
National Headquarters
2501 Avenue J. Box 6109
Arlington, TX 76911
Publication: *The ARC*

The Council for Exceptional
Children
1920 Association Drive
Reston, VA 22091
Publication(s): *Exceptional
Children* (8 per year)

Office for Gifted and Talented
U.S. Office of Education
400 Maryland Avenue, S.W.
Washington, DC 20202

Recreation and Youth Services

Boys Club of America
771 First Avenue
New York, NY 10017

Camp Fire, Inc.
4601 Madison Avenue
Kansas City, MO 64112
Publication(s): *Leadership
Magazine*

Children's Art Carnival
62 Hamilton Terrace
New York, NY 10031
Film: "Learning Through the
Arts"

Girl Scouts of the USA
830 Third Avenue
New York, NY 10022
Publication(s): *Girl Scout Leader*
(quarterly)

Appendix C

Selected Evaluation and Review Media—Sources

Periodicals

AAAS—Science Books and Films. Reviews trade and textbooks, 16-mm films, video cassettes, and filmstrips for elementary through college students, the general public, and professionals. Published by American Association for the Advancement of Science, 1515 Massachusetts Avenue, N.W., Washington, DC 20005.

Appraisal: Science Books for Young People. Children's Science Book Review Committee. Boston University School of Education, Department of Science and Mathematics Education.

The Best Science Books for Children. A selected and annotated list of science books for children ages five through twelve. Compiled by Kathryn Wolff and others for the American Association for the Advancement of Science, 1983.

Bibliography of Books for Children. An annotated listing of fiction, nonfiction, and reference books for children. Published by the Association for Childhood Education International, 3615 Wisconsin Avenue, N.W., Washington, DC 20016.

The Black Experience in Children's Books, 1984. Edited by Barbara Rollock and revised every five years since 1974. Published by The New York Public Library.

The Black World in Literature for Children. Edited by Joyce W. Mills. Published by Atlanta University School of Library and Information Studies, 1978.

Booklist. American Library Association, 50 East Huron Street, Chicago, IL 60611.

Bulletin of the Center for Children's Books. Edited by Betsy Hearne. Published by the University of Chicago Press for the University of Chicago Library School.

Canadian Children's Literature/Literature Canadienne pour La Jeunesse. Published quarterly as a public service by the Canadian Children's Press in cooperation with the Canadian Children's Literature Association.

Catholic Library World. Official publication of the Catholic Library Association, 461 West Lancaster Avenue, Haverford, PA 19041.

Children's Choices. Compiled by a joint committee of the International Reading Association and the Children's Book Council.

Children's Literature Association Quarterly. Publication of the Children's Literature Association. Assisted by a grant from the Growing Child of Lafayette, Indiana.

Children's Prize Books: An International Listing of Children's Literature Prizes. 2nd ed., rev. and enl. (K. G. Saur, 1983).

Film Library Quarterly. Published by the Film Library Information Council, Box 348, Radio City Station, New York, NY 10101–0348.

Growing Point. Contains "review(s) of books of the growing families of the English reading world and for parents, teachers, librarians and other guardians." Six issues annually. Published by Margery Fisher.

The Horn Book Magazine. Published by The Horn Book, Inc., Park Square Building, 31 St. James Avenue, Boston, MA 02116.

Interracial Books for Children Bulletin. Published by the Council on Interracial Books for Children, Inc., 1841 Broadway, New York, NY 10023.

JOYS, the official Journal of *ALSC.*

The Junior Bookshelf: A Review of Children's Books. Published by the Stanley Press, Ltd, Bretton Street, Dewsbury, England WF 129BL.

Language Arts. The official journal of the elementary section of the National Council of Teachers of English.

Let's Read Together: Books for Family Enjoyment. Edited by Harriet Quimby. Published by the Association for Library Services to Children/American Library Association, 1981.

The 1982 U.S.A. Children's Books of International Interest. Compiled by the International Relations Committee of ALA/ALSC.

"Notable Children's Trade Books in the Field of Social Studies."

Compiled by a joint committee of the Children's Book Council and the National Council for the Social Studies. Published in *Social Education* (April 1984).

"Outstanding Source Trade Books for Children." Compiled by a joint committee of the Children's Book Council and the National Science Teachers Association. Published by *Science and Children* (March 1984).

Parents' Choice: A Review of Children's Media. Includes books, television, movies, music, story records, toys and games. Published by Parents' Choice Foundation, Box 185, Waban, MA 02168.

Publishers Weekly. Published by R. R. Bowker Company, 1911 Rowland Street, Riverton, NJ 08017 (Subscription address).

School Library Journal. Published by R. R. Bowker Co.

School Library Media Quarterly. The official journal of ALA/ALSC.

Stone Soup. Children send stories, pictures and reviews. Mailed to members of the Children's Art Foundation.

Stories: A List of Stories to Tell and Read Aloud, 7th ed. Edited by Marilyn Iarusso. Published by The New York Public Library, 1977.

A Treasury of Books of Family Enjoyment: Books for Children from Infancy to Grade 2. Compiled by Elouise Daniel. Published by Blue Engine Express, 173 East Iroquois, Pontiac, MI 48053, 1983.

Voice of Youth Advocates (VOYA). Published by Voice of Youth Advocates, Inc. % Scarecrow Press, 52 Liberty St., Metuchen, N.J. 08840.

Wilson Library Bulletin. Published by the H. W. Wilson Company, 950 University Avenue, Bronx, New York 10452.

Young Viewers. Published by the Media Center for Children (MCC).

Books

Beilke, Patricia F. and Frank J. Sciara. *Selecting Materials for and about Hispanic and East Asian Children and Young People* (Hamden, CT: Library Professional Publications, 1986).

Bernstein, Joanne E., *Books to Help Children Cope with Separation and Loss,* 2nd ed. (New York: R. R. Bowker, 1983).

Baskin, Barbara H., and Karen H. Harris, *Books for the Gifted Child* (New York: R. R. Bowker, 1980).

Field, Carolyn W. and Jaqueline Shacter Weiss, *Values in Selected Children's Books of Fiction and Fantasy (Hamden, Conn.: Library Professional Publications, 1987).*

Flemming, Carolyn, and Donna Schate, *Choices: A Core Collection for Reluctant Readers* (Evanston, IL: J. G. Burke Publishers, 1983).

Freeman, Judy, *Books Kids will Sit for* (Hagerstown, MD: Alleyside Press, 1984).

Hearne, Betsy, *Choosing Books for Children: A Commonsense Guide* (New York: Delacorte, 1981).

Larrick, Nancy, *A Parent's Guide to Children's Reading: How to Introduce Your Children to Books and the Joys of Reading*, 5th ed. (New York: Bantam, 1982).

Hymn, Ruth Nodelman, *Fantasy for Children*, 2d ed. (New York: R. R. Bowker, 1983).

Polette, Nancy, *Picture books for Gifted Programs* (Metuchen, NJ: Scarecrow Press, 1981).

Schon, Isabel, *A Hispanic Heritage: A Guide to Juvenile Books About Hispanic People and Cultures* (Metuchen, NJ: Scarecrow Press, 1980).

Tway, Eileen, *Reading Ladders for Human Relations*, 6th edition (Urbana, IL: National Council of Teachers of English, 1981).

Appendix D

SERVICES TO CHILDREN & YOUNG ADULTS
Diana Young, Editor
North Carolina State Library

It is predicted that 60 percent of American children born today will spend some time in a single-parent home before their eighteenth birthday. In some states preschoolers are the fastest growing segment of the child population, yet more mothers than at any previous time in our history are in the work force. Correspondingly, more children than ever before are in some form of organized child care.

In recognition of the trends the Hennepin County Library Task Force on Library Service to Children in Groups was impaneled and chaired by Vicki Oeljen. This article is excerpted from a task force report and uses insofar as possible the exact text. Questions or comments about the study should be addressed to Gretchin Wronka, Senior Children's Librarian, Hennepin County Library System, 12601 Ridgedale Dr., Minnetonka, Minnesota 55343-5648; (612) 541-8530.

Service to Children in Groups

The Report

Planning recommendations and staff discussions over several years have shown children in groups to be a rapidly growing phenomenon in need of expanded public library service. Statistics project a large increase in the number of children, ages 0–4, in suburban

Hennepin County, from 37,338 in 1980 to 41,594 in 1990, an increase
of 11.1 percent.

There is an even greater growth in the numbers of children
enrolled in group care facilities. Nationally, more than 70 percent of
all children between the ages of 3 and 5 attend some form of
preschool education.[1] Statistics published by the Minnesota Department of Public Welfare in October 1983 indicated that approximately
12,000 children, age 6 weeks to 14 years, are cared for in an estimated
1,000 nursery schools, day-care centers and licensed day-care homes
in suburban Hennepin County. The number of children in care
facilities has increased by 3,455, or 40 percent, since 1979 while the
number of facilities has grown by 200, or 38 percent, in the same
period. State officials indicate that this trend is continuing. In addition, an estimated 2,000 children, ages 5 to 14, are enrolled in school
district latchkey programs offering before- and after-school care.[2]

Adult statistics are also changing. In addition to the many single
parent families today, many more mothers are working outside the
home. In 1983, for the first time, half of all mothers with children
under age 6 were in the labor force.[3]

These changing forms of modern society create a need for changes
in library service as well. Traditionally, the individual child has been
well served through reference and reader's advisory services, story
time, and programs. Now, many children do not come to the library
by themselves because they are enrolled in some type of group care.
The groups often do not take advantage of library services because of
lack of awareness, times at which services are offered, and/or lack of
transportation.

Society has placed an increased emphasis on the educational,
social, and cultural growth of children. For example, the ALA *Reali-*
ties: Education Reform in a Learning Society designates as its number
one reality, "Learning Begins before Schooling." It emphasizes a
variety of ways library services to parents and day-care staff can
support preschool learning and suggests coalition building, with the
library staff acting as information providers to community groups.

Realities also urges public officials to appropriate funds for parent
education and early childhood education in public libraries and to
establish state and federal regulations requiring books and library
resources in child-care programs.[4] The *Minnesota Long Range Plan for*

Library Service, 1985 addresses services to children including school media center funding and communication with child-care staff.[5]

Also of interest is a recent survey of adult users in small public libraries from upstate New York that shows an 85 percent correlation between those who visited libraries as children and continue to do so as adults. "Once the library habit has been introduced, it tends to continue throughout the rest of childhood and adult life."[6]

The public library has the opportunity to become a key element in providing services to a segment of the population that is growing rapidly, is recognized as of primary importance, and is greatly in need of the diversity of materials and services necessary to becoming responsible, productive, knowledgeable members of a fast-changing, pluralistic society.

Task Force Activities

In the course of establishing recommendations the task force conducted a literature search; gathered and studied statistics; collected input from HCL children's librarians and suburban Hennepin County child-care providers through questionnaires, meetings, and informal conversations; conducted a six-month survey to determine current service being offered to children in groups in HCL; and studied projects undertaken by other library systems throughout the country. Two notable examples of the latter are the King County Traveling Library Center and the Library Child Care Link of the South Bay Cooperative Library System.

Statistics gathered from September 1984 through February 1985 showed that 18,293 children and 2,585 adults in child-care groups were served through HCL programs. This was accomplished with no direct library-initiated contact. Inequalities are inherent in service based on patron request rather than library initiation in that only child-care staff who are aware of services and materials make contact. While story times are generally considered to be service to the individual child, the survey showed that 40,000 children who were part of an identified child-care group participated in story times during the six-month period. The group requests that could not be accommodated usually failed due to reference desk and other programs commitments.

Charge

The Task Force was asked to prepare the following documents:

1. A three-year plan of service, 1985–1987, including recommendations, prioritized when applicable, for utilization of staff, collection, and other resources. Recommendations should be evaluated
   and prioritized with regard for what is realistically feasible in
   balance with all other services that HCL should continue to
   provide.
2. Policy recommendations—library board or administrative.
3. Procedures relating to both policies and practices.
4. A 1984 LSCA grant proposal.

To expand on the above: Recommendations are listed in four categories of priorities—very high, high, medium, and low. The task
   force intends that those appearing in the very high category be
   established in 1985, those in high be established in 1986, and
   those in low be reexamined in 1987 to evaluate feasibility and
   desirability at that time. Adoption of the recommendations must
   not diminish the responsibility to serving the individual child.
   [Editor's Note: Only very high and high recommendations are
   included in this article].

The task force has drafted the Library Board Policy on Service to
   Children in Groups and has recommended the rewriting of the
   Library Board Policy on Programming to minimize disparity of
   programming between groups and individuals.

For the task force, procedures evolved for incorporating into each
   recommendation the action that should take place and the person
   who should be responsible for that action. Most of the recommendations assume the development of system guidelines, by agency
   size, for service to children in groups. See guideline below.

Rather than prepare a grant proposal, the task force investigated
   grant sources and selected those that seemed the most suitable
   sources of funds for recommendations. Many of the task force
   recommendations are suitable for outside funding.

Note: The task force focused almost exclusively on preschool children, as it is in this age range that the proliferation of groups has
   occurred. However, survey results indicated that half of the
   groups served during the six-month survey were full-time school
   students. While the task force set one goal with three attendant
   recommendations relating to school group service, it should be
   stressed that school group service was not addressed in depth,

but further study is essential. Therefore, it is the strong recommendation of this task force that guidelines for service to school groups be established immediately.

Recommendations Section

Policy

Policy is needed as a framework for building a plan of improved service to children in groups. *The task force recommends that the following policy be adopted:*
Hennepin County Library is committed to the provision of quality library service for children and seeks to provide equal access to individuals and those in groups. In recognition of the increase in the number of children and the number of children in groups and the difficulty in reaching persons in groups as effectively as individuals, HCL will actively share information, expertise, materials, and services with children in groups, child-care workers, and the organizations and networks serving those children. Guidelines and sufficient support will ensure fair and uniform service to individuals and groups throughout the library system.

Guidelines

The task force cannot create a system for assigning the responsibilities toward groups in the individual agencies. A process must be implemented for distributing responsibility fairly within HCL and ensuring that all groups receive quality service throughout the system. Guidelines should be developed and adopted according to the following suggestions. These guidelines must precede the implementation of most of the recommendations.

The task force recommends that guidelines for service to children in groups be established according to the size of library (community library 1, 2, 3, and area). Representatives responsible for children's services from each library will meet in groups according to library size with the senior children's librarian and a PSD coordinating librarian. Guidelines will be developed to reflect the service that can be offered by libraries of similar size.

In preparing the guidelines the following factors should be addressed to minimize inequitable service resulting from local option.

Ratio of adults to children:

• take into account ages of children

Services that can be provided:

- take into account group size, age of children, notification time, age range within the group, staff complement, frequency of visits, initial and follow-up visits

Availability of the library during nonpublic service hours
Size of group that can be accommodated
Staffing patterns required to respond to groups:

- take into account group size, service requested.

Notification time requested:

- take into account service requested

Visit frequency:

- take into account service requested, number of groups served

Visit duration:

- take into account service requested

Creation of service priorities:

- take into account visit duration, visit frequency, services requested, group size, geographic distance, access to transportation, type of group

Visits by children's librarian to group locations:

- take into account visit frequency, geographic distance, access to transportation

Limits on local option
Extended loan
Establishment of a referral process within HCL for groups that cannot be accommodated at individual agencies

Guidelines should be adopted by December 31 and should be reviewed annually.

Priorities

Many factors must be considered in choosing how best to implement the recommendations. Those that follow suggest some specific means for implementation, but practical application necessitates carrying them out in a variety of ways or to varying degrees. Adoption of some recommendations depends on the completion of others and some cover activities that are currently done at some agencies or that have been tried experimentally. It must be kept in mind that a commitment to serving children in groups will affect the entire library.

As stated in the policy section, providing quality service to children in groups requires the aid and cooperation of child-care staff. Therefore, workshops, printed materials, and network contacts are given high emphasis. This sharing of information, expertise, and materials includes child-care group leaders and staff, networks, group umbrella organizations, HCL staff, and librarians outside HCL.

Whenever practical, library services should be offered within the library setting. Transportation problems of child-care groups require that some services be offered outside the library. The goal is optimal library service to children and the adults working with them, not the number of people in the library.

Some group child-care staff members have expressed a willingness to pay for certain HCL services. Because the danger of creating unequal service patterns and because charging fees is strongly opposed by the children's librarians, this suggestion was rejected.

The priorities were assigned according to the suggested time of implementation. They are based on suggestions from the HCL children's librarians and group child-care staff. Cost, ease of implementation, current budget, current staffing, and degree of controversy were considered, but the overriding concern was service to children.

GOAL *Regularly inform child-care providers of materials, services, and facilities available at Hennepin County libraries and encourage their use.*

RATIONALE *The difficulty of reaching a child in a group as effectively as an individual child requires that librarians work through child-care providers. Many providers are unaware of all that HCL has to offer. Survey information collected by the task force shows that currently all group visits to the library are initiated by child-care staff rather than by librarians.*

Very High Priority

Recommendation 1 A committee of children's librarians working with the senior children's librarian and public information office (PIO) will develop brochures explaining services available at HCL for child-care groups and staff.

Recommendation 2 Children's librarians will initiate and annually renew contact with child-care leaders by personal visits, mail, and/or telephone to acquaint them with services and materials available. Contact procedures will be determined by individual children's librarians. These contacts will increase demand and agency staff and collection. This recommendation is dependent on the completion of recommendation 3.

Recommendation 3   The senior children's librarian will annually produce an updated list of child-care providers and parenting groups for use by children's librarians.

Recommendation 4   Children's librarians will provide regularly scheduled workshops on an area basis for child-care providers covering such topics as orientation to the library and search strategy. A lower priority option is to videotape presentations. These require considerable effort to produce and are less effective. In addition, child-care facilities generally lack playback equipment. Once created, howeer, they are a readily available alternative.

Recommendation 5   The senior children's librarian will identify newsletters of appropriate child-care organizations and will solicit items and information from children's librarians and others, which will be submitted on a regular basis to these newsletters through public information office. Information will be provided about pertinent materials, book sales, programs, and workshops.

Recommendation 6   Children's librarians with the help of PIO, senior juvenile selection librarian, and the senior children's librarian will regularly create materials lists ranging from simple bibliographies to full annotations. Child-care providers indicate that materials lists are a high priority and have requested lists by age level, subject, and currency (last five years). This recommendation will have a significant impact on the materials budget.

Recommendation 7   The senior children's librarian will establish and maintain a staff speaker bureau file consisting of names of staff members who have prepared presentations and their outlines and materials lists. These speakers and materials may be used to provide similar workshops to avoid duplication of effort.

Recommendation 8   Children's librarian will offer formal and informal book talks individually or via speaker's bureau, panels, or video presentations to child-care providers. Costs are high for staff preparation time and impact on materials collections.

GOAL *Provide quality service, sufficient materials, and a welcoming atmosphere to children in groups while maintaining current levels of service to individuals.*

RATIONALE There is a need to increase the awareness of the importance of service to children in groups to all library staff. To serve groups as fully as possible, while maintaining current levels of service, additional staff dedicated to children's services and an increase in the materials budget are necessary.

Very High Priority

Recommendation 16 Staff time devoted to children's work will be increased. Options include additional agency staff, additional professional staff assigned to provide service throughout each area, realignment of agency staff responsibilities to support the increase in children's services, and additional substitute funding.

Recommendation 17 Juvenile materials budget will be increased in response to use and circulation.

Recommendation 18 Use of the survey designed by the task force to measure service to children in groups will be continued after revision by the children's librarians. Results of the survey, along with demographic information, will enable the senior children's librarian to make future budget recommendations.

Recommendation 19 Children's librarians will discuss task force recommendation and their impact on all staff via agency meetings.

Recommendation 20 Professional staff will be encouraged and given the opportunity to attend continuing education programs to enhance their knowledge of children's materials and services.

Recommendation 21 Children's librarians, agency heads, and lead clerks will meet annually to set agency goals for the year for service to children in groups.

Recommendation 22 Agency heads will be responsible for maintaining a positive staff attitude toward service to children in groups.

Recommendation 23 Staff training and development committee will provide assistance to inform, motivate, and encourage staff in serving increased numbers of groups.

GOAL *Provide improved access to programming for children in groups.*

RATIONALE Groups are often discouraged from attending programs because of space limitations, staff availability and program costs.

High Priority

Recommendation 24 Additional cultural activities programs will be provided with the schedule based on the guidelines that will be established, individual library's facility and staff, number of groups in the community, frequency of requests, and size of groups. Agency children's librarians will communicate this information to the program librarian. In addition to an increase in the cultural activities budget, staff costs will be affected.

Recommendation 25 Agencies will provide additional in-house programming, e.g., films, puppet shows, and story times, based on the factors outlined in the recommendation above. Additional staffing will be required.

Recommendation 26 Library board policy on programming will be rewritten to minimize disparity of programming between groups and individuals.

GOAL *Clarify roles and increase cooperation between HCL and local school districts.*

RATIONALE Policies and practices of school media centers and public libraries are often mutually misunderstood and conflicting. Some schools view the public library as a substitute rather than a supplement to the school media center, and heavy and inappropriate demands are being placed on HCL staff and materials.

Very High Priority

Recommendation 31 HCL administrators will initiate discussion with school administrators to clarify the role of each institution and encourage school administrators to allocate adequate funding for materials and staff in their school media centers.

Recommendation 32 Administrative policy and guidelines for practice will be written defining HCL's role in supporting the school's curricula, assignments, and special programs, e.g., Book Nook.

Recommendation 33 Children's librarians will regularly contact school personnel in their community by attending faculty meetings, making visits, or telephoning in order to facilitate communication and cooperation.

GOAL *To foster excellent communication with child-care staff and their organizations and to better understand their needs for service.*

RATIONALE Libraries and child-care groups do not always clearly understand one another's goals, needs, communication systems, or bureaucracy.

High Priority

Recommendation 35   Establish an advisory board made up of child-care staff from a variety of types of cares, which will meet on a regular basis with children's librarians to make suggestions and monitor progress. The senior children's librarian will select the board with input from children's librarians, chair meetings, and produce written reports of these meetings.

GOAL   *Evaluate HCL's response to these goals and recommendations.*

RATIONALE   In light of societal changes and the library's response to this report the task force feels a responsibility to assess recommendations and note progress.

High Priority

Recommendation 36   Representatives from the task force will be reconvened by the associate director for public services in eighteen months to prepare a written progress report assessing implementation of the recommendations, evaluating the response of the child-care community and recommending realignment of priorities where necessary.

Implementation

In her letter of January 29, 1986, Wronka lists the following accomplishments.

At this point, $10,000 from the 1986 budget had been allocated for substitute funds to support children's services. Requests for funds will be funneled through the office of the senior librarian for children's services. The money will be used to support

1. service to groups;
2. special services *new* to a particular library, e.g., toddler story time, evening story time, book talking in elementary or junior highs, etc.;
3. special projects such as collection development; and
4. development of new and innovative programs for a particular library of the system.

The library is also sponsoring a day-care providers workshop. A direct mailing was sent to licensed groups and family day-care providers in the area we wanted to reach. The program will be planned and presented by children's librarians; in-service training credits will be offered through the county day-care licensing agency. The goal is to provide day-care providers with information about the library services and materials available to them for use with their children or as part of their own professional development.

Based on last year's workshop, a fourteen-minute videotape was produced for use by day-care providers as a basic orientation/introduction to the Hennepin County Library. It can be used in the library or the center. The attempt was to give "rock bottom" information to providers who may not be familiar with library services.

A workshop to inspire the staff is also planned. It will include a prominent child advocate, a member of the Governor's Council on Children, Youth, and Families, and a practical approach to how library systems can improve services to day-care providers, both family and group.

References

1. Will Manley, *Snowballs in the Bookdrop* (Hamden, Conn.: Library Professional Publ. 1982), p. 51.
2. Roz Anderson, School District 281, Community Education Latch Key Program, interview with Holly McDonnell, Crystal, Minnesota, February, 1985.
3. Sheila Kammerman, "Child Care Services: A National Picture," *Monthly Labor Review* 106:35 (Dec. 1983).
4. American Library Association Task Force on Excellence in Education, *Realities: Educational Reform in a Learning Society* (Chicago: American Library Assn., 1984), p. 3.
5. Issued as *Minnesota Libraries* 27, no. 11 (Autumn, 1984).
6. Barbara Will Razzano, "Creating the Library Habit," *Library Journal* 110: 114 (Feb. 15, 1985).

Notes

1. Library Services for Children: A Historical Perspective

1. Caroline Maria Hewins, "Work With Children in Connecticut," in *Library Work With Children*, ed. Arthur E. Bostwick (New York: H. W. Wilson Company, 1917), 55.

2. Clara Whitehill Hunt, "Values in Library Work With Children," in *Library Work With Children*, ed. Bostwick, 136–37.

3. Anne Carroll Moore, "Library Membership as a Civic Force," in *Library Work With Children*, ed. Bostwick, 115.

4. Ibid., 117.

5. Henry Edward Legler, "Library Work With Children," in *Library Work With Children*, ed. Bostwick, 105.

6. Mary Wright Plummer, "The Work for Children in Free Libraries," in *Library Work With Children*, ed. Bostwick, 85.

7. Moore, "Library Membership As a Civic Force," in *Library Work With Children*, ed. Bostwick, 125.

8. Harriet G. Long, *Rich the Treasure*, (Chicago: ALA, 1953), 15.

Additional References

Arthur E. Bostwick, *The American Public Library* (New York: D. Appleton and Company, 1929), 87–106.

Elizabeth H. Gross, *Children's Services in Public Libraries*, (Chicago: ALA, 1963).

Alice M. Jordan, "Chapter on Children's Libraries," in *Library Work With Children*, Alice I. Hazeltine (New York: H. W. Wilson Company, 1917).

Effie L. Power, *Library Service for Children* (Chicago: ALA, 1930).

Frances Clark Sayers, "The American Origins of Public Library Work With Children," *Library Trends* 12 (July 1963): 6–12.

Lillian H. Smith, *The Unreluctant Years* (Chicago: ALA, 1953).

2. The Impact of Four Studies/Reports on Library Services for Children

1. Robert D. Leigh, *The Public Library in the United States: The General Report of the Public Library Inquiry* (New York: Columbia University Press, 1950).
2. Ibid., 100.
3. Ibid., 101.
4. Ibid., 103.
5. *Report of the Commissioner of Education's Committee on Library Development, Albany* (Albany: The State University of New York, 1970).
6. Ibid., 25–30.
7. The National Commission on Libraries and Information Science, *A National Program for Library and Information Sciences, Final Draft* (Washington, DC: March 10, 1975), 4.
8. Ibid., 2.
9. Lowell A. Martin, Faith McDowell, and Nancy Magnuson, *The Free Library and the Revitalization of Philadelphia: A Program for the 1980s* (Philadelphia: Free Library, 1981), 18.
10. Ibid., 49.
11. Ibid., 99.
12. Ibid., 74.
13. "San Francisco Public Library Heeds Martin's Advice and Closes Branches," *Library Journal* 107 (June 15, 1982): 1166.

Additional References

J. Q. Benford, " 'Philadelphia Project': 10,000 Students Tell What's Wrong and What's Right About Their School and Public Libraries," *Library Journal* 96 (June 15, 1971): 2041–47.

J. G. Burke, "Where Will All the Children Go?" *American Libraries* 2 (January 1971): 56–61.

J. Gordon Burke, and Gerald R. Shields, *Children's Library Services* (Metuchen, NJ: The Scarecrow Press, 1974).

John Mackenzie Cory, and Anne R. Izard, "Children's Librarians in 1970," *American Libraries* 2 (October 1971): 973–76.

Carolyn Field, "Student Library Needs," *Library Journal* 95 (January 15, 1970): 105.

Lowell A. Martin, *Library Response to Urban Change: A Study of the Chicago Public Library*. (Chicago: ALA, 1969).

Lowell A. Martin, "The Philadelphia Project: The Action Library, Its Purpose and Programs" in *Total Community Library Service*, ed. Gary Garrison (Chicago: ALA, 1973).

Helen R. Sattley, "Run Twice as Fast: Service to Children," *American Libraries* 2 (September 1971): 943–49.

3. Management Concerns: External, Non-Library Issues

1. *Estimates of Public Costs For Teenage Childbearing*. Report issued by The Center For Population Options, Washington, DC, 1986.

2. Marion Wright Edelman, "What Society Does to and for its Children." Address to the Association for Library Service to Children, ALA, June 26, 1979.

3. Survey reported by Dan Rather on the CBS Evening News, September 2, 1987.

4. National Commission on Excellence in Education. *A Nation At Risk: The Imperative for Educational Reform* (Washington, DC: U.S. Department of Education, 1983).

5. William J. Bennett, Secretary of Education, *First Lessons: A Report on Elementary Education in America* (Washington, DC: U.S. Department of Education, 1986).

6. Marguerite Baechtold, and Eleanor R. McKinney, *Library Service for Families* (Hamden, CT: Library Professional Publications, 1983).

7. Danny Cunningham, "Population Shifts Demand Library Response," *American Libraries* 13 (September 1982): 505.

8. Corrie Player, "Smooth Move," *Parents Magazine* (April 1986).

9. *Report of the Task Force on Library and Information Services to Cultural Minorities* (Washington, DC: NCLIS, 1983).

10. Patricia F. Beilke and Frank J. Sciara, *Selecting Materials for and about Hispanic and East Asian Children and Young People* (Hamden, CT: Library Professional Publications, 1986).

11. Pauline Wilson, "Children's Service and Power, Knowledge to Shape the Future," *Top of the News* 37 (Winter 1981): 117–18.

12. Regina Minudri, "The Management Perspective," in *Libraries Serving Youth: Directions for Service in the 1990s* ed. Judith Rovenger (New York: NYLA, 1987).

4. Management Concerns: External Professional Factors

1. Ethel Ambrose, "National Survey of Support for Children's Services at the State Level," in "Services to Children," ed. Diana Young, *Public Libraries* 20 (Winter 1981): 123–25.

2. Barbara Will Razzano, *Public Library Services to Children and Young Adults in New Jersey* (Trenton, NJ: New Jersey State Library, 1986).

3. Ibid.

4. New York Library Association Task Force on Standards for Youth Services, *Standards for Youth Services in Public Libraries of New York State*, 1984.

5. Ohio Library Association, Children's Services in Libraries and School Media Centers Division, *A Guideline to Planning Public Library Service to Children in Ohio*, 1984.

6. Michigan Library Association Children's Services Division, *Standards for Public Library Service to Children and Competencies for Children's Librarians* (Draft), 1985.

7. Vernon E. Palmour et al., *A Planning Process for Public Libraries* (Chicago: ALA, 1980).

8. Douglas Zweizig and Eleanor Jo Rodger, *Output Measures for Public Libraries: A Manual of Standardized Procedures* (Chicago: ALA, 1982).

9. Charles R. McClure et al., *Planning and Role Setting for Public Libraries: A Manual of Options and Procedures* (Chicago: ALA, 1987).

10. Wisconsin Department of Public Instruction, Division for Library Services, *Wisconsin Public Library Standards* (Madison, WI: Wisc. Dep. Pub. Instr., 1987).

11. Razzano, *Public Library Services*.

12. *Wisconsin Public Library Standards*.

13. Razzano, *Public Library Services*.

14. *Wisconsin Public Library Standards*.

15. McClure, quoted in ibid.

16. Patrick M. O'Brien, "An Administrator Speaks of Services to Youth," *Top of the News* 37 (Spring 1981): 243–46.

17. Wisconsin Division for Library Service, *Output Measures for Children's Services in Wisconsin Public Libraries, A Pilot Project—1984–85*.

18. Robin R. Gault and the PLA Committee on Services to Children, "Planning for Children's Services in Public Libraries," in "Services to Children and Young Adults," ed. Diana Young, *Public Libraries* 25 (Summer 1986): 60–62.

19. Ibid.

20. Bennett, *First Lessons*.

21. Rovenger, *Libraries Serving Youth*.

22. NYLA, *Standards for Youth Services*.

23. *Becoming A Nation of Readers* (Washington, DC: National Academy of Education, National Institutes of Education, Center for the Study of Reading), 1985.

24. Nat'l. Comm. Excellence in Educ., *A Nation at Risk*.

25. ALA Task Force on Excellence in Education, *Realities: Educational Reform in a Learning Society* (Chicago: ALA, 1984).

26. Minudri, "Management Perspective" in Rovenger, *Libraries Serving Youth*.

27. Evelyn Shaevel, YASD Executive Director, personal notes Nov., 1987 and Leslie Edmonds, conference organizer for the sponsoring University of Illinois, conversations and notes. Nov., 1987.

5. Management Concerns: Internal and Operational

1. Baker, D. Philip, *The Library Media Program and the School* (Littleton, CO: Libraries Unlimited, 1984).

2. Linda Silver, "Show Me—A Management Approach to Programs for Children," *School Library Journal* 38 (Summer 1982): 113.

3. O'Brien, "An Administrator Speaks of Services to Youth,": 246.

4. "Public Libraries Show 12 percent Spending Jump." *American Libraries* 8(7) (July/August 1977).

5. Collin Clark, "The Impact of Proposition 13 on California's Public Libraries," *Public Libraries* 18 (Spring 1979): 7–9.

6. David J. Blum, "Stacks of Trouble: Public Libraries try to Maintain Services in the Face of Budget Cuts," *The Wall Street Journal* 6 August 1981, p. 6.

7. "A Review of Issues Affecting Children's Services in Selected Urban Public Libraries" Unpublished report (prepared by the children's coordinators of fifteen large library systems, 1976).

8. Charles Robinson, "Why Bother?" *Public Libraries* 18 (Fall 1979): 50–51.

9. Margaret Mary Kimmel, "Baltimore County Public Library: A Generalist Approach," *Top of the News* 37 (Spring 1981): 297–301.

10. American Library Association, Children's Services Division/American Association of School Librarians, "Recruitment and Training of Volunteers to Work with Young Children and Library Materials: Guidelines," n.d.

11. Peggy Sullivan, "Deja Vu from the Bridge," *School Library Journal* 25 (April 1979): 19–23.

12. *Wisconsin Public Library Standards.*

6. Cooperation, Networking, and Community Outreach

1. Emerson Greenaway, "New Developments and Goals in Service to Students," in *Proceedings of the Conference on School–Public Library Relations, New York City* (Albany, NY: SUNY. State Education Department Division of Library Development, February 8–9, 1968), 7–12.

2. Benford, "The Philadelphia Project," 2041–47.

3. Ibid., 2041.

4. Diana Young, "School/Public Library Cooperation" in *Public Libraries* 18: (Winter 1979) 104–05.

5. "Stimulating Reading and Library Use by Children through Involvement in Quality Arts Experiences, in *Top of the News* 38 (Summer 1982): 286.

6. Young, "School/Public Library Cooperation," 104–5.

7. Information furnished by the Division of Library Programs, U.S. Department of Education, Summer 1987.

8. Ibid.

9. Ibid.

10. "Stimulating Reading and Library Use," 286.

11. Theodore C. Hines, "Children's Access to Materials," in *Children and Books* by Zena Sutherland, 5th ed. (Glenview, IL: Scott Foresman, 1977), 625.

12. *Meeting Information Needs of the 80s: Report of the Commissioner's Committee on Statewide Library Development* (Albany, NY: SUNY, State Education Department, New York State Library, 1981).

13. Marilyn L. Miller, "Children's Access to Library Systems" in *Library Quarterly* 51 (January 1981): 38–53.

14. *Report of the Commissioner of Education's Committee on Library Development* Albany, NY: SUNY, (1970).

15. Alice E. Fite, "Report of the [NCLIS] Task Force on the Role of the School Library Program in Networking," *School Media Quarterly* 7 (Winter 1979): 89–114.

16. Young, "School/Public Library Cooperation," 104–5.

17. Information furnished by the Division of Library Programs, U.S. Department of Education, Summer 1987.

18. Miller, "Children's Access to Library Systems."

19. Joan Neumann, "Intershare: A View from the Hole, or Building the Foundation for a Regional Network for Intersystem Cooperation," *The Bookmark* 30 (Spring 1980): 394–97.

20. Fite, "Report of the [NCLIS] Task Force," 89–114.

21. *Report of the Commissioner of Education's Committee on Library Development*, 1970.

7. Children's Services and the New Technology

1. Robert Grover and Mary Kevin Moore, "Print Dominates Library Service to Children," in Mediatmosphere," *American Libraries* 13 (April 1982): 268–69.

2. Carol A. Emmens, "The Fourth Basic: Courses in Viewing Television Critically," in "SLJ/Video Watch," *School Library Journal* 28 (February 1982): 45.

3. *Critical Television Viewing: A Language Skills Work-A-Text* (New York: WNET).

4. Emmens, "The Fourth Basic," 45.

5. Michael Miller, "Video Learning Centers Enrich Rural Libraries," in "Mediatmosphere," *American Libraries* 12 (February 1981): 103.

6. Barbara Webb, "Maryland Creates First Video Production Network," in "Mediatmosphere," *American Libraries* 12 (May 1981): 287–89.

7. " 'Read More About It' Begins Second Season," in "The Source," *American Libraries* 12 (January 1981): 46–47.

8. Bertha M. Cheatham, "Library News of the Year in Retrospect," *School Library Journal* 26 (January 1980): 33.

9. Patrice K. Andrews, "Children's Broadcasting Information Online KIDSNET Database Gives Tips on Radio and TV Programming," in Youthreach," *American Libraries* 17 (January 1986): 76, 78.

10. Richard Moses, "Steam Engines in the Public Library, or Computers, Children and Library Services," *Emergency Librarian* 10 (January–February 1983): 13–16.

11. Patrick R. Dewey, "Computers, Fun and Literacy," in "SLJ/Practically Speaking," *School Library Journal* 29 (October 1982): 118.

12. Edward B. Fiske, "An Analysis: Schools Enter the Computer Age," in "Spring Survey of Education," *New York Times* (25 April 1982): sec. 12, p. 38.

13. Ibid., 38.

14. Robert Chapman, *Dictionary of American Slang* (New York: Harper & Row, 1987).

15. Barbara Dimisk, "The Microcomputer in the Public Library: A Children's Room Experience," *Top of the News* 39 (Spring 1983): 253–59.

16. Barbara Harvie and Julie Anton, "Is There A Microcomputer in Your Future? Computertown Thinks the Answer is 'Yes,' " *Top of The News* 39 (Spring 1983): 275–81.

17. Jenne Britell, "Social Consequences Beyond School," *New York Times*, (April 25, 1982): sec. 12, p. 42.

18. "Kenneth B. Clark Launches N.Y. Series Featuring Educators, Psychologists," *Library Journal* 108 (April 15, 1983): 782.

19. Frances Grandy, "A Major Gain for the Disabled Computers in the Classroom," *New York Times* April 25, 1982: sec. 12, p. 42.

20. Theodore C. Hines, Lois Winkel, and Rosann Collins, "The Children's Media Data Bank," *Top of the News* 36 (Winter 1980): 176–80.

21. Susan Spaeth Cherry, "The Moving Finger Accesses," *American Libraries* 12 (January 1981): 14–16.

22. "Children's Book Review Project," *American Libraries* 14 (June 1983): 405.

8. The Multifaceted Services of the Children's Department

1. *Webster's New Collegiate Dictionary* (Springfield, MA: Merriam, 1977).

2. Jim Trelease, *The Read Aloud Handbook* (New York: Penguin Books, 1982).

3. Glen Collins, "Reading to Children—It Runs in Families," *New York Times* (January 11, 1982): sec. B, p. 6.

4. Dorothy Butler, "Reading Begins at Home," part I, *The Horn Book* 59 (October 1983): 545–52.

5. Ann Weiss Schwalb, "Puppets for Loan," *School Library Journal* 24 (February 1978): 27–29.

6. Marilyn Berg Iarusso, "Children's Films: Orphans of the Industry," *Films Library Quarterly* 9 (1976): 5–7.

7. Martha Barnes, "Six Years Later: A Re-examination of Trends and Developments in Children's Film since 1976," *Film Library Quarterly* 15 (1982): 1, 9–14.

8. Maureen Gaffney, *More Films Kids Like* (Chicago: ALA, 1977).

9. "Reading and Learning is His Game: ABC-TV Cap'n O. G. Readmore," *American Libraries* 14 (June 1983): 405.

10. "CBS Keeps Eye on Reading," *American Libraries* 12 (March 1981): 157.

11. Carl A. Emmens, "Cable Casting: Tips from Lancaster County Library," in SLJ Videowatch," *School Library Journal* 28 (April 1982): 40.

12. "Roll Tape, Red Lights On, Smile!" *NYLA Bulletin* 30 (October 1982): 8.

13. Don R. Smith, "Library Clout in Local Cable," *American Libraries* 12 (September 1981): 500–3.

14. Carl A. Emmens, "Kidvid," in "SLJ Videowatch," *School Library Journal* 28 (December 1981): 36.

15. Smith, "Library Clout in Local Cable," 500–3.

16. Emmens, "Kidvid," 36.

17. "Reading Rainbow Links TV and Books," *School Library Journal* 29 (March 1983): 78.

18. Kathy Wendling, "Porter PL Makes the Cable TV Connection," in "SLJ Videowatch," *School Library Journal* 29 (April 1983): 19–22.

19. "Public Library Services to Preschoolers," *Cognotes* ALA 99th annual conference Newsletter, June 1980.

9. Early Childhood, Preschool, and Parent Education Programs

1. Information from the "Reading Resources for Sesame Street" files of the National Book Committee archives.

2. Elizabeth Ogg, "Preparing Tomorrow's Parents," New York: Public Affairs committee, 1975.

3. Statistical Abstract of the United States, 102nd Ed, (Washington, DC: 1981). Bureau of the Census.

4. Nancy Rubin, "Learning How Children Learn farom the First Moments of Life," *New York Times* (January 10, 1982): sec. 13, p. 36–37.

5. Sally Reed, "Chicago's Early Focus on Learning Problems," *New York Times*, Ed. (January 10, 1982): sec. 13, pp. 36–37.

6. Ferne O. Johnson, *Start Early for an Early Start* (Chicago: ALA, 1976).

7. Frances A. Smardo, "Are Librarians Prepared to Serve Young Children?" *Journal of Education for Librarianship* 20 (Spring 1980): 274–84.

8. Ann D. Carlson, *Early Childhood Literature Sharing Programs in Libraries* (Hamden, CT: Library Professional Publications, 1985).

9. J. Piaget and B. Inhelder, *The Psychology of the Child* (New York: Basic Books, 1969); J. Piaget, *The Origins of Intelligence in the Child* (New York: Norton, 1963); J. Piaget, *Play, Dreams and Imitation in Childhood* (New York: Norton, 1962).

10. Erik Erikson, *Childhood and Society*, 2nd rev. ed. (New York: Norton, 1964).

11. R. R. Sears, E. Maccoby, and H. Levin, *Patterns of Childhood Rearing* (New York: Harper & Row, 1957); R. R. Sears, *Identification and Child Rearing* (Stanford, CA: Stanford U. Press, 1965); R. R. Sears and S. S. Feldman, *The Seven Ages of Man* (New York: Kaufman, 1973).

12. A. Gesell, F. Ilg, and L. Ames, *Infant and Child in the Culture of Today*, rev. ed. (New York: Harper & Row, 1974); L. Ames et al. *The Gesell Institute's Child from One to Six* (New York: Harper & Row, 1979).

13. Jerome Kagan, *The Second Year: The Emergence of Self-Awareness* (Cambridge, MA: Harvard U. Press, 1986); *The Nature of the Child* (New York: Basic Books, 1984); *The Growth of the Child: Reflections on Human Development* (New York: Norton, 1978).

14. Jerome S. Bruner, *The Process of Cognitive Growth: Infancy* (Worcestor, MA: Clark Press, 1968); *The Relevance of Education* (New York: Norton, 1971).

15. Kenneth B. Clark, *Prejudice and Your Child* (Boston: Beacon Press, 1963).

16. Urie Bronfenbrenner, *Is Early Intervention Effective? A Report on Longitudinal Evaluation of Preschool Programs*, vol. 2 (Washington, DC: Office of Child Development, U.S. Department of Health, Education and Welfare, 1974).

17. Bruno Bettelheim, *The Uses of Enchantment: The Meaning and Importance of Fairy Tales* (New York: Knopf, 1976).

18. Burton L. White, *The First Three Years of Life* (Englewood Cliffs, NJ: Prentice-Hall, 1975).

19. Ferne O. Johnson, "Library Services Benefit Preschoolers," *Catholic Library World* 50 (December 1978): 212.

20. *A Nation At Risk*.

21. ALA Task Force, *Realities*.

22. Bennett, *First Lessons*.

23. Lilian G. Katz, "Mothering and Teaching: Significant Distinctions" (Speech presented at the New York State Home/School/Community Partnership Conference, February 6–7, 1980).

24. Carlson, *Early Childhood Literature Sharing*.

25. Juliet Markowski, "Toddler Storytime Possibilities" (Westchester Library system children's services meeting, November 20, 1979).

26. Susan Zwick, "Storytime Ideas for Preschoolers," in "SLJ/Practically Speaking," *School Library Journal* 28 (January 1982): 36.

27. Kathleen Englehart, correspondence, September 1981.

28. Nancy Elsmo, *handbook for Parents* developed for the Racine Public Library.

29. Frances E. Millhouser, "Two's Company," *School Library Journal* (May 1979).

30. Virginina Richey, personal communication, November 1987.

31. Julie Cummins, ed., *New York Library Systems' Children's Consultants' Newsletter* (Rochester, NY: Rochester Public Library, April 1978).

32. Martha Barnes, "Library Service to Very Young Children and Their Parents in Westchester County," *The Bookmark* 37 (Summer 1978): 111–17.

33. Canadian Association of Toy Libraries, *Toy Libraries 2: The Many Uses of Toy Lending* (Toronto: Canadian Association of Toy Libraries, 1980).

34. Frank Self, Nancy De Salvo, and Faith Hektoen, *Materials for Adult Use from Birth to Three* (Farmington, CT: Farmington Public Library, 1983).

35. "Allen County, Indiana, Made 1982 Brighter for Its Patrons," *Library Journal* 108 (May 1, 1983): 864.

36. Burton L. White, "The Year in Review," *The Center for Parent Education* 3 (December 5, 1980).

37. Karen Ponish, " 'Babywise' and Toys Develop Literacy Skills," *American Libraries* 18 (September 1987): 709–10.

38. Barbara Barstow and Linda Silver, "Your Young Child and the Library," *American Libraries* 18 (September 1987): 10–11.

39. Judy Vanke, *Parenting Programs: Four Library Models* (Cleveland, OH: Cuyahoga County Public Library, (April 1980).

40. Micki Nevett, "A Children's Literature Course for Parents," *School Library Journal* 27 (March 1981): 105–6.

41. Janet Gourley and Nancy De Salvo, "Parent Support Services in Glastonbury and Farmington," *School Library Journal* 26 (April 1980): 26.

42. Dorothy T. McDonald and John H. Ramsay, "Awakening the Artist: Made for Young Children," *Young Children* 33 (January 1979).

43. Cummings, ed., *New York Library Systems' Newsletter*.

44. Pat Cook, "American Library Association: The Big Apple 1980," *Emergency Librarian* 7 (July–August 1980): 9.

45. Barnes, "Library Services," 111–17.

46. Kent Garland Burtt, "New Center: Antidote for a Mother's Isolation," in "Living," *Christian Science Monitor*, (March 12, 1979).

47. Urie Bronfenbrenner, "Is Early Intervention Effective?" *Day Care and Early Education* 2 (November 1974): 14–18, 44.

48. Brian Sutton-Smith, "Play Pays Off" in "SR Reviews," *Saturday Review of Education* 1 (January 1973): 49.

49. Sylvia F. Johnson and Core Villegas, "Mother and Child Programs for Adults," correspondence, 1981.

50. Leslie Edmonds, correspondence, October 1982.

51. Faith Hektoen, "Parent Support Programs," *Public Libraries* 16 (Winter 1977): 16–18.

52. "Unique Outreach Projects Seek Youngsters in Day Care Centers," *American Libraries* 14 (June 1983): 375.

53. Virginia Richey, children's librarian of the Monroe County Public Library, Bloomington, Indiana, correspondence November 1987.

54. "Unique Outreach Projects Seek Youngsters in Day Care Centers," *American Libraries* 14 (June 1983): 375.

55. Personal involvement by the author.

10. Some Other Matters in Summary

1. John Rowe Townsend, "A Sense of Story: Essays on Contemporary Writers for Children," *The Horn Book* (1977): 15.

2. Ibid.

3. Alice R. Brooks, "Developmental Values in Books," in *Youth Communication and Libraries*, ed. Frances Henne et al. (Chicago: ALA, 1949), 49–51.

4. "Island Trees School Board Lifts Seven Year Book Ban," *Library Journal* 107 (September 15, 1982): 1694.

5. Nancy Larrick, "The All-White World of Children's books," *Saturday Review* 40 (September 11, 1965): 63–65.

6. August Baker, "Guidelines for Black Books: An Open Letter to Juvenile Editors," *Publishers Weekly* 1 (July 14, 1969): 131–33.

7. Isabel Schon, "Recent Detrimental and Distinguished Books About Hispanic People and Cultures," *Top of the News* 38 (Fall 1981): 79–85.

8. Gloria Blatt, "The Jewish-American Experience: The View from Children's Fiction," *Top of the News* 35 (Summer 1979): 391–98.

9. "Jake and Honeybunch Go To Heaven: Children's book Fans Smoldering Debate," *American Libraries* 14 (March 1983): 130–32.

10. Kornei Chukovsky, *From Two to Five*, trans. and ed. Miriam Morton (Berkeley: University of California Press, 1963), 124.

11. Sam Sebasta, "Why Rudolph Can't Read," *Language Arts* 58 (May 1981): 545–48.

12. Bruno Bettelheim, and Karen Zelan, *On Learning to Read: The Child's Fascination with Meaning* (New York: Knopf, 1982).

13. Anne Carroll Moore, "My Roads to Childhood," *The Horn Book* (1961): 211.

14. Penelope Lively, "Bones in the Sand," *The Horn Book* 57: (December 1981): 646.

15. "Children's Books for a Better World: An IBBY Statement for the International Year of the Child," *IBBY U.S. National Section Newsletter* vol. 3, no. 2 (Summer–Fall 1978).

16. Alice Geradts, "Children's Literature Research Collections: Services and Research for Children's Libraries," *Bookbird* (February 19, 1981): 15–19.

17. Irenemarie Cullinane, "Children's Books International—A total Library Experience," *Top of the News* 32 (January 1976): 131–34.

18. Marilyn Louis Schontz, "Selected Research Related to Children's and Young Adult Services in Public Libraries," *Top of the News* (Winter 1982): 125–42.

19. Ibid., 129, 135.

20. Shirley Fitzgibbons, "Research on Library Services for Children and Young Adults: Implications for Practice," *Emergency Librarian* 9 (May–June 1982): 10.

21. Karen Perry, "Research in Children's Services in Public Libraries: A Group Project in North Carolina," in "Services to Children," ed. Diana Young, *Public Libraries* 19 (Summer 1980): 58–60.

22. Ibid.

23. Mary Kohler, "The Rights of Children—An Unexplored Constituency," *Social Policy* (March–April 1971).

24. *Report to the President, White House Conference on Children*, Washington, DC: 1970.

25. *White House Conference on Families: New York State Recommendations*, Vol. 3, no. 2 (Albany, NY: Council on Children and Families, June 1980).

26. "Resolutions Passed at The White House Conference" (NYPL Memorandum, 31, December 1979, pp. 1–22).

27. Virginia Mathews, manager of American Indian Libraries lobbying effort, 1974 to 1984, conversation. November 1987.

28. Lana Hostetler, "Putting Our Child Care Skills to Work in Advocacy," *Child Care Information Exchange* 29 (January–February 1983): 25–27.

Bibliography

Books

Aaron, Shirley L. *A Study of Combined School-Public Libraries.* Chicago. ALA, 1980.

American Library Association. *Restricted Access to Library Materials: An Interpretation of the Library Bill of Rights.* Chicago: ALA, 1982.

Baechtold, Marguerite, and Eleanor Ruth McKinney. *Library Service for Families.* Hamden, CT: Shoe String, (Lib. Prof. Pubns.) 1983.

Bader, Barbara. *American Picturebooks from Noah's Ark to the Beast Within.* New York: Macmillan, 1976.

Baker, Augusta and Ellin Greene. *Storytelling: Art and Technique.* 2nd edition. New York: Bowker, 1987.

Baker, D. Philip, and David R. Bender. *Library Media Programs and the Special Learner.* Hamden, CT: Shoe String, Lib. Prof. Pubns., 1981.

Baskin, Barbara H., and Karen H. Harris. *Books for the Gifted Child.* New York: Bowker, 1980.

Bator, Robert. *Signposts to Criticism of Children's Literature.* Chicago: ALA, 1983.

Bauer, Caroline Feller. *Handbook for Storytellers.* Chicago: ALA, 1977.

———. *This Way to Books.* New York: Wilson, 1983.

Berger, Melvin. *Computers in Your Life.* New York: T. Y. Crowell, 1981.

Bettelheim, Bruno. *The Uses of Enchantment: The Meaning and Importance of Fairy Tales.* New York: Knopf, 1976.

Bodart, Joni. *Booktalk!* New York: Wilson, 1980.

Boyle, Deirdre. *Children's Media Market Place.* Hamden, CT: Gaylord Prof. Pubns., 1978.

Bracken, Jeanne, Sharon Wigutoff and Ilene Baker. *Books for Today's Young Readers.* Old Westbury, NY: Feminist Pr., 1981.

Broderick, Dorothy M. *Image of the Black in Children's Fiction.* New York: Bowker, 1973.

————. *Library Work With Children.* New York: Wilson, 1977.

Butler, Dorothy. *Cushla and Her Books.* Boston: Horn Book, 1980.

Butler, Dorothy, and Marie Clay. *Reading Begins at Home: Preparing Children for Reading Before They Go to School.* Portsmouth, NH: Heinemann Ed., 1982.

Carr, Jo. *Beyond Fact: Nonfiction for Children and Young People.* Chicago: ALA, 1982.

Cass-Beggs, Barbara. *Your Baby Needs Music.* New York: St. Martin, 1980.

Chambers, Aidan. *Introducing Books to Children.* rev. ed. Boston: Horn Bk., 1983.

————. *The Reluctant Reader.* Oxford: Pergamon, 1969.

Chambers, Nancy, ed. *The Signal Approach to Children's Books.* Metuchen, NJ: Scarecrow, 1981.

Chen, Ching-chich, and Stacey Bressler, eds. *Microcomputers in Libraries.* Metuchen, NJ: Neal-Schuman, 1983.

Cianciolo, Patricia Ann. *Picture Books for Children, 2d ed., rev.* Chicago: ALA, 1981.

Clay, Katherine, ed. *Microcomputers in Education: A Handbook of Resources.* Phoenix: Oryx Pr., 1982.

Conroy, Barbara. *Library Staff Development and Continuing Education: Principles and Practices.* Littleton, CO: Libs. Unl., 1978.

Cooperman, Paul. *The Literacy Hoax: The Decline of Reading, Writing, and Learning in the Public Schools and What We Can Do About It.* New York: Morrow, 1980.

Costa, Betty, and Marie Costa. *A Micro Handbook for Small Libraries and Media Centers.* Littleton, CO: Libs. Unl., 1983.

Cott, Jonathan. *Pipers at the Gates of Dawn*. New York: Random, 1983.

Crago, Maureen, and Hugh Crago. *Prelude to Literacy*. Carbondale, IL: S. Ill. U. Pr., 1983.

Cullinan, Bernice E., Mary K. Karrer and Arlene M. Pillar. *Literature and the Child*. Harcourt, Brace Jovanovich, 1981.

DeSalvo, Nancy, and others. *Resource List for Adults of Materials to Use the Very Young Child*. Farmington, CT: Farmington Village Library, 1982.

Dizer, John T. *Tom Swift and Company: "Boys" Books by Stratemeyer and Others*. Jefferson, NC: McFarland & Co., 1982.

Duke, Judith S. *Children's Books and Magazines: A Market Study*. White Plains, NY: Knowledge Indus., 1979.

Durkin, Dolores. *Children Who Read Early*. New York: Columbia U. Tchrs. Coll., 1966.

Egoff, Sheila, G. J. Stubbs, and L. F. Ashley, eds. *Only Connect: Readings on Children's Literature*. 2nd ed. Toronto: Oxford U. Pr., 1980.

Field, Carolyn W., ed. *Special Collections in Children's Literature*. Chicago: ALA, 1982.

Fisher, Margery. *Matters of Fact: Aspects of Non-fiction for Children*. New York: T. Y. Crowell, 1972.

FitzGerald, Frances. *America Revised*. New York: Vintage, 1979.

Fraser, James H., ed. *Society and Children's Literature*. Boston: Godine, 1978.

Gaffney, Maureen, ed. *More Films Kids Like*. Chicago: ALA, 1977.

Gaffney, Maureen, and Gerry Bond Laybourne. *What To Do When the Lights Go On*. Phoenix: Oryx Pr., 1981.

Gillespie, John, and Christine Gilbert. *Best Books for Children: Pre-School Through the Middle Grades*. 2nd ed. New York: Bowker, 1981.

Gillespie, John, and Diana L. Spirt. *Administering the School Library Media Center*. New York: Bowker, 1983.

Glazer, Susan. *How Can I Help My Child Build Positive Attitudes Toward Reading?* Newark, DE: Int'l. Reading Assn., 1980.

Graves, Michael, and others. *Easy Reading: Book Series and Periodicals for Less Able Readers*. Newark, DE: Int'l. Reading Assn., 1979.

Greenfield, Howard. *Books: From Writer to Reader*. New York: Crown, 1976.

Gross, Elizabeth H. *Public Library Service to Children*. Dobbs Ferry, NY: Oceana, 1969.

Gross, Beatrice, and Ronald Gross. *The Children's Rights Movement: Overcoming the Oppression of Young People*. New York: Anchor, 1977.

Haviland, Virginia. *Children's Books of International Interest: A Selection from Four Decades of American Publishing*. 2nd ed. Chicago: ALA, 1978.

————, ed. *The Openhearted Audience: Ten Authors Talk About Writing for Children*. Washington, DC: Lib. Cong., 1980.

Hearne, Betsy. *Choosing Books for Children: A Commonsense Guide*. New York: Delacorte, 1981.

Herbert, Frank, and Max Barnard. *Without Me You're Nothing: The Essential Guide to Home Computers*. New York: Pocket Books, 1981.

Holt, John. *Escape from Childhood: The Needs and Rights of Childhood*. New York: Ballantine, 1975.

Huck, Charlotte. *Children's Literature in the Elementary School*. New York: Holt, Rinehart and Winston, 1979.

Hunt, Tamara, and Nancy Renfro. *Puppetry in Early Childhood Education*. Austin, TX: Nancy Renfro Studios, 1982.

Inglis, Fred. *The Promise of Happiness: Value and Meaning in Children's Fiction*. New York: Cambridge U. Pr. 1982.

Katz, Bill, and Ruth Fraley. *Reference Services for Children and Young Adults*. New York: Haworth Pr., 1983.

Keniston, Kenneth, and the Carnegie Council on Children. *All Our Children*. New York: Harcourt Brace Jovanovich, 1977.

Kimmel, Margaret Mary, and Elizabeth Segal. *For Reading Out Loud! A Guide to Sharing Books with Children*. New York: Delacorte, 1983.

Lanes, Selma G. *The Art of Maurice Sendak*. New York: Abrams, 1980.

————. *Down the Rabbit Hole: Adventures and Misadventures in the Realm of Children's Literature*. New York: Atheneum, 1971.

Larrick, Nancy. *Encourage Your Child to Read: A Parent's Primer*. New York: Dell, 1980.

Lesser, Gerald. *Children's Television: Lessons from Sesame Street.* New York: Random, 1974.

LiBretto, Ellen V. *High/Low Handbook: Books, Materials, and Services for the Teenage Problem Reader.* New York: Bowker, 1981.

Lima, Carolyn W. *A to Zoo: Subject Access to Children's Picture Books.* New York: Bowker, 1982.

Lystad, Mary. *From Dr. Mather to Dr. Suess: 200 Years of American Books for Children.* Boston: G. K. Hall, 1980.

Mancall, Jacqueline C., and M. Carl Droti. *Measuring Student Information: A Guide for School Library Media Specialists.* Littleton, CO: Libs. Unl., 1983.

Meek, Margaret, A. Warlow and G. Burton. *The Cool Web: The Pattern of Children's Reading.* New York: Atheneum, 1978.

Miller, Bernard S., and Merle Price, eds. *The Gifted Child, the Family, and the Community.* New York: Walker & Co., 1981.

Morse, Jane Crowell, ed. *Beatrix Potter's Americans: Selected Letters.* Boston: Horn Book, 1982.

Newcomb, Horace. *Television: The Critical View.* New York: Oxford, 1979.

Newman, Joan E. Girls are People Too! *A Bibliography of Non-Traditional Female Roles in Children's Books.* Metuchen: Scarecrow, 1982.

Papert, Seymour. *Mindstorms: Children, Computers and Powerful Ideas.* New York: Basic Books, 1980.

Parker, Robert P., and Frances A. Davis, eds. *Developing Literacy: Young Children's Use of Language.* Newark, DE: Intl. Reading Assn., 1983.

Paulin, Mary Ann. *Creative Uses of Children's Literature.* Hamden, CT: Shoe String, Lib. Prof. Pubns., 1982.

Perino, Sheila C., and Joseph Perino. *Parenting the Gifted: Developing the Promise.* New York: Bowker, 1981.

Peterson, Linda Kauffman, and Marilyn Leathers Solt. *Newbery and Caldecott Medal and Honor Books: An Annotated Bibliography.* Boston: G. K. Hall, 1982.

Polette, Nancy. *Books and Real Life.* Jefferson, NC: McFarland & Co., 1984.

———. *Picture Books for Gifted Programs*. Metuchen, NJ: Scarecrow, 1981.

———. *3 R's For the Gifted: Reading, Writing and Research*. Littleton, CO: Libs. Unl. 1982.

Polette, Nancy, and Marjorie Hamelin. *Exploring Books with Gifted Children*. Littleton, CO: Libs. Unl. 1980.

Pulaski, Mary Ann Spencer. *Your Baby's Mind and How It Grows: Piaget's Theory for Parents*. New York: Harper & Row, 1978.

Reasoner, Charles. *Bringing Children and Books Together: A Teacher's Guide to Early Childhod Literature*. New York: Dell, 1979.

Renfro, Nancy. *Puppertry, Language and the Special Child*. Austin, TX: Nancy Renfro Studios, 1984.

Rees, David. *Painted Desert, Green Shade: Essays in Contemporary Writers of Fiction for Children and Young Adults*. Boston: Horn Book, 1984.

Richardson, Selma K., ed., *Proceeding* of 23rd Allerton Park Institute, Champaign-Urbana, Illinois, University of Illinois, Graduate School of Library Science, 1977.

Rudman, Masha. *Children's Literature: An Issues Approach*. Lexington, MA: Heath, 1976.

Sadker, Myra, and David Sadker. *Now Upon a Time: A Contemporary View of Children's Literature*. New York: Harper & Row, 1977.

Sebesta, Sam Leaton, and William J. Iverson. *Literature for Thursday's Child*. Chicago: Science Research Assocs., 1975.

Simon, Sidney B., Leland W. Howe, and Howard Kerschenbaum. *Values Classification: A Handbook of Practical Strategies for Teachers and Students*. rev. ed. New York: Dodd, 1985.

Singer, Dorothy G. *Teaching Television: How to Use TV to Your Child's Advantage*. New York: Dial, 1981.

Smardo, Frances A. *What Research Tells Us About Storyhours and Receptive Language*. Dallas: Dallas Public Library, 1982.

Sommerville, c. John. *The Rise and Fall of Childhood*. Beverly Hills: Sage Pubns., 1982.

Spencer, Donald A. *Computer Dictionary for Everyone*. New York: Scribner, 1974.

Sutherland, Zena, and Diane L. Monson. *Children and Books*. 6th ed. Chicago: Scott, Foresman, 1981.

Sutherland, Zena, ed. *Children in Libraries: Patterns of Access to Materials and Services in School and Public Libraries*. Proceedings of the 41 st Conference of the Graduate Library School. Chicago: U. of Chicago Pr., 1981.

Townsend, John Rowe. *Written for Children*. rev. ed. New York: Lippincott, 1983.

Vail, Priscilla L. *The World of the Gifted Child*. New York: Walker & Co., 1979.

Vandergrift, Kay E. *Child and Story: The Literary Connection*. New York: Neal-Schuman, 1980.

Velleman, Ruth. *Serving Physically Disabled People: An Information Handbook for All Librarians*. New York: Bowker, 1979.

Vygotsky, L. S. *Thought and Language*. Cambridge: MIT, 1962.

Wadsworth, Barry J. *Piaget's Theory of Cognitive Development:An Introduction for Students of Psychology and Education*. New York: Langman, 1979.

White, Dorothy. *Books Before Five*. Portsmouth, NH: Heinemann Ed., 1981.

White, Virginia, and Emerita Schulte. *Books About Children's Books*. Newark, DE:Intl. Reading Assn., 1979.

Wilkin, Binnie Tate. *Survival Themes in Fiction for Children and Young People*. Metuchen, NJ: Scarecrow, 1978.

Wilson, Jane B. *The Story Experience*. Metuchen, NJ: Scarecrow, 1979.

Winick, Mariann, and Charles Winick. *The Television Experience: What Children See*. People and Communications Series, vol 6. Beverly Hills: Sage Pubns., 1979.

Winn, Marie. *Children Without Childhood*. New York: Pantheon, 1980.

Woods, L. B. *A Decade of Censorship in America: The Threat to Classrooms and Libraries, 1965–1975*. Metuchen, NJ: Scarecrow, 1979.

Woolard, Wilma. *Combined School/Public Libraries: A Survey with Conclusions and Recommendations*. Metuchen, NJ: Scarecrow, 1980.

Yolen, Jane. *Touch Magic: Fantasy, Faerie and Folklore in the Literature of Childhood*. New York: Putnam Pub. Group, Philomel Bks., 1981.

Zweizig, Douglas, and Eleanor Jo Rodger. *Output Measures for Public Libraries*. Chicago: ALA, 1982.

Articles

Applebaum, Judith. "Marketing the Active Backlist." *Publishers Weekly* 217 (January 18, 1980): 81.

Baker, D. Philip. "School and Public Library Programs and Information Dissemination." *School Media Quarterly* 5 (Winter 1977): 119–27.

Banbury, Mary M. "Remediation and Reinforcement: Books for Children with Visual Perceptual Impairments." *Top of the News* 37 (Fall 1980): 41–46.

Beckman, Judy. "Turning Reluctant Readers into Lifetime Readers." *English Journal*, 73 (January 1984): 84–86.

Benne, Mae. "Educational and Recreational Services of the Public Library for Children." *Library Quarterly* 48 (October 1978): 499–510.

———"Leavening for the Youth Culture." *Wilson Library Bulletin* 52 (December 1977): 312–18.

Bowie, Melvin. "Tips from Local A-V Production from SESAME STREET Research." *School Library Media Quarterly* 10 (Winter 1982): 156.

Brink, Mary L. "Role of the Children's Consultant in a Cooperative Library System." *The Bookmark* 39 (Fall 1980): 25–29.

Broderick, Dorothy. "Censorship Re-evaluated." *Library Journal* 96 (November 15, 1971): 3816–18.

Broderick, Dorothy M. "Racism, Sexism, Intellectual Freedom, and Youth Librarians." *Top of the News* 33 (Summer 1977): 323–32.

Burch, John L. "Computers, Humanistic Values, and the Library." *Public Libraries* 18 (Winter 1979): 89–92.

Crowley, Ginny McKee. "Children's Services: The Role of the State Children's Services Consultant." *New Jersey Libraries* 13 (December 1980/January 1981): 4–6.

Darkatsh, Manuel. "Who Should Decide on a Book's Merit?" *Elementary English*. 51 (March 1974): 353–4.

Davie, Judith F. "Resources, Referral and Reassurances: The Library and Parents of the Gifted and Talented." *Top of the News* 38 (Summer 1982): 331–36.

Dyer, Esther, and Daniel O'Connor. "Crisis in Library Education." In "Inside our Schools." *Wilson Library Bulletin* 57 (June 1983): 860–63.

Dyer, Esther, and Concha Robertson-Kozan. "Hispanics in the U.S.: Implications for Library Services." *School Library Journal* 29 (April 1983): 27–29.

Edmonds, Leslie. "Taming Technology: Planning for Patron Use of Microcomputers in the Public Library." *Top of the News* 39 (Spring 1983): 247–51.

Elsmo, Nancy, and Micki Nevett. "The Public Library: A Resource Center for Parents: A Drama in Three Acts." *Public Libraries* 22 (Fall 1983): 96–98.

Erbeck, Diane. "Television and Children: A ProCon Reading List." *Top of the News* 37 (Fall 1980): 47–53.

Fasick, Adele. "Research and Measurement in Library Services to Children." *International Library Review* 12 (June 1976): 262–69.

Fassler, Joan, and Marjorie Janis. "Books, Children, and Peace." *Young Children* (September 1983).

Kimmel, Margaret Mary. "Children's Rights, Parents' Rights—A Librarian's Dilemma." *School Library Journal* 27 (October 1980): 112–14.

Kingsbury, Mary E. "Keeping Out of Trouble: Research and Children's Services of Public Libraries." In *Children's Services of Public Libraries*, edited by Selma K. Richardson, 131–47. Urbana, IL: U. of Ill., 1978.

Klein, Norma. "Some Thoughts on Censorship: An Author Symposium." *Top of the News* 39 (Winter 1983): 137–53.

Lanes, Selma G. "A Case for the Five Chinese Brothers." In "SLJ/Up for Discussion." *School Library Journal* 24 (October 1977): 90–91.

Lathrop, Ann. "Microcomputer Courseware: Selection and Evaluation." *Top of the News* 39 (Spring 1983): 265–74.

Lesser, Gerald S. "Stop Picking on Big Bird." *Psychology Today* 12 (March, 1979): 57–60.

Liehn, Robert. "The Computer (Inter) Faces Life." *Media & Methods* 19 (November, 1982): 14–15.

Lopez, Antonio M. "Microcomputers: Tools of the Present and Future." *School Media Quarterly* 9 (Spring 1981): 164–67.

Lucas, Linda. "Volunteers: Altruistic Prima Donnas?" In "Research in Action," edited by Mary Grace Donnelly. *Public Libraries* 19 (Fall 1980): 87–89.

MacCarry, Bert W. "Shadow and Substance: Puppets in the Library." *School Library Journal* 26 (February 1980): 17–20.

McCormick, Edith. "Librarians Hate Us, But the Public Loves Golden Books." *American Libraries* 12 (May 1981): 251–57.

"Making Kids Computer-Wise: Plattsburgh Buys Apple II." *Library Journal* 107 (March 15, 1980): 669.

Malette, Phyllis. "The Children's and Young Adult Librarian: A Power Profile." *Emergency Librarian* 7 (March–June 1980): 12–15.

Manley, Will. "Facing the Public." *Wilson Library Bulletin* 58 (October 1983): 124–25.

May, Jill P. "Walt Disney's Interpretation of Children's Literature." *Language Arts* 58 (April 1981): 463–72.

Miller, Inabeth. "The Micros are Coming." *Media & Methods* 16 (April 1980): 33–34, 72, 74.

"NCLIS Task Force on Cultural Minorities Reports . . ." *Library Journal* 108 (December 1, 1983): 2190–92.

Nicklin, R. C., and John Tashner. "Micros in the Library Media Center." *School Media Quarterly* (Spring 1981): 168–72, 177–81.

Noble, Grant. "What Parents Should Know About Children and Television." *Young Viewers* 6 (1983): 5–7.

Patte, Genevieve. "Children's Libraries in France." *International Library Reviewers* 6 (October 1974): 435–48.

Plaiss, Mark. "New Librarians Need Skills, Not Philosophy," In "On My Mind." *American Libraries* 14 (October 1983): 618.

Prentice, Ann E. "The Lingo of Library Finance." *American Libraries* 8 (November 1977): 530–52.

Russell, Ann N. "A Public Library in Television." *Public Libraries* 18 (Winter 1979): 92–95.

Sager, Donald J. "Public Library Service to the Microchip Generation." *Top of the News* 39 (Summer 1983): 307–14.

Shapiro, Lillian L. "Media Centers: Rare and Well-Done." *Library
Journal* 99 (November 1974): 3011–17.

Siegfried, Pat. "Computers and Children: Problems and Possibilities." *Top of the News* 39 (Spring 1983): 241–46.

Silver, Linda R. "Standards and Free Access—Equal but Separate."
School Library Journal 26 (February 1980): 26–31.

Simmons, Barbara, and Paula Smith Lawrence. "Beginning Reading:
Welcome Parents." *Childhood Education* 57 (January/February 1981):
155–60.

Singer, Jerome L., and Dorothy G. Singer. "Come Back, Mister
Rogers, Come Back." *Psychology Today* 12 (March 1979): 56, 59–60.

Skiff, Margaret S. "A Great New Edition of a Great Old Classic:
Children's Books, A Critical Evaluation." *Top of the News* 33 (Summer 1977): 346–50.

Smardo, Frances A. "Perception, Pictures and Puzzles: Challenging
Children's Books." *Catholic Library World* 55 (October 1983): 128–33.

Strickland, Charlene. "Puppets Need Personalities." In "Practically
Speaking." *School Library Journal* 29 (March 1983): 124–25.

Sullivan, Peggy. "Burnout, Renewal, and Gore: An Overview." *Illinois
Libraries* 64 (December 1982): 1147–48.

———. "Library Service to Children: Celebration and Survival." *Horn
Book* 52 (June 1976): 262–69.

Taitt, Henry A. "Children—Libraries—Computers." *Illinois Libraries*
62 (December 1980): 901–03.

Tashner, John H. "Using a Computer with Gifted Students." *Top of
the News* 38 (Summer 1983): 318–24.

Thorndill, Christine Maltby. "The Skeltons in the Closet: Revision of
Racial, Ethnic and Sexual Stereotypes in Series Books." *Top of the
News* 34 (Spring 1978): 345–48.

Todaro, Julie. "Public Librarianship in Library Education: What Are
We Doing:" In "Keep on Learning," edited by Mary Beth Babikow.
Public Libraries 21 (Winter 1982): 158–62.

Troutner, Joanne. "Microcomputer Books for Core Collections."
School Library Journal 30 (September 1983): 41–44.

Verrone, Robert J. "Why Books Cost So Much." *School Library Journal* 25 (February 1979): 20–22.

Walsh, J. A. "How to Arrange a Meeting Between Dr. Freud and Dr. Seuss." *The Unabashed Librarian* 24 (1977): 29–30.

Warwick, Ellen D. "A Singular View: Non-Series Books on the Third World." In "SLJ/Up for Discussing." *School Library Journal* 28 (September 1981): 40–41.

White, Herbert S. "Defining Basic Competencies." *American Libraries* 14 (September 1983): 519–25.

Wigutoff, Sharon. "Junior Fiction: A Feminist Critique." *Top of the News* 38 (Winter 1982): 113–24.

Wilson, Pauline. "Children's Service and Power: Knowledge to Shape the Future." *Top of the News* 37 (1981) 115–23.

———. "Children's Services in a Time of Change." *School Library Journal* 25 (February 1979): 24.

Wood, Irene " . . . While Children's Films Struggle for Innovation." *American Libraries* 10 (June 1979): 345.

Young, Diana. "Library Service to Children—A Job or a Profession?" *Public Libraries* 20 (Spring 1981): 24–26.

———. "Materials Selection." In "Service to Children." *Public Libraries* 19 (Fall 1980): 84–85

———. "Reaching for Tomorrow Today." In "Service to Children." *Public Libraries* 19 (Winter 1980): 119–21.

Index